Democracy, social resources and political power in the European Union

Manchester University Press

Democracy, social resources and political power in the European Union

NIILO KAUPPI

∼

Manchester University Press
Manchester and New York

distributed exclusively in the USA by Palgrave

Copyright © Niilo Kauppi 2005

The right of Niilo Kauppi to be identified as the author of this work has been asserted by him in accordance with the Copyright, Designs and Patents Act 1988.

Published by Manchester University Press
Oxford Road, Manchester M13 9NR, UK
and Room 400, 175 Fifth Avenue, New York, NY 10010, USA
www.manchesteruniversitypress.co.uk

Distributed in the United States exclusively by
Palgrave Macmillan, 175 Fifth Avenue,
New York, NY 10010, USA

Distributed in Canada exclusively by
UBC Press, University of British Columbia, 2029 West Mall,
Vancouver, BC, Canada V6T 1Z2

British Library Cataloguing-in-Publication Data is available

Library of Congress Cataloging-in-Publication Data is available

ISBN 978 0 7190 7059 4 paperback

First published by Manchester University Press in hardback 2005

This paperback edition first published 2013

The publisher has no responsibility for the persistence or accuracy of URLs for any external or third-party internet websites referred to in this book, and does not guarantee that any content on such websites is, or will remain, accurate or appropriate.

Printed by Lightning Source

The nether sky opens, and Europe is disclosed as a prone and emaciated figure, the Alps shaping like a backbone, and the branching mountain-chains like ribs, the peninsular plateau of Spain forming a head. Broad and lengthy lowlands stretch from the north of France across Russia like a grey-green garment hemmed by the Ural mountains and the glistening Artic Ocean.

The point of view then sinks downwards through space, and draws near to the surface of the perturbed countries, where the peoples, distressed by events which they did not cause are seen withering, crawling, heaving, and vibrating in their various cities and countries. (Thomas Hardy, *The Dynasts*, Part I, Fore Scene)

To Oona and Caius

Contents

List of figures and tables	*page* viii
Acknowledgments	ix
Introduction	1
1 Some theoretical premises of European Union research	4
2 A structural constructivist theory of politics and of European integration	22
3 France's European policy	51
4 Social and constitutional integration in Finland and France	67
5 French Members of the European Parliament	88
6 European Parliament elections in Finland and France in 1999	117
7 Intellectual politics and Europe	161
Conclusions	184
Bibliography	188
Index	205

Figures and tables

Figures

5.1 The French political field and European institutions   *page* 112

Tables

5.1 Abstention percentages in French European Parliament elections	89
5.2 Seats in the European Parliament	90
5.3 Political experience of French MEPs (1989–94)	92
5.4 European, national and international (including ministerial) experience of MEPs	93
5.5 Alumni of *grandes écoles* and members of *grands corps* in the European Parliament	94
5.6 Social representation indexes of deputies and MEPs	95
6.1 Europeanism in the French campaigns to the European Parliament	129
6.2 Results of the French elections to the European Parliament, 1999	144
6.3 Finnish MEPs, 1999–2004	152
6.4 Results of the Finnish European Parliament elections in 1999 in percentages and seats	154
6.5 Typology of MEPs	158

Acknowledgments

I observed with mixed feelings from across the Atlantic the entry of Finland into the European Union in 1995. A year later, I returned to Europe, first to France and then to Finland. Although pro-European by instinct, like many I soon became concerned about the form European integration was taking. A deepening rift between the people and the elites had developed, which manifested itself in public apathy in the European Parliament elections. As a social scientist, I felt it was time to go beyond the simplifying discussions of the notorious 'democratic deficit' I could read every day in the press. I was convinced that critical, empirical analysis of the political practices and social mechanisms that prevented democratisation would contribute to a more democratic development of the European Union. To help to further critical reflection on Europe in a more practical way, I also co-founded an association of European intellectuals, Helsinki Forum, to promote alternative discourses on Europe. Today, my engagement in the battle for Europe continues to be both intellectual and practical. I hope this book will be read as my modest contribution to this collective endeavour.

Thanks to funding from the Academy of Finland, I was able, like a medieval scholar, to spend long periods working in faraway lands, the United States and France, engaging in extensive fieldwork and conducting interviews. Academic nomadism has taught me that academic disciplines are defined differently in different national and institutional contexts. The academic nomad is constantly forced to take stock of his or her own position and defend his or her scholarly choices and motivations. Yet the interdisciplinarity and self-reflexivity that result also heighten the nomad's sensitivity to seemingly insignificant details and potential comparisons, encouraging him or her to 'think outside the box'.

Conducting this research in very different institutional and intellectual settings in three countries has influenced in many ways the conscious and unconscious choices I have made. In Finland, the Centre for European Studies at the University of Helsinki has been an academic 'oasis', a stimulating environment for scholarly activity. My thanks to the entire staff for creating a unique spirit: *Kiitoksia teille kaikille!* This project began to take shape in the United States in 1995, at Indiana University in Bloomington. I later spent the Fall of 1999 and the academic year 2002–2003 as a visiting scholar at the Minda de Gunzburg Center for European Studies at Harvard University. I profited enormously from the lively discussions of the international community of scholars at the CES and would like to thank Abby Collins, Peter Hall and Charles Maier for making these stays possible. The École des hautes études en sciences sociales (EHESS) in Paris provided a key location at several stages in this project. I am indebted to Monique de Saint Martin who kindly invited me to spend the Spring of 1996 at the Centre de sociologie de l'éducation et de la culture, and the Spring of 1999 at the Centre d'études des mouvements sociaux, both at the EHESS. Most recently, I have found a community of like-minded scholars at the Institut d'études politiques in Strasbourg. I would like to thank Yves Déloye and Didier Georgakakis for inviting me to spend a month there as a *professeur invité* in April 2004. I greatly enjoyed meeting Ph.D. students and French colleagues. At the Institut d'études politiques in Paris, Christian Lequesne and Luc Rouban provided me with valuable information on the effects of European integration in France. I would also like to thank former French MEPs Alain Lamassoure and Adrien Zeller for taking time to answer my questions on France and Europe.

Although he did not live to comment on this manuscript as a whole, my greatest intellectual debt is to the late Pierre Bourdieu who, since I began attending his research seminar at the EHESS in Paris in 1986, was supportive of my research and kind enough to read my texts. In addition, since 1996 I have had fruitful conversations about what Europe is and should be with many individuals on different occasions in Europe and North America. I have presented parts of this manuscript at various conferences (Cini Foundation, Council for European Studies, European Sociological Association, Finnish Political Science Association, Society for French Historical Studies, Theory, Culture, and Society [TCS] and TCS/Cosmopolis,) and as an invited speaker at several institutions (Boston University, Bucknell University, Bryn Mawr College in Avignon, Georgia State University, Jyväskylä University and the University of Minnesota). I wish to thank Marybeth Gasman, Sakari Hänninen, Brigitte Mahuzier, David Swartz and John Westbrook for these invitations. Amongst the numerous scholars whose thoughtful comments moved the project forward I would like particularly to thank Avner Ben-Amos, Leslie Derfler, Jim Ennis, Jari Ehrnrooth, Edward Epstein, Rick Fantasia, Julien Friend, Mihai Gheorgiu, Bert Gordon, Karen Heinze, Tiina Huokuna, Patrick Hutton, Herbert Kalthoff, Marja Keränen, Pia Letto-Vanamo, Hélène Lipstadt, Tapio Lovio, Michel Mangenot, Jean Pedersen, David Schalk, Torbjörn Wandel, Thomas Zittel and Vera Zolberg.

My warmest thanks go to my friends and colleagues Pami Aalto and Henri Vogt who read and gave valuable comments on the entire manuscript. I am also indebted to Willy Beauvallet and Michael Kull for research assistance. The expert editing of Nely Keinanen and Kimmo Absetz, Liz Rosdeitcher, Ivor Stodolsky and Evan Young improved the manuscript immeasurably. My appreciation goes finally to the editorial staff of Manchester University Press for their efficiency in helping bring this project to completion. Translations to English are mine unless otherwise indicated.

Acknowledgments

My dear wife and best friend Anne Epstein helped me in a multitude of ways, too numerous to all be listed here. This work would simply not have been possible without her. I dedicate this work to our children, Oona and Caius, the new generation of Europeans.

Niilo Kauppi
Herttoniemi, Finland

Introduction

> We are not in business at all; we are in politics. (Former President of the EEC Commission Walter Hallstein, quoted in Swann 1990, vii)

There has been a lot of talk about the European Union's so-called 'democratic deficit', by which is meant its lack of legitimacy in the eyes of its citizens. This book provides a critical analysis of the democratic stalemate in European politics. In contrast to most studies, however, this book argues that the root of the 'democratic deficit' has more to do with the domestic political fields of the Union's member-states and the structure of the evolving European political field than with the relationships between supranational institutions. It analyses the complex ways 'Europe' is integrated into domestic politics and shows how domestic political fields and cultures have prevented deepening integration.

This work innovates in two closely connected ways. First, it introduces a new, sophisticated theory that focuses on Europe both as an object of political struggle between groups and individuals and as a political order whose culture and values these actors reproduce. Building on Pierre Bourdieu's social theory and drawing on thought in anthropology, international relations and political science, it outlines a structural constructivist theory of European integration that contrasts with social constructivism and older approaches such as intergovernmentalism. Second, by recentring the analysis of Europe on the political agents – politicians, civil activists, intellectuals, bureaucrats – involved in its construction, this work investigates, through case studies on France and Finland, how agents struggle with the transformations that European integration has brought about, the weakening of the nation-state and the increasing dominance of supranational decision-making. As the European Union is an evolving political field, studying individuals – a neglected aspect of research – is as important for understanding the Union's functioning as is the study of institutional structures. Finland, a small and new member-state of the European Union, provides a contrastive case to France, a leading, large and long-standing member-state. I argue that Europe is essentially a local phenomenon, embedded in specific national cultures, meaning structures and social settings. As the European Union becomes more structured, imposing political practices and habits on the individuals working in its institutions, individuals also apply to European institutions models of behaviour characteristic of their political culture and of their positions in domestic political fields. In accordance with this theoretical point of view, the current work accounts for meaning structures by combining micro- and macro-levels as well as theory and empirical material.

2   Democracy, social resources and political power in the European Union

The domestic effects of European integration are seldom discussed in the popular press of the member-states. To speak critically about Europe is difficult, partly because one is immediately labelled a 'federalist' or a 'sovereignist'. However, the structuration of a European political field is under way, no doubt about it. This involves the constitution of a common subfield of 25 national political fields, a hybrid sector composed of supranational, national and regional elements. European integration comprises two closely connected processes. First, there is a supranational and national monopolisation of political power by European political and bureaucratic agents and national executive political agents, who form strategic alliances. Second, there is the establishment of shared political institutions, such as the European Parliament, and of networks linking local, regional, national and supranational levels. These processes are accompanied by collective symbolic constructions of Europe by political groups and enterprises. I demonstrate here that in order to understand the concrete effects and political signification of integration it is of heuristic advantage to examine the social practices of all of these various political agents.

In this work, the structuration of the emerging European political field is understood as combining two dimensions: the supranational/national dimension and the executive/legislative dimension. Here we will see that the European political field has become more structured in the sense that its elements are, more than before, dependent on one another. Political agents produce and embody this hierarchical space through their political actions and decisions. The macro-transformations I will study are the shift of emphasis from economic to political integration on the one hand and the fusion of domestic and European fields on the other hand. My aim is not to examine all the 'effects of Europe' but to concentrate on specific political groups (MEPs, women politicians, Commissioners) and on relatively neglected aspects of research such as gender, educational background, political experience and intellectual discourse.

Chapters 1 and 2 deal with theoretical issues of European Union research. In Chapters 3 and 4 I analyse European executive legitimacy: French presidential foreign policy ambitions in a changing Europe; the integration of French politicians and technocrats into the European bureaucracy; and the constitutional changes implemented in Finland and France in 2000, seen partly as responses to increasing European integration. Chapters 5, 6 and 7 deal with European legislative legitimacy: European Parliament election campaigns, MEPs (Members of the European Parliament) as a distinct group; and French intellectuals' endeavours, as representatives of civil society, to take stock of European integration. Throughout, I have chosen to focus on areas which illustrate very different dimensions of the transformations in the French political field: foreign policy, political discourse, political careers and intellectual culture as a part of political culture. For example, in Chapter 7, I examine Pierre

Introduction

Bourdieu's intellectual politics as part of the symbolic structuration of French debates on Europe. Chapters 3 and 7 deal mostly with symbolic structuration, whereas Chapters 4, 5 and 6 examine institutional structuration.

In Chapters 1 and 2, I critique current theories of European integration and elaborate an alternative, structural constructivist theory of European integration. Structural constructivism offers a middle-range approach that combines theory with empirical research. By concentrating on the actions of politicians and political groups, it can reveal some of the qualitative transformations brought about by European integration in terms of political identity and power opportunities. I show how this approach avoids the essentialism of social constructivism and the narrowness of older theories such as intergovernmentalism.

In Chapter 3, I examine transformations in French European policy and France's foreign policy rhetoric. I will show how the requirements of the past influence the qresent and determine the future (the post-imperialist syndrome, or 'PIS', Kortunov 2001). In Chapters 4 and 5, I analyse the integration of French politicians and civil servants into European Union institutions, looking particularly at the characteristics of French MEPs compared to other political groups in French politics, and at the status of the European Parliament in the career patterns of French politicians. The increasing interdependence of the French and European polities has led to significant developments at the centre and the periphery of the French political field. New groups of politicians and civil servants, types of political resources, and posts in the administration and political institutions have come into being. Some of these transformations, occurring mostly at the centre, have received scholarly and journalistic attention. Others, such as the formation of marginal groups, have largely gone unnoticed.

The remaining chapters deal with the domestic influence of European Parliament elections. In Chapter 6, I discuss the European Parliament elections of 1999 from the point of view of the challenges they presented to French and Finnish society and state institutions. More than ever before, 'Europe' as a political issue was present in the election campaigns, splitting the field into pro- and anti-European political parties. The elections mobilised social movements and intellectuals, eager to transmit their messages to the public and integrate their demands into the political system. In Chapter 7, I scrutinise how French intellectuals integrate 'Europe' into their discourses. The case of the late Pierre Bourdieu, a leading intellectual, demonstrates that European Parliament elections provided an occasion for intellectuals to renew their public function and influence the agendas of political parties.

Following the above broad outline of the research, I will now examine some of the theoretical premises of European Union research.

1 Some theoretical premises of European Union research

A major obstacle to an adequate examination of European integration is the definition of political phenomena as requiring either a national or an international relations (IR) approach. The 'theology of realism' preached by some intergovernmentalist political scientists (Hoffmann 1982; Moravcsik 1993, 1998) and neorealists in IR-theory (Waltz 1979) leads to misleading oversimplifications, reinforcing the division between national and supranational. In academe, this institutionalised division has prevented scholars from studying European integration in all its complexity. Country specialists have neglected the supranational dimensions of European polity-building while international relations specialists have not been interested in national processes. Projected into theoretical discourse this opposes intergovernmentalism to supranationalism. This division of labour has hampered the analysis of processes that are fundamentally both national and supranational. According to intergovernmentalists the European Union is essentially formed of states, whereas supranationalists assert that supranational structures determine the nature of European integration. In reality, national and European interests merge, as sometimes vehemently chauvinistic policies have been at the same time fundamentally pro-European.

A closer look at both national and European politics reveals that it is misleading to examine one without examining the other because of their increasing fusion (Mény 1996; Wessels 1997; Rosamond 1999; Chryssochoou 2001). The traces of the dichotomy between national and international politics can be seen in the most knowledgeable studies on French politics. For instance, William Safran's textbook (Safran 1995) hardly studies the internal significance of European Union institutions for French politics. Part of the problem is that the European Union's challenge to political science boils down to the fact that it is a political system that defies categorisation (see Christiansen 1994). This epistemological situation forces many to use the nation-state as an anchor to prevent political science from merging into either international relations or sociology. However, the existence of new power structures in Europe requires revising dominant theoretical categories and concepts, which are still tied to the nation-state. Scholars have to overcome thinking within the confines of the nation-state by pointing out that the borders of, say, the French political field do not stop at French national borders: Paris is in Brussels and Brussels in Paris. The relationship between the emerging European political field and its relatively independent sub-areas, the national political fields, is one of partial and dynamic overlapping.

The emerging, multilevelled European political field forms a *dynamic topography* which is not composed of equilibrium states but rather of a series of transformations. The European Union can be conceptualised as being both a politico-economic *convergence structure* that coordinates through various political instruments (structural funds, the *acquis communautaire*, etc.) and institutional configurations (the European Commission, the Council of Ministers, the European Parliament, etc.) the policies of European central institutions and member states ('European governance'), and a source of *divergent transformations* in national politics (see for instance Bulmer 1983 for Great Britain; Lequesne 1993 for France; and Murto et al. 1996, Raunio and Tiilikainen 2002 for Finland). Most of these studies suggest that joining the European Union is one of the most important if not the most significant event of member-states in their recent political history (see also Nousiainen 1992).

European political integration as the emergence of a relatively autonomous and structured European political field is often confused with the modernisation of national economic, social and political lives. It is a complex process of redefining established institutions and practices and has two main effects. First, political integration translates into a series of transformations inside national and regional politics. This includes changes in political and administrative practices. Second, political integration signifies the constitution of a new sector shared with other national and regional polities. This common European sector or Eurosphere is relatively autonomous, centred on European institutions such as the European Parliament, national political institutions such as the Minister of European Affairs, and local institutions such as the civil servants in charge of relations with Brussels. The first effect of political integration is tied to national decision-makers while the second effect leads to the creation of an extra-territorial political authority based in Brussels. The political fields that form the European Union are thus characterised by a dual power base, national and European, and in the case of federal systems like Germany, even a triple power-structure composed of the regions, the national capital and the European centre.

According to Dusan Sidjanski, politicians involved in European affairs can be grouped into four categories depending on the nature of their activities (Sidjanski 1996). The first group, European political leaders, is composed of professionals of Europe who are 'full-time Europeans' (1996, 282). This group includes Commissioners and civil servants of the European Union, MEPs, justices of the European Court of Justice, members of the Economic and Social Committee, and so on. These individuals form the core group of the Eurosphere. A second group consists of the variety of domestic political agents who deal with European Union affairs on either a full- or part-time basis. These politicians range from national ministers to civil servants having competence in European issues. Sidjanski's third group is more heterogeneous than the first two. It includes representatives of multinational companies stationed in Brussels, lobbyists, lawyers, consultants on European issues, and so on. In the fourth group Sidjanski includes all those individuals who might exercise an influence in national and regional political or economical life on European issues and decision-making.

As a result of the formation of a European political field, political resources in European 'postnational' and 'postabsolutist' polities are being redistributed. A simplified example from the French context will illustrate this general transformation. A small commune is seeking finances to construct a bridge. The local officials find out that the European Union has structural funds reserved for this purpose. They hire somebody who has experience in Brussels. The commune receives an important grant from Brussels to construct the bridge. The EU-liaison person communicates directly with Brussels and also gets into contact with individuals in similar positions in neighbouring towns to elaborate similar projects. Quickly, she or he becomes indispensable to the commune. Thanks to new financial means, this individual has access to new political resources which also transform the rules of the local political struggle. The deputy-mayor might find him- or herself in competition with the new arrival.

These political, economic and administrative officials are found on all levels of national political systems, from the national capital to the smallest commune. They have access to European political resources, to European decision-makers and information sources, and to individuals in homologous positions in other European member-states. These individuals also become the vehicles of a simple ideological message: the future is Europe and there is no alternative to European integration.

The emerging, multilevelled European political field forms an increasingly interdependent but still relatively unstable symbolic and institutional area where the European, the national and the regional meet. In it, individuals generate novel political practices and power structures. In this area of intersection, two political cultures meet. On the one hand, a culture characterised by an attachment to national political symbols and their rituals, to national pasts, memories and a collective imaginary ('the French nation', 'la France profonde, républicaine', etc.). On the other hand, a culture that aspires toward something that does not exist yet, a representation of Europe and its future, or of the revival of a regional past, a dream fuelled by pretension, experimentation and bluff. This unstable area is not peripheral, marginal or secondary, as some have argued (Reif and Schmitt 1980, 115–24). These processes of European integration touch equally central and local political institutions. For instance, when France or any other European Union member-state holds the presidency of the European Union, the French president speaks not only in the name of France but also of Europe. The relationship that unites the current president Jacques Chirac to France symbolised by the French flag are transferred to Europe and to the European flag. Chirac becomes the representative of Europe, a political leader playing a global role on equal footing with leaders such as George Bush and Vladimir Putin. Chirac thus represents not only France, but also Germany, Great Britain and the other European Union member-states. In other terms, we are witnessing in the case of the rotating European Union presidency a symbolic transformation of national representation into supranational representation.

For small member-states like Finland, the presidency of the European Union presents a unique occasion to influence European politics. While Finland held the presidency of the European Union in the second half of 1999, the Finnish Prime Minister Paavo Lipponen and President Martti Ahtisaari played politics on a European level, Lipponen in the enlargement of the European Union to the East (the Baltic states) and Ahtisaari as the European Union's representative in the Kosovo war. In the case of the larger European member-states with a colonial and/or imperial past, the UK, Germany, and France, a struggle for supremacy over the European polity is taking place as they are attempting to impose their point of view on the European Union as a whole by transforming it into a common European interest.

In the domestic political game, 'Europe' has become the new trump card in small and large member-states alike. By appealing to France's leading role in Europe, President Chirac was able to lead France into a publicly legitimate war in Kosovo. By openly criticising the poor level of female representation in French politics compared to other European countries, certain groups have succeeded in legitimising the introduction of parity between men and women in political elections. By severely criticising French economic competitiveness in Europe and pointing to the necessities of globalisation, Prime Minister Lionel Jospin propelled forward the privatisation of French companies. In this way, politicians switch the symbolic context of political action from the local, regional and national levels to the European and even global level. Legitimate users of the 'Europe-card' are politicians integrated into the supranational political level – the presidents, members of governments, regional politicians, MEPs, and others who are institutionally part of European institutions.

While holding office in the European Parliament or in other European institutions, politicians acquire new political habits. Through their make-up, European institutions become constitutive parts of national and regional political lives. I will argue that in a certain way, individual actions insert these values into national and regional political registers in terms of preferences and evaluations. The breeding ground of European values has been topographically restricted to certain political locations, like the European Parliament. The localisation of European values has prevented them from spreading into other sectors of national politics, thus hampering Europeanisation. Furthermore, promotion of European political values has been weak because of the structural and situational constraints political activity in the national political fields imposes on value formation (see Chapter 5).

Transformations as adaptations to a new politico-economic architecture are not limited to high politics. On the contrary, I will demonstrate in this study how politicians and civil servants alike have had to adapt and reinvent themselves in this new political regime. Political habituation does not mean the abstract fusion of disparate elements but rather major transformations at the individual level, a fusion of old and new values that leads to changes in political perceptions and evaluations.

Forms of structuration

In Western Europe, the process of integration of national politics has revolutionised the frames of reference of politicians and civil servants (Milward 1994, 224–317; Goetz 2000; Cole 2001; Cowles et al. 2001; Kerwer and Teutsch 2001). Research instruments, however, are still tied to traditional concepts such as the state and the nation. Theories and instruments are desperately needed that take into account this changed reality and enable us to examine a fundamentally transformed political, economic and social reality.

The process of structuration of the European political field can be understood both as involving processes of convergence and divergence. This implies the institutionalisation of new political and economic values and patterns of behaviour that unite national politics into a structurally looser entity, the European political field. This convergence touches institutions, practices and norms, shaping a common attitudinal role (Nye 1968, 865–74) that provides politicians with a shared mental framework, constituting a rudimentary form of *homo politicus europaeus*. Neoliberalism represents one side of the coin; the reverse side includes a myriad of political transformations. Whole national policy sectors are renovated following Brussels directives. Apart from homogenisation and isomorphic changes, the European political field also functions as a divergence architecture. Because national and regional political cultures differ from one another, structuration processes vary from one context to another. They transform domestic political cleavages in both foreseeable and unforeseeable ways. I will demonstrate that in the French case integration into the European political field has enabled certain political groups to challenge traditional French political values.

European integration is always mediated by individual action. For this reason, the impact of European integration on domestic politics is difficult to assess. Theoretically, three modes of structuration can be separated from one another. *Institutional* structuration refers to modifications in institutional configurations, to use Norbert Elias's term (Elias 1978). Domestic politics are structurally transformed when a country enters the European Union and when individuals operating in this context 'domesticate' or integrate the Union. The European Parliament, the European Union's Ministerial Council and other institutions are the most visible signs of this institutional adaptation. At the same time, new political resources are available to some political groups at this supranational level. A second mode of structuration is processual. By *processual* structuration I mean that domestic policies change as a result of European integration. In some cases, Brussels directives and EMU-criteria directly govern national policies. A third mode of structuration could be called symbolic. By *symbolic* structuration I mean that 'Europe' becomes a symbolic element in the legitimation of political action and in the construction of new political identities. Politicians use 'Europe' as a weapon in internal political struggles. In summary, the domestication of 'Europe' or the process of the formation of a symbolic European field of political action takes a multitude of forms in the different European Union member-states.

Structurally, integration into an evolving European political field is a complex process of adaptation of a European Union member-state's political institutions to the pressures of supranational entities. Leading to functional differentiation of both institutions and elites, it creates in national politics a fused sector tied to European institutions and promotes internal fragmentation through regional autonomy ('neofeudalism'). Through elections to the European Parliament transnational political careers become possible (as the example of Daniel Cohn-Bendit, who was both a former assistant mayor of the German city of Frankfurt am Main and a French MEP, demonstrates). While European integration has promoted elite fusion at the level of European executive politics through institutions such as the European Union's Ministerial Council, it has also led to other qualitative transformations. Elite differentiation has divided national elites into two groups, those who participate in fused European networks and those who are excluded from them. Executive elite fusion has also been accompanied by the immunisation of politics to the economy. By transferring economic and political power to the European Union level, decision-makers have promoted economic reform while sheltering this reform from the disrupting interference of democratic, electoral politics. At the same time, the publics in all EU member-states have been split into pro- and anti-Europeans. Integration has triggered often violent public reactions to economic privatisations and public spending cuts.

Supranational structuration connects to one another traditional forms of political organisations tied to the nation-state and new forms of political authority tied to the European Union. The 'post-absolutist' or 'post-national' state does not yet exist in Europe, however. Following Antonio Gramsci, we could say that we are in an interregnum situation, in which 'a great variety of morbid symptoms appear' (Gramsci 1971, 276). Major developments in the economy and the role of the state have been accompanied with less overt, but equally significant transformations in definitions of political legitimacy and authority structures between citizens and officials.

Europe-wide political structuration takes both overt and more subtle forms. In France, it has led to new legislation emanating from Brussels directives, to new government offices and posts involved in relations with the European Union and the administration of structural funds, to new political elites such as MEPs, to important modifications in the political calendar through an extension of the year for the National Assembly and the addition of new elections to the European Parliament every five years (for details, see Lequesne 1993). Integration has also reinforced the regionalisation of domestic politics and the promotion of autonomous regional languages and cultures, such as Breton, through massive programmes such as the Intereg III (2000–6, approximately €5 billion). The qualitative effects of structuration can be dramatic, as the case of the Finnish constitutional reform demonstrates. Until 1999, the Finnish political system was a semi-presidential one, resembling the French system. Since the end of Urho Kekkonen's presidency in 1981, the renovation of the semi-presidential system had been a burning political issue. Joining the European Union in 1995 presented the political establishment with an opportunity to reform the system (Jyränki 2000; Uimonen 2001). Using European integration and the imperatives of European representation as a motive for reform, the Finnish political class decided to curtail the power of the president and strengthen that of the prime minister. Instead of having as the main representative a president whose power is restricted to foreign and security policies, the prime minister is now the main representative of Finland. This example shows that the integration into a broader political field can directly reinforce and legitimise domestic political reform (see Chapter 4 for details).

The processes of structuration of the European political field have also, in more subtle ways, given a boost to certain domestic political processes in France. For instance, especially the development of various movements for women's rights and the electoral strategies of leading politicians in the Socialist party, have been promoted. As I will show in Chapter 6, they have promoted the feminisation of politics institutionally by offering French women politicians posts in the European Parliament. French politicians in the Council of Europe introduced the idea of parity (*parité*) between men and women into the French political debate. Traditionally, women have been weakly represented in French politics. Comparison of women's representation in France to other European countries in the press fuelled a broad movement that has culminated in laws and regulations concerning gender and political representation. Entering French political culture in the second half of the 1990s, politicians can today back parity as much by idealism as by pragmatism (see Chapter 5 for a fuller analysis).

While European integration empowers certain groups like regional politicians to challenge national authorities by providing them with symbolic and material supports in European institutions, it also paradoxically institutionalises anti-European ideologies on the right and left. It was in the European parliament elections that the extreme right led by Jean-Marie Le Pen got its first electoral success. By openly challenging the European Agenda 2000-programme pushed for by the French minister for environment Dominique Voynet, the regionalist 'hunters' list' *Chasse-Nature-Pêche-Tradition* (CNPT) succeeded in getting several of its candidates elected to the European Parliament in the 1999 elections. The case of the hunters demonstrates that European integration also indirectly connects political elections to civil society. Since 1979 the elections to the European Parliament have presented an occasion for various movements and lists outside the control of political parties to bring their message to the public, thus pressuring parties to modify their political agendas well after the elections. By widening the basis of civic activism, I will show that the European Parliament elections link intellectual politics to democratic politics through the examples of intellectuals such as Bernard-Henri Lévy in 1994 and Pierre Bourdieu in 1999. While the elections gave a voice to those who do not have one, they also reasserted the role of intellectuals in French public debate.

With neoliberalism and anti-globalisation, ideology has become an important weapon in European politics. Integration triggers locally embedded actions based on cultural perceptions of the changes taking place. These actions can be violent, as the actions of French farmers demonstrate. Repeated until it has become a mantra, politicians used 'European cooperation' to legitimise a variety of measures, most often those associated with cutting public spending to fulfil the European Union's EMU-criteria. At the level of national and subnational elites inserted into transnational networks, elite socialisation has developed affinities and a common economic and political outlook. This differentiation of elites and elite culture enables concerted European political and economic action to take place.

Social and economic transformations and the decline of the nation-state have dramatically altered the nature of European politics. Structurally, some sectors of the domestic fields such as the economy are more integrated and more structured, and individuals in these sectors have adapted themselves to the supranational institutionalisation of political careers and values. Historically, new institutions modify policy aims and means. Symbolically, 'Europe' becomes a key element in the construction of new identities and in internal political skirmishes. The locations where European issues are elaborated and the kinds of resources politicians are able to activate, accumulate and transform in these sites determine the forms Europeanisation take in national politics. There does not seem to be any viable alternative to integration into a larger European political field.

Structuration, agency and political order

> We must define precisely what these changes consist of: that is, substitute for an undifferentiated reference to *change* – which is both a general container for all events and the abstract principle of their succession – the analysis of *transformations*. (Foucault 1997, 172)

The main problem any social scientific research dealing with the European Union has to face is that scholars are trying to make sense of a unique historical process by using theories and concepts that were invented to describe wholly other historical contexts and circumstances. Concepts always carry with them previous semantic choices and empirical problems. When scholars reuse concepts in new circumstances, they redefine them. Conceptual change does not only refer to nominal changes but also to changes in the substance of the concept.

Nobody knows for sure to what European construction is going to lead. Political scientists have been busy trying to determine 'the nature of the beast' (Risse-Kappen 1996, 53). They assume that the process of European integration has an essence. However, as there is only movement toward something the telos of which is unknown, what might be needed is a focus on the convergence/divergence processes and the qualitative and quantitative transformations of European integration, not the supposed essence of a beast that keeps transforming itself. Naturalism, essentialism and substantialism prevent scholars from seeing the process-aspect of European construction. A concentration on ontology detracts scholars from more complex studies on the European Union as a dynamic topography, a complex set of transformations without a telos, transformations that are institutionalised to various degrees. Due to an intricate game of affinities and complicities and to synchronisation of various actions involved, the research locus necessary for the understanding of a particular process is not always the nation-state (intergovernmentalism) or the supranational institution (functionalism). Sometimes research might have to examine individuals who occupy specific institutional locations. In the transformational view of European integration, the European Union is a topographical landscape with actors, institutions and values that are embedded in different temporal structures, actualised through situated actions. These temporal structures are tied to, for instance, institutional time, electoral cycles, terms in offices, and – forming the *longue durée* – identities and values. The European political field thus forms a context for political action whose chronotopic – temporal and structural, or diachronic and synchronic – properties radically differ in terms of complexity from those of national political fields. From a politician's point of view, the European Union as the central market of the European political field is a set of institutions and temporalities that transforms the ideational or symbolic and material context of political action tied to national or regional contexts. Transformations are not teleological (Foucault 1997), and they contain elements from concepts such as system change or system substitution. Theoretically speaking, an examination of situated action can reveal – through an analysis of a series of qualitative transformations – the formal aspects of the 'essence' of European integration.

The theory of structural constructivism I propose in this book fuses French structural theories of politics (Bourdieu 1996a; Gaxie 2000) and a 'bottom-up' approach to European integration (Bulmer 1983; Abélès 1992). In this alternative conceptualisation of integration, the shaping of Europe involves low politics most of the time, not high politics. It involves individuals and groups embedded in various institutions and activating capacities in specific situations. Contrary to social constructivist accounts (see for instance Diez 1999, 598–613), this construction of Europe is not only discursive or symbolic but also material. That is, it is realised through innumerable actions such as, in the case of an MEP, for instance, taking the bus to one's office in Brussels, sitting in the cafeteria of the Strasbourg hemicycle chamber with colleagues, discussing issues with lobbyists, composing a report on a specific issue, etc. In order to grasp what the construction of Europe means in practice, the scholar has to go down to the field and see for him- or herself what is happening and what this changing reality means for politicians engaged in a web of activities and discourses. In the end, political transformations involve first and foremost changes in political meaning and value that have a determining impact on the individuals. For instance, the first 'ecoloparade' organised by the European Green parties at the Bastille in Paris in June 1999 took part in the construction of a 'green' Europe through the synchronised activities (marches, games, songs, etc.) of Green social movements from several European member-states, inspiring its participants to imagine new forms of transnational political cooperation (see Chapter 6). The observer has to unite micro- and macro- levels to understand European construction in its complexity.

In contrast to Pierre Bourdieu's structural theory of politics (see for instance Bourdieu 2000), a structural constructivist theory of European integration emphasises the dynamics of political life. Bourdieu's concept of field as a relational entity does not take sufficiently into account individual and situational factors (Kauppi 2000). Relations between individuals can not be reduced to a position in a social space, and political stances to the principle of sociomimesis, according to which social positions and political opinion are homologous and the former has the upper hand over the latter. Individuals do not have common interests only on the basis of homological or structurally equivalent social positions. Often, common experiences draw people together and create a bond that transcends other considerations. Bourdieu's theory also neglects situational factors. A key concept in the analysis of political action is that of *kairos*, or *the opportune moment*. For Stoic philosophers like Cicero (106–43 BC) (see Cicero 1997, 47), an art like politics requires from its practitioner a sense of the occasion. According to this conception of political action, a politician adjusts his anticipations and his actions to modifications in the larger political context. Hazard and chance are essential elements in the politics of the opportune moment and in a structural constructivist theory of European integration.

The idea of *situated action* introduces temporality into the analysis of action. Action is not merely an actualisation of an individual's potentialities, as Bourdieu claims in an Aristotelian fashion, but rather a complex, often conflicting process of actualisation and reaction through improvisation in a specific situation, a fusion of existing and emerging properties. A situation might create through windows of opportunity the possibility for certain actions which are not actualisations of a potential, but rather improvised creations of the moment. It can be difficult to separate one from another. In practice, individuals do not always activate a potential as the situation might require the bracketing of some potentialities. The idea of *dynamic topography* is also central to structural constructivism. It keeps from Bourdieu's theory the idea of social space as a structured entity. But in distinction to Bourdieu, and closer to Max Weber's ideas of spheres of life, it emphasises the role of non-teleological, qualitative transformations and of various temporalities. For an analysis of European integration, Bourdieu's concept of field is too rigid, referring to a relatively closed arena of social activity. Through the idea of dynamic topography as an open structure, the analysis of political action is brought closer to the politician's conception of a concrete situation (Abélès 1992), while the scope of political action is connected to more general cleavages (Lipset and Rokkan 1967) within often dislocated and unevenly developing institutional configurations, which are not totally reducible to the perception individuals have of a situation. The example of the Kohl–Mitterrand–Delors entente is particularly revealing in this context.

With the nomination of Jacques Delors to the presidency of the European Commission in 1995 at the instigation of French President François Mitterrand, the dynamic relationship between Delors, Mitterrand and German Chancellor Helmut Kohl became, in many ways, the main engine of deepening European integration. Mitterrand's close contact with Kohl and Kohl's willingness to let

Mitterrand take the initiative in European affairs made the nomination of Jacques Delors possible. The synchronisation of institutional time (the appointment of a new Commission) and the strategies of major players like Kohl enabled Mitterrand, seeing a window of opportunity, to seize the moment and push forward major integration policies (Olivi 1998). Understanding that Socialism in one country was no longer an option, he realised that Europe presented a political opportunity for Socialism and for France. With this realisation he was on his way to becoming a European statesman. This event was simultaneous with the transformation of a subjective vision based on certain facts and a certain interpretation of reality into an objective state of affairs, to be materialised in institutional configurations and political programmes. This example highlights the role of situational factors in the examination of political action and creative statecraft.

Through the idea of *kairos* or the opportune moment, political action is related to more or less codified, structured situations. Structured situations imply that all political resources cannot be utilised, but rather that some of these resources are bracketed. For instance, in a negotiation where all participants are fluent English-speakers but not native speakers, their native languages are bracketed and the possible advantage their knowledge might bring them is made void. The more a situation is socially structured, the more predictable behaviour will be. The concept of *kairos* enables the scholar to study statecraft while taking into account the structural and temporal constraints imposed by specific political situations (the electoral cycle, for instance) and the interpretations individuals themselves have of them. *Topographical time* is the basis of situated action, the opportune moment being situated at the intersection of temporal and spatial processes. Political action at the opportune moment utilises trends already existing and adds new dimensions to them. For instance, for intellectuals and social movement leaders, European Parliament elections present a window of opportunity for creative political action. I will discuss in this study several examples that illustrate these new possibilities. Before concluding this chapter, I will discuss the relationships between resources and power.

Locations and resources

> The only card game in town is in a town called Brussels and it is a game of poker where we have got to learn the rules and learn them fast. (British trade union leader Ron Todd in 1988, quoted in McIlroy 1995, 313)

According to one observer of French politics, 'It is increasingly difficult to deal with the French polity in isolation from the European regional context' (Safran 1995, 319). For politicians at the turn of the millennium, Europe takes more time than ever before. It fills their political calendar, provides them with new circles and networks, and transforms their global political status. To the question of how much time taking care of European issues concretely takes, former French minister of finance Dominique Strauss-Kahn replied:

> Because of my duties and convictions, a considerable amount of time! Europe in the strict sense of the term – bilateral meetings, the Council of the Ministers of Finance, sessions in Brussels – takes between a third and a quarter of my time. My colleagues and I meet with one another and call one another all the time. So much that we have asked the European Commission to install a video conference system between the eleven ministers of the Euroland. But there is also Europe viewed from the outside. When I go to the G7-meetings, to Japan or the IMF, I do not go there only for France, but for France and Europe. When I attend the meeting of the Council of ministers of the franc zone in Dakar, I represent Europe because the CFA franc is attached to the euro. All in all, Europe in the wide sense of the term takes perhaps half of my time. My predecessors have contributed to the creation of the euro. But they have not experienced its consequences in terms of management and timetable. My colleagues and I have often the feeling of living through something radically new. (Fréchet and Gilson 1999, 35)

For politicians like Dominique Strauss-Kahn, integration into the evolving European political field – with its institutions and procedures – presents new fora for the accumulation of a distinct type of political resource. On a macropolitical level, European institutions and practices constitute an incrementally expanding alternative market for political resources in the various European national political fields that compose it. Europeanised national politics transcends traditional boundaries to incorporate institutions that are situated on foreign soil but that are integral parts of the national systems of political mandate and reward. With this structural opportunity for creative statecraft the set of codified and legitimate political resources is transformed simultaneously with the formation of groups of politicians professionally and psychologically tied to the process of European unification. MEP Sir James Goldsmith's running for Parliament in Great Britain in 1995 demonstrated how an extra-territorial institution, the European Parliament, could be used as a power base for domestic political action. National boundaries were partly overcome through innovative political action.

For top-level politicians in European Union member-states, the making of a European polity with its own resources and networks signifies that they can use supranational resources in the domestic political game and, depending on the political weight of their member-state, domestic resources in the supranational political game. For instance, specific national political resources such as those linked to labour unions that are available to Socialist and Communist politicians have been used by these politicians to 'modernise' trade unionism by appealing to the imperatives of European integration and globalisation. As more and more European firms do business abroad, relations with national political decision-makers give way to relations with bureaucrats in Brussels. Following the logic of re-territorialisation of political decision making from the national to the supranational level, numerous areas such as scientific research and agriculture have been relocated from national to European level, providing politicians and national civil servants with new career opportunities. In specific contexts such as the European Commission, individuals from some of the member-states have more political weight than others and, inevitably, the larger member-states and those that have been in the Union the longest will be favoured in the European political market. Small member-states may expect to play a significant role only in specific, strategic policy areas such as telecommunication policies for member-states like Finland and Sweden. Symptomatic of these authority structures was French Prime Minister Lionel Jospin's comment after the Danish people delivered a 'no' in a referendum on the euro: 'I have a lot of respect for this country, but its size for the European economy is not major' (quoted in Marsden and James 2000).

In this book I will use the concept 'political resources' to signify the main object and means of struggle in politics. They consist of knowledge, reputation, competence and prestige (Gaxie and Offerlé 1985, 105–38; Bourdieu 1989, 2000). 'Legitimacy', 'power' and 'status' (Weber 1978) are closely related terms. The concept of political resources includes elements such as official and unofficial status in political parties or other legitimate political institutions (such as labour unions and other pressure groups in national and local political institutions such as parliaments, regional councils, Senates, and so on); in unofficial circles created around ambitious politicians (for instance, the *rocardiens* grouped around the Socialist politician Michel Rocard) and pressure groups (for instance, the *Confédération Générale du travail*, CGT). To varying degrees, politicians can use all these institutions as political resources. Formally, in French politics the most important institutional sources of political power are the presidency, the government and the two houses of the Parliament, in this order (Lavroff 1979) (following the constitutional changes relative to the presidency in 2000, see Chapter 4).

Formally speaking, the main source of political power in all democratic countries is the democratic process and its result, a political mandate. Other assets, such as social connections (networks), economic means (money and other financial resources) and education (diplomas), complement the democratic process to varying degrees and depending on the political context. Politicians aim to transform these resources into votes, and then retransform this acquired political legitimacy into other resources. In contrast to this legislative source, in France executive legitimacy stemming from membership in specific social groups overrides legislative legitimacy (Mény 1996). Social connections are crucial in view of access to the most important decision-making centre, the entourage of the President of the Republic, and other equivalent milieus, like the cabinets of the prime minister and other ministers. This executive fast-track leads from an adviser's post in a minister's cabinet to one in the president's cabinet and eventually to a minister's portfolio. It provides a parallel track to the electoral avenue that is regulated by electoral cycles and the posts linked to elections, municipal and regional councillors, mayors, deputies, senators and MEPs. Membership in prestigious clubs (for instance, *Club de l'Horloge* or *Club du polo de Paris*) and family relations are examples of social connections (on the influence of these on the beginnings of Jean Monnet's career, see Duchêne 1994, 32–5). These provide the ambitious individual with certain psycho-social characteristics necessary for competent interaction with peers. The most important of these psycho-social characteristics is trust.

Money and other financial means are quite flexible resources. In certain specific time frames such as during the campaigns to the European Parliament, candidates can try to transform money into electoral success through increased media visibility, for instance. The French European Parliament elections of 1994, in which millionaires like the late Sir James Goldsmith (candidate on the anti-Maastricht list *L'autre Europe* led by Philippe de Villiers) used their private funds to finance their campaigns, demonstrate this possibility. In France, education is especially important for access to the political elite, with institutions such as the *École nationale d'administration* (ENA) and the *École polytechnique* having a quasi-monopoly in the training of top politicians and executives (see Birnbaum et al. 1978; Birnbaum 1985). This specific type of contextually defined educational excellence enables certain individuals to accumulate additional social and cultural resources, provided situational barriers and unexpected events are overcome. Through the system of *pantouflage*, that is, from a transfer of civil servants from the relatively poorly paid public sector to the more lucrative private domain, politicians can transform educational resources into financial means.

With European integration and the adoption of the euro, we are witnessing a major political regime transformation from one based on national political resources to one based on a combination of national and supranational political resources. What do European political resources consist of? They are socially constructed in relation to the European Union and its institutions: they stem from the holding of positions in various European Union institutions; from knowledge of Union affairs and issues in other European member-states; from access to information channels relative to European decision-making, for instance to powerful, European business organisations (e.g., the European Employers Organisation, UNICE), labour unions (e.g., the European Trade Union Confederation, ETUC) and other sectoral organisations (see Streeck and Schmitter 1991, 133–46; Sidjanski 1992, 341); and from personal relationships with deputies and Commissioners from other member-states, and with European bureaucrats and other top officials. As a rule, executive politicians from large European Union member-states such as France and Germany, which form the core group of the evolving European political field, have more of these resources than do politicians from smaller member-states like Finland.

A differentiation of European political resources into an executive, hegemonic type, and a weaker, legislative type, has taken place. European political resources evolve in relation to specific networks, sites of power and prestige that are monopolised by certain social groups occupying certain positions. As a consequence of this complex re-territorialisation process, positions have been created at the intersection of the French administration and politics. The most visible of these include a French ambassador and permanent representative to Brussels, a deputy minister in charge of European affairs, various specialists in ministerial cabinets and ministries, and an inter-ministerial committee that serves as a national coordinating body (*Service général de coordination interministériel*, SGCI) (Safran 1995, 320; see also Lequesne 1993, Middlemas 1995, 294). European integration has also affected the work and routines of French public and private life at all levels, high and low. Conversion to Europe has led to the revival of old, but updated ambitions. The aroma of Europe has stimulated political ambition, such as that of becoming the President of Europe, a dream long harboured by the former French President Valéry Giscard d'Estaing, currently president of the European constitutional convention. Likewise, some members of the most powerful group of Euro-politicians, the Commissioners, are eager to play a global political role, with or without France, a role which has not been easily accepted by French national political leaders (for Delors's case, see Ross 1995).

The European hegemonic type of political resources, European executive political resources, is institutionally linked to state executives, the national and European administrations, and the Commission. It is dependent on EU policies and practices, on the political and social practices that regulate the distribution of structural funds, decision-making in European institutions, the forging of a common defence policies, the creation of relations with countries that are not members of the European Union, the rules distributing votes to member-states in the Council of Ministers and to political parties in the European Parliament, and so on. Tied to the structuration of the European political field, to neoliberal economic doctrine, and to the marriage of big politics and big business, this hegemonic techno-economic type of political resources dominates over weaker types of political resources, the legislative type of political resources as well as those political resources tied for instance to national grass-roots movements unconnected to European supranational networks.

National political fields can be subdivided into the central political market and marginal markets, sites of high political resources versus sites of low political resources, high social codification versus low social codification, and so on (see Gaxie 2000). In this conceptualisation, the central political market is characterised by important political resources, relatively strict codification of practices and controlled resource transformation strategies. Thus, the fact that the social composition of the marginal sectors of national political fields, including European Union institutions such as the European Parliament, differs in important ways from that of the central political market, is due most of all to the characteristics of national politics and the structuration of a European political field takes in it. A low level of codification enables politicians to improvise and recruit a relatively heterogeneous group of candidates for the elections. As political practices are not thoroughly institutionalised, a certain looseness in the rules that govern resource transformation can be detected. For instance, the use of economic means for political purposes might be more tightly regulated in the central political market than in the marginal market in which European Parliament elections are located. In fact, I will show that because they are situated at the margins of national political fields, some European institutions provide politicians with the possibility to create alternative political loyalties and networks. Whole groups of politicians are given the opportunity to bypass, to a certain extent, the national central political market, and get connected to European networks.

It goes without saying that the means and ways that can legitimately be used to accumulate political power are themselves the subject of controversy. But this relative instability differs depending on the sector examined, as I pointed out above. Areas of struggle coexist with areas of agreement. For instance, politicians constantly argue over the meaning and political value of 'Europe', as well as over its legitimate political uses. Because of these struggles over definitions and boundaries, symbolic shifts of legitimacy occur. For instance, the fact that the European Parliament has become more powerful transforms the relationships of the parliament to other Union institutions and to national political institutions. A modification in the relationship between national and European institutions can incite national politicians to re-evaluate their opinions of these institutions, and perhaps to see opportunities there where they previously saw only restrictions. This transformation is reminiscent of the famous butterfly effect: minute changes in a remote corner of the earth can have significant effects on the opposite side of the globe. Obviously, accounting for all these transformations is not possible in the context of this study.

In contrast to some theories of national politics that concentrate on institutional settings (for instance Suleiman 1978, 9–10), structural constructivism examines both social characteristics and institutional status. Political power is best examined by connecting these two variables to the degree of structuration of the area studied. This degree of structuration will determine whether social characteristics, previous political experience and other 'personal' qualifications will be more important than formal position in an institution in explaining political strategies and behaviour. For instance, because of the increasing political role of the Commission, offices in this institution have become, as a result of nearly five decades of political and economic integration, increasingly structural parts of the national political fields of the member-states. More controlled, more structured, they have requirements of their own, imposed on newcomers.

Conclusion

Scholars agree that the European Union is a unique political formation. However, in its study most commit themselves to outdated theories and concepts still tied to the nation-state. Drawing on analytical tools developed by the late Pierre Bourdieu, I elaborate a structural constructivist theory of European integration. The European Union is seen as constituting a more and more homogeneous, multipolar and multilevelled political field with its own dividing lines and legitimate resources.

In the following chapter, I will contrasts structural constructivism to older theories of European integration, including those of functionalism, neofunctionalism, intergovernmentalism, as well as newer theories, the multigovernance model and social constructivism. The main advantage of the structural constructivist model will be seen in the fact that it sides neither with state-centric nor Commission-centric approaches. It conceptualises the European Union as a field of forces, where actors endowed with various resources struggle to impose on the others their definitions of legitimacy and value. In this scenario, the values embodied in European institutions are objectified forms of resources that some groups have successfully transformed into general values (such as the *acquis communautaire*). This struggle for dominance is the focus of the structural constructivist approach to European integration.

2 A structural constructivist theory of politics and of European integration

In this chapter, I explore in detail structural constructivism as a theory of European integration. By structural constructivism I refer to a mostly French research tradition that develops some of Pierre Bourdieu's theoretical tools (Bourdieu 1989, 14–25; Ansart 1990; Katshanov and Shmatko 1996, 90–104; Kauppi 1996, 53–68, 2000). Bourdieu's structural constructivist theory of politics offers powerful instruments for a critical analysis of political power. In European studies, the theory of social constructivism has over recent years provided an alternative to traditional approaches such as intergovernmentalism and neofunctionalism. Structural constructivism remedies some of the weaknesses of most versions of social constructivism, such as their diffuse conception of power and ideational notion of culture. Moving beyond this, a developed structural constructivist approach examines the European Union as a multilevelled and polycentric evolving political field.

Pierre Bourdieu never himself studied the European Union, which was for him politically and morally condemnable in its current, neoliberal form (Bourdieu 1998a). Until recently, the growing secondary literature on his work has largely neglected his theory of politics. However, several scholars have adapted some of Bourdieu's analytical tools to the study of political phenomena (Gaxie 1973, 1978, 2000; Gaxie and Offerlé 1985; Muel-Dreyfus 1996) and, more recently, of the European Union (Kauppi 1997, 60–3; Mangenot 1998, 7–32; Georgakakis 2002; Beauvallet 2003). In what follows, I will first review, very briefly, my critical interpretation of Bourdieu's structural constructivist political theory through a discussion of his analysis of domination and the political field, contrasting these with other theories, especially Max Weber's. In the second part, I will present some elements for a structural constructivist approach to European integration.

Bourdieu's structural constructivist theory of politics offers a powerful vision of society and new instruments for the study of domination and electoral politics. Drawing mostly on Max Weber and Karl Marx, but also on Émile Durkheim and Robert Michels, Bourdieu elaborated a complex but pessimistic and disenchanted view of politics. Indeed, towards the end of his life, he became a prominent political figure in the anti-globalisation struggle. Bourdieu's theory of politics can be divided into three components: a general analysis of the social aspects of the political (*le politique*) and domination, a more specific analysis of politics (*la politique*), and the political practice that he developed at the end of his career.[1] The first component elaborates chiefly on Weber's sociology of domination and its analysis of the political. In Bourdieu's framework, which is clearly also inspired by Marx, the struggle for domination takes place between the dominant and the dominated. The second component restricts political action to a specific location, the political field. Here, in contrast to the first component, and following Weber's phenomenological idea of life spheres, Bourdieu sees politics as forming an area of activity that can be separated from other areas of activity such as the economy, religion, education and culture. For Bourdieu, the division of society into social classes forms the explanatory basis for the analysis of political activity, and the world of political representation is one site of the struggle between the dominant and the dominated.

Domination

> To conferre all their power and strength upon one Man, or upon one Assembly of men, that may reduce all their Wills, by plurality of voices, unto one Will ... this done, the Multitude so united in one Person, is called a COMMON-WEALTH, in latine CIVITAS. (Hobbes 1991, 120)

In Bourdieu's mind, the right that citizens have to formulate political opinions and propound political judgements is the fundamental characteristic of any democratic regime. In theory, democracy is composed of citizens who, with certain age limits, are all equal. However, as Bourdieu demonstrates in his numerous studies on political opinion (for instance Bourdieu 1984, 397–465), the ability to produce a political opinion and to emit a political judgement is unequally distributed socially. The technical competence that has to do with political judgement is actually a social competence. This ability varies with educational qualifications and age, among other factors. Those endowed with cultural and economic resources will also be more likely to make political judgements. As in other areas of activity, in politics a concentration of the objectified or embodied instruments of production of political opinions can be observed. In this sense, Western democracies are already selective democracies, as only part of the population has the symbolic means to produce a political opinion, to access the order of political discourse, and thus to partake fully in political culture.

Not every answer to a question considered political is necessarily the product of a political judgement. Bourdieu differentiates three modes of production of opinion (Bourdieu 1984, 417–18). The first depends on *class ethos*, which enables the opinion provider to formulate coherent, common-sense answers that follow the logic of everyday existence. Political principles, 'slant' or *logos* provide the grounding for the second mode of production of political opinion.

Both first and second modes are amenable to logical control and reflexive scrutiny. A third mode of production of political opinion consists of *delegation* of the formulation of political opinions to an organisation providing a political line, such as a party, trade union or other such political organisation. This delegation can be based on either the first or the second mode of production of opinion.

What differentiates the first mode of production from the second and the third is that in the case of class ethos the principles of production of political judgement are implicit. The relationship between class and opinion is direct and unconscious. In Bourdieu's mind this is very problematic as 'dispositions without consciousness are self-opaque and always exposed to seduction by false recognitions' (Bourdieu 1984, 420). In contrast, the relationship between social class and political opinion is indirect in the second and third modes, mediated by the logos of either a specific political axiomatics or a political organisation.

Bourdieu provides a complementary division in the analysis of political opinion, with 'production by proxy' opposed to 'first-person production'. He designates as production by proxy the delegation to a party or other political organisation that represents the individual of the power to produce political opinions. By first-person production Bourdieu means that individuals use their own resources to formulate political opinions.

As the ability to formulate political opinions is unequally distributed, those with more educational resources are more likely to be able to formulate them than those who have none. In Bourdieu's words, 'The probability of producing a political response to a politically constituted question rises as one moves up the social hierarchy (and the hierarchy of incomes and qualifications)' (Bourdieu 1984, 427). Bourdieu also analyses the *mechanisms* that influence the ability to produce an answer to a 'political question' (Bourdieu 1977, 55–89). Variations in this ability depend less on technical expertise or on knowledge of politics than on the social competence that translates into the feeling of having the right to have a political opinion (Champagne 1991). In other words, the ability to imagine the political is as unequally distributed as political competence.

Bourdieu is interested in the role played by faith and trust in political judgement, especially in the case of production by proxy. An element of implicit faith is inscribed in the logic of political choice. Selecting representatives involves choosing not only among programmes and ideas, but also among personalities. The first element of uncertainty concerns the object of judgement: is it a person or is it a set of ideas? Because a person is endowed with a certain habitus, he or she embodies certain ideas that might not be expressed at the moment of choosing the representative. These inexpressed ideas and opinions exist in an implicit mode. On the one hand, the representative expresses the already formulated ideas of his or her electors, and, on the other hand, he or she follows his or her own 'internal programme – or the specific interests associated with his position in the field of ideological production' (Bourdieu 1984, 424). In some cases, there is a high level of correspondence between speech and spokesperson. However, even in these cases usurpation is possible, as the representative might bring into existence opinions that were not previously expressed and thus were not known by those providing the mandate at the moment they made their choice.

In surveys, the least competent persons in matters of political opinion must choose between answers that take on their meaning in relation to a political issue, that is, to a political position in the field of ideological or symbolic production. Because these individuals can produce a 'yes' or 'no' answer to a question but cannot necessarily grasp the political meaning of the question asked, those asking the questions can impose on them a political position. In this way, 'the respondents are dispossessed of the meaning of their response' (Bourdieu 1984, 428), a response which is totally alien to their own opinion but which is nevertheless presented as being their opinion. These least competent persons either then respond to an alien question or answer the question as they understand it, retranslating it into their own language. Thus, '"rationalization of budgetary options" becomes "not wasting money"' (Bourdieu 1984, 428). Through this mechanism, the respondent resorts to his or her class ethos and its unconscious presuppositions. Bourdieu underlines the conservative nature of these predispositions, tied to the world by practical logic. The task of formulating revolutionary political stances is left to political organisations.

The field of ideological production is the realm of professional politicians, an area from which the laymen are excluded. It is in this realm that political problems, programmes and ready-made solutions are produced. This production of political opinion and judgement attempts to achieve collective mobilisation around common problems, to universalise certain particular interests by making their particular condition appear universal. However, part of the problem of the translation of the implicit into the explicit is that there is a radical discontinuity between condition and discourse, between ethos and logos. That is, the unconscious character of practical logic, its inscription in bodily hexis – in everyday schemes of perception and appreciation and in the implicit political underpinnings of class habitus – do not necessarily translate into definite political stances or opinions understood as positions in the field of ideological or symbolic production. It is precisely because of the indeterminacy of the relationship between ethos and logos that professional political agents of all kinds – politicians, journalists, publicists, etc. – play such a key role in the production of political opinion, shaping the world of the politically imaginable and the structures and dividing lines of the field of ideological production.

Bourdieu's theory of electoral and democratic politics concentrates on the analysis of political representation and symbolic political struggles. Following

Thomas Aquinas, Bourdieu discusses the delegation of political power by the people to a representative as a form of alienation (Bourdieu 2000, 101). The people alienate their original sovereignty to a plenipotentiary representative, a party or an individual. An isolated individual cannot make himself heard in politics unless he or she transforms this isolated voice into a group voice. But this means he or she must dispossess him- or herself of a voice in order to escape total political dispossession. In a landmark study *Delegation and Political Fetishism*, Bourdieu analysed the power of delegation as a purely political power that enables a group to form by delegating power to a representative (Bourdieu 1981b, 49–55; 1991, 203–19). In very Durkheimian fashion, the process of delegation becomes a case of social magic in which a person such as a minister, a priest or a deputy is identified with a group of people: the workers, the nation, believers, etc. The group no longer exists as a collection of individuals but rather, through this representative, as a social agent. In this case, delegation signifies alienation implicitly consented to by those represented, and dissimulated usurpation by the representative. As Robert Michels put it, 'le parti, c'est moi' (Michels 1962, 220). Bourdieu reveals the double process of recognition and misrecognition inscribed in political delegation: 'A symbolic power is a power which presupposes recognition, that is, misrecognition of the violence that is exercised through it' (Bourdieu 1991, 209).

The representative exists in a metonymical relationship with the group. He or she is a member of the group, that is, a part of it, but at the same time he or she stands for the group as a whole, is a sign of the group. The representative represents the group and speaks in its name (Bourdieu 1981b, 50), the relationship between representative and represented being similar to that between signifier and signified. But at the same time, those represented have a *fides implicita* in the representative. He or she is given a blank cheque. Bourdieu seems to say that this separation of rulers and ruled means that democracy is impossible. The paradox of the monopolisation of collective truth is for Bourdieu the principle of all symbolic imposition: a person speaks in the name of the group and manipulates the group in its own name (Bourdieu 1981b, 52) and thus the organisation quickly supplants the group. 'People are there and speak. Then comes the party official, and people come less often. And then there is an organisation, which starts to develop a specific competence, a language all of its own' (Bourdieu 1981b, 52).

In his discussion of how groups function, Bourdieu sketches two approaches to the problem of political opinion and competence. The first type centres on markets, votes and polls. In such approaches, individuals are demobilised and groups are reduced to aggregates (Bourdieu 2000, 85). In the case of individual speech or of *voice*, to use Albert Hirschman's term (Hirschman 1970), the mode of aggregation is statistical or mechanical. It is independent of the individuals and the group does not exist politically, that is, as a political entity. Bourdieu contrasts this conception, which he calls liberal (Bourdieu 2000, 82), with Émile Durkheim's corporatist conception of political opinion. According to Durkheim (1950, 138) – and before him Jean-Jacques Rousseau – individual votes would ideally be animated by a collective spirit. They would express the community's opinion, will, and constitute a relatively permanent and coherent group. The Elementary Electoral College should be not a collection of isolated individuals but rather a permanent and integrated group, a body with a spirit animated by tacit accord founded on complicity. For Bourdieu, this corporatist philosophy is the implicit philosophy of 'true' electoral democracy (Bourdieu 2000, 83).

Bourdieu analyses political action as consisting mostly or even exclusively of symbolic action: speeches, writings and other symbolic interventions. A key concept in Bourdieu's sociology of domination is that of symbolic violence, the imposition of a cultural code. Here he is not referring to symbolic systems *à la* Durkheim. Symbolic power does not stem from the illocutionary force of speech, as it does for Austin or Searle. Rather, words have an effect when they confirm or transform the vision people have of the world. Behind the words is belief in the person who utters them and in the legitimacy of the words being uttered. 'Who is speaking?' is the first question that should be asked when the legitimacy of a political message is being evaluated. Symbols make visible and make invisible. They reveal certain aspects of reality while hiding others. For instance, the working class does not exist as a physical entity, it is a symbolic construction that has become real because it has become an accepted part of political reality. The same goes for the state and most concepts that form part of political reality. These entities exist to the extent that representatives feel authorised to speak in their name, thus giving them real political force.

Symbolic violence is the basic mechanism by which domination is unconsciously reproduced by the dominated. In Bourdieu's theory, the dominated have to participate in the domination that is exerted on them, otherwise it would not be legitimate. Reproduction of domination takes place with the consent of those dominated. Symbolic violence is transmitted in language and in social practices, and can be found in all human interaction. It is everywhere. Theoretically, at least, it can be contrasted with actions performed voluntarily. In practice, however, it is difficult to separate the two. The concept of symbolic violence can also be contrasted with that of physical violence, which is the monopoly of the state. In contrast to Michel Foucault's work (Foucault 1977), Bourdieu rarely talks about physical violence and mastery over bodies (Bon and Schemeil 1980, 1203), though the public control of this kind of violence is a key feature of state formation. Instead, Bourdieu emphasises the symbolic aspects of domination and the symbolic violence exercised by the schooling system, art, law and culture more generally.

In Bourdieu's vision, political action means acting on the social world, often by attempting to break with the world as a natural entity. Radical political action invokes a radical epistemology (Bachelard 1983) that questions the world as it is usually interpreted. For Bourdieu, the object of politics *par excellence* is knowledge of the social world and the struggle for the legitimate definition of reality. In the political arena, the value of an idea depends less on its truth value than on its power to mobilise. Bourdieu states, following nineteenth-century French social philosopher Alfred Fouillée (Fouillée 1893), but without ever citing him, that in politics ideas are power-ideas (*idées-forces*) (Bourdieu 2000). Power-ideas like 'liberty' or 'equality' cannot be proven true or false. The only way for opponents to refute them is to oppose to them some alternative power-ideas. The political weight of power-ideas will depend on their capacity to mobilise, or to universalise, which is the precondition for mobilisation. In politics, 'saying is doing' only to the extent that a political agent is capable of guaranteeing that the group will carry out the actions the agent suggests. Only then will political agents consider a political statement to be equivalent to an act. But the truthfulness of power-ideas is not verifiable or falsifiable when the ideas are expressed. Only if a statement such as 'I will win the elections to the presidency' is realised in the future, will it be considered true and politically effective.

Bourdieu's analysis of political opinion, delegation and the symbolic aspects of politics reduce politics to a struggle for domination. However, this conflict model is constructed on a harmony model of the social characteristics (class, habitus) of the agents involved in the struggle and their structural positions in various fields. The social field functions as the base structure of politics, the political game being the superstructure. In this vision, politics is about fetishism and the world of appearances (see also Derrida 1993). The real game is 'backstage' in the social field, connected to the political field by any number of homologies or structural equivalences. In the social field, as in any field of social activity, social class is the ultimate determinant of success or failure for any individual. Instead of the Marxist dichotomy of the economic versus the cultural, one finds in Bourdieu's theory of politics the dichotomy of the social versus the symbolic or the political.

Although some might say that modern Western states keep a monopoly over physical violence through the army and the police, it is an exaggeration to say that the state holds the monopoly over symbolic violence. This is because while physical violence can be monopolised and its existence empirically verified, the same cannot be said of symbolic violence (Addi 2001, 950–4). The power over bodies is of a different nature than the power over minds, which cannot be dominated by just one institution. Families, religions, companies, the media, and various kinds of associations and organisations compete with the state and other public institutions for control of this kind.

The political field

> There are general laws of fields: fields as different as the field of politics, the field of philosophy or the field of religion have invariant laws of functioning. (That is why the project of a general theory is not unreasonable and why, even now, we can use what we learn about the functioning of each particular field to question and interpret other fields.) (Bourdieu 1993, 72)

It is perhaps in Bourdieu's concept of the political field that his debt to Max Weber is the clearest, as he acknowledges himself: '[Max Weber was] the scholar who came the closest to the notion of 'field', yet at the same time never reached it' (Bourdieu 1996a, 7). Following Max Weber in his *Zwischenbetrachtung* (Weber 1922, 542; Gerth and Mills 1991, 323–62), Bourdieu analyses politics like any other area of social activity such as the economy, religion or education (Bourdieu 1971a, 3-21; 1971b, 295–334). Political capital is symbolic capital in the field of politics, a type of capital that the agents involved in this field compete for. The political field has its own, autonomous logic, a formal binary logic that is substantiated by the historical development of political ideas, ideologies and practices. Agents at the autonomous pole of the political field possess the most legitimate type of political capital, whereas agents at the heteronomous pole of the political field possess alternative types of political capital. The dominant have a lot of capital, the dominated relatively little. Through a process of political mimesis, agents' political stances and political strategies follow their positions in the political field. According to Bourdieu, 'It is the structure of the political field, that is, the objective relation to the occupants of other positions, and the relation to the competing stances they offer which, just as much as any direct relation to those they represent, determines the stances they take, i.e. the supply of political products' (Bourdieu 1991).

In contrast to Weber's social spheres (Weber 1922, 542), Bourdieu's concept of the field is structural and relational. In his political theory, he conceptualises politics topologically. The political field constitutes a space that is structured such that the value of each constituent element is formed through the network of relationships this element entertains with the other elements in the field. Following Saussurean precepts, value is relational and not substantial. In theory, then, the relative value of an element is determined by this set of relationships and not by any external factors, such as international politics or the state of the economy in the case of the political field. For this reason, distinction does not imply a search for distinction, as in Torstein Veblen's theory of the leisure class. An existing element is always distinctive, that is distinguishable in theory and practice from other elements in a structure. If it was not, it would not exist. For this reason, intentionality is not an issue in Bourdieu's field theory, or in his theory of the political field.

Like any field, the political field is subject to some general principles. The most important of these *modi operandi* is the field's organisation around two opposite poles: the protagonists of change and the apostles of law and order, the progressives and the conservatives, the heterodox and the orthodox. This binary logic not only structures political parties and ideologies; it permeates the political field as a whole, from political parties and other political organisations between the progressive and conservative wings, all the way down to the habitus of an individual who might have evolved from a radical youth into a conservative party official. The tension between order and change is present in the activities of revolutionary movements at all times: for instance, in the hesitations of their leaders about using violence against their own supporters in order to effectively combat state authorities. As the political field becomes more autonomous, these struggles become institutionalised, eventually forming part of the objectified and materialised social unconscious. Each political organisation and the field as a whole develop their own esoteric cultures that are alien to outsiders.

The main resources in the political field are political capital (as the specific resource of the political field), economic capital and cultural capital (Gaxie 1973; Caro 1980, 171–97). 'Political capital is a form of symbolic capital, credit founded on credence or belief and recognition or, more precisely, on the innumerable operations of credit by which agents confer on a person (or on an object) the very powers that they recognize in him (or it)' (Bourdieu 1991, 192). Individuals are distributed throughout the field first according to the overall volume of capital they possess and, secondly, following the composition of their capital (Bourdieu 1991, 231). Those who succeed in accumulating the most political capital will be the dominant, while those who have the least capital will be the dominated (Bourdieu 1984, 451–3). The position of an individual in this structure determines his or her forms of capital and discourses. The structure is also a set of power relationships between individuals and groups in the political field. Moving beyond Saussure and Lévi-Strauss (who developed the dominant social scientific interpretation of Saussure's theory), Bourdieu innovates by adding power to structures. Relationships are not only linguistic or symbolic but also social, involving power relations.

Like rational choice theorists, Bourdieu emphasises that agents maximise utility. He assumes goal-oriented behaviour that is directed toward the accumulation of status and power in the field. But Bourdieu's approach is more flexible. Utility is field-specific, that is historically and socially constituted, and socially defined. Agents can be individuals, groups, institutions, firms, and so on. Not all agents succeed in accumulating status. Some resign themselves to subordinate status. Further, an agent's self-interest also serves the general interest because it reinforces the legitimacy of the field's values. In distinction to economic rationality, individuals often commit themselves to values, such as academic excellence, that can lead, for instance, to reduced living standards. Yet another difference between rational choice and Bourdieu's field-theory is that in the latter, individuals are not necessarily consciously choosing between different alternatives. Rather, guided by their habitus in their actions, they just know what the right thing to do (or not to do) is.

In a way, Bourdieu's logical framework for explaining the rationale of actions in a field shares some of the features with Simon's concept of bounded rationality (Simon 1982). Individuals do not have complete information and they also have limitations of perception. In the framework provided by Bourdieu's theory these limitations of perception can be attributed to three factors: the characteristics of fields, of positions and of socio-cultural factors. In a field, certain aspects of reality are considered less important and are for that reason neglected. In some cases, their neglect might be a condition of possibility of the field as a whole, its 'illusio'. For instance, the rejection of worldly values can be considered as being a condition for the existence of the religious field. Limitations might also be due to an agent's position in a field. The agents and groups occupying the dominant positions in a field might not see the effects of their actions on the dominated agents, for instance. Limitations might finally be linked to what Simon calls subjective aspects. In a structural constructivist framework, these could be called factors having to do with upbringing, class or more broadly habitus.

In his text 'Champ politique, champ des sciences sociales, champ journalistique' (1996a), Bourdieu discussed the political field as a microcosm of the social macrocosm. Like other areas of social activity it has its dominant and dominated, its 'rich' and 'poor', its right and left. As in other areas of social activity, the more autonomous a field is, the more closed off it is from the outside world. In a relatively autonomous political field, the position of an individual will correlate with his or her political stances. Political agents attempt to monopolise the legitimate means of manipulating the social world (Bourdieu 1981a, 13). They compete with journalists and social scientists in the struggle for the 'monopoly of legitimate symbolic violence' (Bourdieu 1981a, 19), a phrase borrowed from Weber's discussion of the priesthood having the monopoly over the legitimate manipulation of the means of salvation and the state's monopoly over legitimate violence (Weber 1966, 27–8).

The political field is 'understood both as a field of forces and as a field of struggles aimed at transforming the relation of forces which confers on this field its structure at a given moment' (Bourdieu 1981a, 3; 1991, 171). It is composed of producers who have monopolised the production of political goods offered on the political marketplace. Ordinary citizens are reduced to the role of consumers. The political stances of the moment, as seen, for instance, in electoral outcomes, are the result of an encounter between supply and demand. Both legitimate supply and legitimate demand are historically formed through social struggles between different groups to define them. Political supply consists of political goods offered by political enterprises, parties, trade unions, political clubs, and so on. These goods can be either symbolic, consisting of ideas and programmes, or material, such as posts in the party hierarchy. The same applies to demand, which has been collectively and historically conditioned to take certain forms. Citizens have to choose among different types of political goods, problems, programmes, analysis, concepts, events, and so on. Formally, consumers have equal access to political goods. In practice, however, social factors such as education and wealth limit access. Those who do have access to these resources become knowledgeable consumers, while those who lack these resources have no alternatives, and abstain in elections or rely totally on their political representatives.

The influence of Weber's discussion of the priesthood is also evident in Bourdieu's analysis of the relationship between political professionals and amateurs. As the political field gains in autonomy, the laymen become increasingly dispossessed of the properly political means of production. In France, professional politicians who have gone through elite French schools like the *Instituts d'études politiques* or the *École nationale d'administration* gradually replace amateur political activists (Bourdieu 1996b). This way the criteria that regulate entry into the political field also change. Bourdieu does not theorise the levels of autonomy, but it clearly follows that as the field becomes more autonomous in a society, its internal mechanisms play a more central role in political activity (Weber 1978, 608). To understand the specific meaning of a political stance, one must situate it in a relational network composed on the one hand of the other stances formulated at the time in the political field and, on the other hand, of the structure of the demand.

As political capital becomes objectified into posts in the party apparatus, relative independence from electoral sanction develops. For individuals in normal times, the temptation to integrate into the political apparatus grows as the material and symbolic spoils accumulated by the party are redistributed to the followers (Weber 1966, 63–4; Bourdieu 1981a, 19–21). Conversely, in exceptional or revolutionary times staying in the political apparatus can be risky.

Political agents are always, though to varying degrees, involved in a double game, the first internal to the political field and the second external to it, in the larger social field. In the political field itself professionals seek recognition from peers, whereas in the social field they seek support from the voters in elections. A political agent's power in the political field depends on his or her capacity to speak in the name of those exterior to it, the laymen. A political agent's dependence on

A structural constructivist theory of European integration

the political apparatus varies according to his or her capital structure and volume. The less of other social resources such as education and personal wealth political agents have, the more dependent they are on the resources provided by delegation. The more they invest in the political apparatus, the more they become dependent on it (Michels 1962). Bourdieu has analysed the social effects of this *dispossession* in the case of the French Communist party (Bourdieu 1981a). In contrast to intellectual groups or an aristocratic club, this type of political organisation is built on both objective characteristics such as the posts it offers to its followers, and on subjective dispositions such as fidelity to the party and the convergence of its followers' vision of the world and that of its leaders and militants. As political parties get more professional and more bureaucratic, professionals enter into competition among themselves for control over the political apparatus (Gaxie 2000). 'The struggle for the monopoly of the development and circulation of the principles of the division of the social world is more and more strictly reserved for professionals and for the large units of production and circulation, thus excluding de facto the small independent producers (starting with the 'free intellectuals')' (Bourdieu 1981a, 19; 1991, 196). Thus, according to the logic of monopolisation of the supply of political goods, the relatively limited access to these political goods of those most deprived of economic and cultural resources is reinforced. The more socially incompetent agents are in politics, the more they will depend on the supply of political goods and the more readily will they delegate their power to political entrepreneurs and organisations. This mobilisation requires from professional politicians a double game: one in relation to the citizens and the other aimed at their competitors. Bourdieu assimilates political parties to military organisations that mobilise their resources to defeat their competitors on the battlefield of political life:

> In parliamentary democracies, the struggle to win the support of the citizens (their votes, their party subscriptions, etc.) is also a struggle to maintain or subvert *the distribution of power over public powers* (or, in other words, a struggle for the monopoly of the legitimate use of objectified political resources – the law, army, police, public finances, etc.). The most important agents of this struggle are the political parties, combative organisations specially adapted so as to engage in this *sublimated form of civil war by mobilizing in an enduring way*, through prescriptive predictions, the greatest possible number of agents endowed with the same vision of the social world and its future. So as to ensure that this enduring mobilisation comes about, political parties must on the one hand develop and impose a representation of the social world capable of obtaining the support of the greatest possible number of citizens, and on the other hand win positions (whether of power or not) capable of ensuring that they can wield power over those who grant that power to them. (Bourdieu 1991, 181; italics in original)

The main object of struggle among professionals in the political field is recognition from peers, or political capital as a specific type of symbolic capital. Bourdieu differentiates between two types of political capital, that acquired by the individual and that acquired by delegation. Individual political capital is the result either of slow accumulation, as in the case of French notables, or of action in a situation of institutional void and crisis (Bourdieu 1981a, 18), in which case the concept is close to Weber's charismatic legitimacy. Personal political capital disappears with the physical disappearance of the person holding this power. He or she is recognised and known for characteristics that are considered his or her own. On the other hand, political capital is acquired by delegation through 'investiture' by an institution – such as a political party or other political enterprise. A person such as a priest, a professor or any official receives from the institution a limited and provisional transfer of collective capital composed of recognition and fidelity (Bourdieu 1981a, 19). Through this process the capital is partly transformed from the collective to the individual. Political capital becomes institutionalised in the form of posts and positions. Those in the service of political enterprises are their delegates.

Political capital by delegation thus refers to a situation where the power of a politician depends on the power of his or her party and of his or her position in the party. The leader of the party becomes, through investiture, a banker (Bourdieu 2000, 65) and the party a bank specialised in political capital. The banker controls access to this collective capital, which is bureaucratised and certified by the party's bureaucracy. Citing Antonio Gramsci, Bourdieu writes that political agents such as trade union representatives are 'bankers of men in a monopoly situation' (Bourdieu 1991, 194; Gramsci 1978, 17).

In Bourdieu's analysis of social classes and representation we are reminded that the struggles of the representatives offer nothing but mimesis of the stances of the social groups or social classes they represent (Bourdieu 1991, 192). Representatives are thus simultaneously conditioned by their positions in the political field and their positions in the social field, at times miming one, at times the other, or even both at the same time. The homology between their positions in the political field and the social field, and their locations in the political field and the field of production of political stances explains why they satisfy the needs of their electors without even consciously attempting to do so. As the congruence between representative and represented is of a semiotic nature, resembling the relationship between signifier and signified, congruence between what the representative says and what the electors think is necessary for representation to exist. This congruence also explains why, while competing with other politicians or political enterprises in the political field, representatives also satisfy the interests of those they represent. They serve themselves while serving others.

A structural constructivist theory of European integration

As a theory of politics Bourdieu's theory is Durkheimian and functionalist in its holistic analysis of the political field, and Weberian in its attempt to think of social and political processes using economic terms as models. Following Durkheim, Bourdieu sees the political in functionalist terms as forming a whole that is more than the sum of its parts. The logic of the whole conditions the role of the parts, and the whole takes on a life of its own that is independent of the parts. The logic of the political field as a whole determines the stances taken by political agents (Bourdieu 1991, 184). Bourdieu also sees political activity in terms of rituals, institutions and symbolic action. As we have seen, a central ritual in his theory is that of investiture, whereby an individual is chosen to represent and constitute a group. Like in Weber, for whom the modern state is an 'enterprise' or a 'business' (*Betrieb*) (Weber 1978), in Bourdieu the offer and demand of political goods and the monopolisation of capital are the main processes of political activity. As a result, sociology and political science paradoxically become subfields of economics (types of minor economics) miming economic terms and thought schemes. Political action becomes an inferior, because less 'rational', form of economic action. In Bourdieu's theory of the political field, politics is seen as the realm of groups fighting for domination. Phenomena usually seen as political, such as the public sphere (Habermas 1989) and the rule of law, have no place in Bourdieu's theory. Incorporating them would require distinguishing politics from other human activities in qualitative terms.

From the 1960s onward, Bourdieu increasingly studied the state, and specifically the French state. In Bourdieu's theory of politics, the genesis of the state is

> [t]he culmination of a process of concentration of different kinds of capital; capital derived from physical force or instruments of coercion (the army, the police), economic capital, cultural, or better still informational capital, symbolic capital; a concentration which, as such, translates into possession of a sort of meta-capital giving the bearer power over all the other kinds of capital and those who possess them. (Bourdieu 1994, 109)

Through a process of privatisation of public power prior to the existence of the state, certain social groups succeed in monopolising various kinds of public authority. The new authority that emerges becomes responsible for setting the rules and deciding about the relative value and exchange rates of social resources. The state participates in a decisive manner in the production and reproduction of the instruments of construction of reality. In Bourdieu's formulation, the state seems to be a kind of grand organiser that 'constantly exercises a formative action of durable dispositions', of *Dauerhabitus* to use Weber's term (Weber 1922, 541). It imposes fundamental principles of classification – sex, age, competence, and so on, on everybody (Bourdieu 1997b, 209). Its influence is everywhere. In the family, it controls the rites of institution; in the schooling system, it creates divisions between the chosen and the rejected. These are durable, often definitive symbolic divisions that are universally recognised and that often have determining effects on the future of individuals. The individual's 'voluntary servitude' to the state order is the result of the harmony between cognitive structures, either collective or individual, and the objective structures of the world to which they apply. It seems to be total.

As we have seen, in Bourdieu's theory of politics public authority is thus always private authority disguised as public authority which has succeeded, through symbolic violence, in transforming itself and presenting itself as representing the collective whole. Competition and symbolic violence among various groups – *homo homini lupus* – are endless, instituted by society in a Rousseauist manner but lacking the positive basis Rousseau's theory of primitive man has. There is no end to the struggle, no light at the end of the tunnel. In fact, it seems that in Bourdieu's theory the state, if understood as genuine shared public authority, does not play any role.

Bourdieu's account of political capital emphasises its objectified nature. This is only one side of the story, however. Political capital as a symbolic resource has also to be *used* in order for it to be valuable. Capital gains are relatively modest and value is not just retrieved from a treasury. In this sense political action, which is curiously under-theorised in Bourdieu's political theory, is the necessary condition for the existence of this type of resource. As political capital is less objectified than certain types of economic capital such as money on a bank account, its analysis has to concentrate on the political practices through which is it accumulated, and on the symbolic aspects of the political order. This poses problems for the objectification of political capital. As symbolic interaction contains to varying degrees emergent properties and elements of chance, the exact amount of political resources an agent has in his or her possession is difficult to determine. Further, as political action often involves bluff and, to varying degrees, the imposition of values ('symbolic violence'), value is to a large extent created through social interaction. Political reality is not just reproduced by agents, it is also created by them. In certain conditions the bluff is successful and reality is transformed to correspond to the goal of an action that initially was considered impossible or unlikely to be realised.

In Bourdieu's version of structural constructivism, social transformation takes place through reproduction of the social order in time. However, in certain conditions, individuals as political entrepreneurs can change this reality. A recent solution to the problem of accounting for creative action is the concept of social skill (Fligstein 2001, 105–25). But it is difficult to see how the concept of social skill differs from Bourdieu's concept of habitus (which includes skills) as they are both still embedded in a Aristotelian logic of potentiality/activity that does not take sufficiently into account the social and interactional qualities of symbolic resources.

Bourdieu's analysis of political capital as a type of symbolic capital suffers from other weaknesses that a developed structural constructivist approach must address. In his general theory of fields, Bourdieu did not draw qualitative differences between different types of fields, between types of capital, or between politics and other human activities. For instance, what I would call 'generic fields', such as the social field, have to be separated in terms of their properties from 'specialised fields', such as the European political field. Social fields will exist as long as human societies do. Consequently, generic social resources such as social capital, valid (to various degrees of course) in all areas of human activity and in all human societies, do not have the same properties as more specialised resources such as European political capital that exist only at certain times and in certain places. Generic resources also can be more easily converted than more specialised resources into other resources. Moreover, fields have to be differentiated from one another in non-abstract terms. For instance, the political field contains specific inventions such as elections as a means of allocating political power that differentiate it from other fields like the literary field.

Bourdieu's formal field-theoretical model enables comparison of different fields or a field at different stages. However, it is an ideal-typical construction in Weber's meaning of the word. In reality, fields are always in formation in the sense that they are dynamic, incomplete entities subject to varying degrees of external influence. In reality, value is never totally Saussurean, that is, endogenously formed.

Bourdieu studied the public domain as an area where various private interests, masquerading as group interests, try to grab the public interest for themselves, or transform their particular interests into the public interest. Perhaps because politics is assimilated to power struggle, other crucial aspects of modern politics are not taken into account. Bourdieu's version of a structural constructivist theory of politics does not elaborate on the specificity of democratic politics as a specific area of social activity. Bourdieu does not, for instance, reflect on the specific historical meaning of elections and political representation. This is curious because, after all, as opposed to the electoral process, the student does not choose his professor, children do not choose their parents and workers do not choose their bosses. By law, public officials are supposed to further the public interest, although they sometimes use their legitimacy to further their particular ends. Political power is public power, and the state is the guarantor of public order. In contrast to Weber, whose approach was historical, Bourdieu does not distinguish among different kinds of political fields. For Bourdieu, the mechanism of power delegation operated the same way in the totalitarian Soviet Union as in democratic France (Bourdieu 2000, 101) and in the religious and political domains. In the manner of Rousseau, he overemphasises the laymen's blind belief in and total submission to the delegate. But people are not as easily duped as Bourdieu would have us believe, and the media regularly denounces politicians for their wheeling and dealing. Thus we may be justified in arguing that Bourdieu's analysis of the state, to which he devotes a considerable amount of energy, is handicapped by insufficient analysis of the concept of the public.

In Bourdieu's theory of the political field, politics is a game. In many ways, Bourdieu's pessimistic analysis of politics is reminiscent of Plato's critique of the Sophists. Politics is the realm of the arbitrary and the symbolic: it is deceit and cannot be the realm of the true and the beautiful. Perhaps for this reason he saw himself until the end as a critical intellectual, as a man of science among the people, at a distance from the political establishment. Bourdieu's underlying ideal model of the political seems to be based on direct democracy in a polis composed of critical individuals, without parties or political organisations. Delegation of power and political representation logically lead to usurpation and manipulation, not to real democracy.

Bourdieu's model for analysing delegation, the monopoly of production of political goods and political power as symbolic power comes from Weber. So does his conception of politics as a separate life sphere (Weber 1922, 542; Ben-David and Collins 1966, 451–65) or field, which he developed using linguistic models adopted from Saussure and Lévi-Strauss. Political value is Weberian in the sense that it is fiduciary value that is dependent on the legitimacy attributed to a person, organisation or idea and Saussurean in the sense that it is relational value. But Karl Marx's (and Louis Althusser's) influence is also apparent. Apart from Bourdieu's analysis of political fetishism, which duplicates in another semantic register Marx's analysis of fetishism and merchandise circulation (Marx [1867] 1954, 72), and his presentation of social value in terms of modes of production and capital, the division of society into social classes is the ultimate explanatory device by which Bourdieu analyses the political. Class struggle in the social field takes a sublimated form in the political field (Bourdieu 1991, 182). Social classes structure the social field, a kind of super-field that is present in various forms in other spheres of social activity, including in politics. The social field and the political field are united by a pre-established qualitative harmony consisting of structural homologies. This harmony enables agents operating in different fields to find common interests tied to their relative positions in these fields. Thus for instance, those dominated in the field of power, the intellectuals, can, in certain historical circumstances, find common interests with those dominated in the social field, the working classes.

The analysis of European integration requires the modification and adaption of Bourdieu's original formulations.

Structural constructivism as an approach in European integration studies

The political reality of the European Union is Janus-faced. On the one hand, it is an emergent system of governance that is networked, not hierarchical, and open, not closed (Zeitlin and Sabel 2003). On the other hand, the European Union is far from being a power-free institutional and discursive space. Integration has produced new power-centres, hierarchies and political resources. Structural constructivist political theory systematises some of Weber's ideas by underlining the construction of reality by agents who, constrained and empowered by structures that are material and symbolic, struggle to accumulate political resources and increase their own power. Structural constructivist scholars are interested in revealing the hidden power mechanisms behind European integration. The key question of a structural constructivist approach to European integration is through what mechanisms political agents reproduce and transform the European political order. Research inspired by Bourdieu's theory concentrates on specific objects, on groups such as MEPs or European civil servants, for instance, and on connecting political strategies to structural location and social resources such as gender, class and education, and then linking these to broader processes such as the professionalisation of Europe and the construction of a European political field (Kauppi 1997; Mangenot 1998; Georgakakis 2002; Beauvallet 2003). These scholars develop some of Bourdieu's theoretical concepts, such as the field as a structured entity of analysis, structural homology as a tool that enables to connect fields to one another, and social resources as instruments of political struggles. They construct their objects of research through a critique of preconceptions, combining statistical data with in-depth interviews, and linking habitus to the structures of fields.

Until the 1990s, two models dominated scholarly discussion on European integration. The state-centric model emphasises the role of nation-states in their attempts to strengthen and augment their power. According to some proponents of this intergovernmentalist and neorealist model (for instance, Moravcsik 1983) the process of European integration has, in many ways, strengthened rather than weakened European nation-states, which are still the key players in European politics. A second model, propagated by a variety of scholars, is called the multigovernance model. According to this model, nation-states are losing ground in the face of growing supranationalisation and regionalisation of decision-making. According to these scholars, the European Union has already become the main decision-maker in Europe (see, for instance, Schneider and Aspinwall 2001).

New institutionalisms of rationalist, historical and sociological persuasion (March and Olsen 1984, 734–49; Powell and DiMaggio 1991; Hall and Taylor

1996, 936–57; Kato 1996, 553–82) have recently provided a third way opposed to both the neofunctionalist/multilevel governance and intergovernmentalist approaches. Institutions are understood as rules and shared meanings that enable social interaction. From the 1990s onward, a version of the new institutionalism, social constructivism or sociological institutionalism, has presented a social scientific alternative for the study of European integration. By introducing Anthony Giddens's social theory into international relations theory and European studies (Wendt 1992, 391–425), social constructivism opened new paths for scholarly work that emphasise socialisation and the social construction of reality, following in spirit Berger and Luckmann (1966). In contrast to previous approaches, social constructivism underlines the symbolic aspects of European integration, that is, of discourses, norms and, more generally, the power of words and symbols to construct two distinct political ontologies or legitimate political orders relative to Europe: a Europe of nation-states and a Europe of supranational processes.

According to some social constructivists (Christiansen, Jørgensen and Wiener 1999, 528–44; Checkel 1999, 545–60), the purpose of their research programme is to study relatively neglected areas of the integration process, such as polity formation through rules and norms, the transformation of identities, the role of ideas and the uses of language. Social constructivism focuses on what practitioners call social ontologies, which include such diverse phenomena as intersubjective meanings, cultures of national security and symbolic politics. By emphasising social interaction, they are able to examine the structure of the international system and the dialectics between states and the international order in a new way. According to some scholars (Jepperson et al. 1996), social constructivism is situated between rationalism, represented by such approaches as neorealism and neoliberal institutionalism, and reflectivism, which includes postmodernism and poststructuralism (Christiansen, Jørgensen and Wiener 1999).

Other approaches have supplemented and, to a certain extent, challenged these policy-oriented, high politics approaches to European integration. Some of these anthropological and sociological institutional approaches look at integration processes from 'the bottom up', to use Simon Bulmer's term, or at the level of everyday political life. French political anthropologist Marc Abélès has studied the European Parliament and the European Commission from the inside, analysing the internal dividing lines and tensions of these institutions. By mapping the contradictions of supranational political representation, Abélès strives to present European political institutions as they reveal themselves to an outside observer (Abélès 1992). An MEP has to represent both the national interests of his or her country and those of the supranational institution he or she serves (Katz 1999). The European parliamentarian is thus seen as a new type of politician who can be contrasted with both the traditional nationally-elected politician and the international politician appointed to an international organisation. In his study of the cabinet of the former head of the European Commission Jacques Delors, George Ross scrutinises the strategies of Delors's cabinet in the Commission, and the numerous practical questions that arise when national politicians and civil servants end up serving common, European interests (Ross 1995).

While presenting an alternative approach, social constructivism also has its weaknesses. A major one is the absence of a theory of agency (Checkel 1999). While social constructivism concentrates on the agency–structure interaction, giving priority to structure, it neglects political action as situated action, that is, action in specific institutional settings. Another weakness of social constructivism is that, despite its stated aims to study the social fabric of European politics, it is only weakly sociological. Its protagonists are eager to examine the discursive processes informing European integration, identity, norms of behaviour, and so on, leaving largely untouched the key issue of the social characteristics of the individuals and groups who, through their activities, construct this symbolic and material entity.

Compared to other approaches in European integration studies, one of the advantages of structural constructivism as an alternative to social constructivism is that it does not commit itself to either a state-centric or a supranational point of view. As the European Union is a changing political reality that unites supranational and national elements, a scholar's sticking to one or the other approach introduces a significant bias in research (Mörth and Britz 2002), a bias which prevents him or her from accounting for the 'nature of the beast' (Risse-Kappen 1996, 53–80). Structural constructivism as a holistic approach requires painting with broad strokes the structural features of the emerging political field in which political agents act. In contrast to the traditional nation-state theorised by Bourdieu which forms a unipolar political field, the European Union should be analysed as a more or less structured multipolar political field where supranational, intergovernmental, national and regional, public, semi-public and private institutions share power. In the following, I present a preliminary outline of the European Union using an adapted structural constructivist framework to be fleshed out in this book.

Currently the European Union is a multilevel emerging political field structured around two poles: European Union institutions where supranational political resources are concentrated and which provide institutional sites in which these resources can be acquired, and national/regional decision-making centres. The main structural tension in the European Union is between these supranational and the national poles, an opposition that takes a multitude of forms: institutional structures, ideas of the political order (confederation or federation), economic policy (regulated capitalism or neoliberalism) (Marks, Hooghe, Blank 1995), political careers (European or national) (Kirchner 1984; Scarrow 1997, 253–63; Georgakakis 2002), and so on. The process of European Union integration is one of supranational political stratification where certain interests have been favoured at the expense of others – business at the expense of labour, consumers at the expense of citizens, elites at the expense of the general populace. The groups occupying central positions in the 'Eurosphere', as Dusan Sidjanski has called the groups and interests tied to European decision-making (Sidjanski 1996), are mostly civil servants, experts, technocrats and nongovernmental agents both from business and lobby groups.

While the supranational-national dimension forms the first axis of the European political field, political legitimacy constitutes its second. Collective European symbolic political resources consist of two subtypes that correspond homologically to two types of national political legitimacy: executive and legislative legitimacy, or output and input legitimacy (Mény 1996; Scharpf 1999, 6). Executive legitimacy is held by agents in institutions such as the European Commission and the Council of Ministers, institutions that hold partially differing conceptions of the European Union's future. Legislative legitimacy is located in institutions such as the Council and the European Parliament, and, at the national level, in national governments and legislative bodies such as the lower chambers (Norton 1996). The dominance of executive legitimacy over legislative legitimacy in the European political field is manifested by the dominance of institutions such as the Council (an assembly of member-state executives), the European Commission (a supranational bureaucracy) and national governments over elected bodies such as the European and national parliaments. The Commission, which can be considered the European Union's main executive body (Marks, Hooghe and Blank 1995) presents itself as the privileged caretaker of the European interest (see, for instance, the European Commission 2001). This evolving political authority structure is isomorphic or structurally similar to the political structures of the established and homogeneous national political fields, where the real decision-making centres have for some time been outside the direct control of elected institutions (Mény 1996; Wessels and Katz 1999).

Incrementalist strategies (the Monnet method) applied by political agents at all levels of the European polity have legitimised the double political stratification process between supranational/intergovernmental and national/regional levels, on the one hand, and between executive and legislative legitimacy, on the other hand. Reversing symbolically this European political authority structure can prove to be very difficult. The supranational and executive poles have developed in close symbiosis, reinforcing one another, creating new networks of power, furthering democratic erosion and becoming more autonomous vis-à-vis national and legislative processes. At the same time, European integration is deepening and widening as decision-making becomes more communitarian through qualified majority voting and as new policy areas come into the sphere of the European Union and new countries join the Union.

The European Union has taken over some of the functions of the nation-state, but a European civil society and an effective European democracy have not yet developed. In its current form, the European Union is undemocratic, a polity without a civil society, either dispensing law without legitimacy or providing some amount of output legitimacy and little input legitimacy to use Fritz Scharpf's terms (Scharpf 1999; Moravscik and Sangiovanni 2002). From a structural constructivist point of view it seems a division of political labour has developed in which the Commission and the Council provide output legitimacy and the state executives input legitimacy. While the European Union does not possess the traditional attributes of a state, such as the monopoly of legitimate violence, or of a federation, such as a constitution and taxation and spending powers, it is nonetheless both a supranational political authority in the narrow sense of the term (the European Union as a synonym for 'Brussels') and a relational power structure (the European Union as a multilevelled political field) in which certain supranational groups and interests increasingly dominate the more established social-political units that compose parts of it. In the framework provided by structural constructivism, nation-states and federal states are embedded in this larger political unit, becoming ever more disjointed and fragmented as they transfer, willingly or unwillingly, some of their traditional privileges to a supranational bureaucracy and the organised interests that have developed around it. The European Union as a constitutional order rests on a concept of sovereignty divided between European Union institutions seeking constitutional legitimacy through the Convention led by Giscard d'Estaing, and the national constitutional orders that compose the Union.

At the same time, struggles over the definition of Europe and over the value of European political resources are taking place. The European field of political stances is organised around the issue of federalism/confederalism. At the supranational level of the European Union bureaucracy, various powerful supranational interest groups (for instance industrial groups) and the political representatives of smaller member-states oppose the attempts by political representatives of some of the larger member-states to keep the European Union a confederation of nation-states. The European Commission increasingly determines the rules of the supranational political game through institutional configurations (for instance, by reinforcing its position vis-à-vis the Council), the imposition of new principles of social classification (through directives, for instance), rulings of the European Court of Justice, initiatives and alliances with public and private actors, and so on.

This supranational concentration of resources, the networks it creates and the technocratic decision-making it reinforces also transform the political cultures of the national and regional political fields. The case of the European Parliament demonstrates this (see also Chapter 5 and Chapter 6). In Finland, for instance, a member of the European Union since 1995, this supranational concentration of resources and the European Union's dual authority structure have reinforced the power position of political institutions such as the office of the prime minister in the national state machinery. Dominated in the emerging European political field, national and European parliaments and elections still do play a significant role in the legitimation of political authority and in societal mobilisation around common issues. Nevertheless, as the European Union has become more institutionalised, and European governance has developed, the groups included at the supranational level have become more aware of their common interests, and thus have become more and more reluctant to change the political order on which their power is based. As long as this 'European ruling class' does not have an interest in democratising the system, it is difficult to see how the system could be democratised. In this light, the European Union is a regime of political domination in which certain interest groups have succeeded in stacking the cards, regularising interactions favourable to them and delegitimising others, while maintaining unequal resource distribution.

Although European Parliament elections have relatively little political meaning in the sense that there is no government formation that would depend on their results (Reif and Schmitt 1980), their effects may lie elsewhere. In Finland, the elections to the European Parliament have enabled individuals who would not normally succeed politically to gain an electoral position. At the same time, the last European elections in 1999 were characterised by a total lack of interest from top politicians, testifying to a more systematic strategy of delegitimisation of European electoral legitimacy, which was intended, from a structural constructivist point of view, to safeguard the interests of a 'cartel of elites', to use Ralf Dahrendorf's term (Tsinisizelis and Chryssochoou 1998), and the value of the European executive resources it controlled. For former Finnish Prime Minister Paavo Lipponen, what mattered was the executive level, the European Council and the Council of Ministers of the European Union. This indifference toward the European electoral institution reinforced the structural marginality of the European Parliament in Finnish politics. However, it also enabled television celebrities, former sports stars and other citizen-electors known to the general public, to win seats in the European Parliament and, paradoxically caused a real public discussion concerning European issues to emerge.

In France as in other domestic political fields the picture is not totally different. There too, the European Parliament is a marginal political institution that attracts a variety of political novices, mavericks and upstart politicians. While the European Parliament has become a viable political alternative for some (Katz and Wessels 1999; Beauvallet 2003), the majority of the political class and the public considers it still a relatively insignificant institution – an unidentified political object. In France, women politicians have been successful in these elections, as have regional politicians unknown to the national audience. The success of women politicians can be explained through looking at the strategies of politicians like François Mitterrand, by the strong presence of women in parties such as the Socialist party, and by a political desire to show that France is, like other European countries, a modern democracy where women play a significant political role. But many of the women initially elected to the European Parliament – where they could be out of the way and do as little damage as possible – eventually found their way to other, more central sectors of the French political field, even becoming ministers. For regional politicians the European Parliament has, likewise, presented an alternative avenue of access to top national positions in the Paris Senate and the lower chamber, enabling them to further their cause, a Europe of regions. The European Parliament functions as a relatively weakly regulated access point to national political fields.

In Finland and France, the effects of European integration are formally or functionally the same. European elections provide a certain number of new electoral positions. The national political order has been integrated into a larger, supranational space, a space whose hierarchies and power structures politicians reproduce through their political strategies and career choices, as I will show in this work. In this political order, European deputies resemble technocrats more than politicians (Katz 1999). The denationalising effect of European integration on political habitus is weak. For Finnish and French politicians alike, working in Brussels does not present an alternative to a national political career, and they do not all become federalists after having worked in the European Union. In this sense, the European Parliament is not an identitive institution. For many, a supranational political career becomes an additional alternative to more traditional prospects at the national, regional and local level. Supranational career patterns are thus still dominated by domestic structures, testifying to a strong path-dependency. Of course this does not mean that integration has not affected parliamentary careers in Europe (Stolz 2001). In general the political value of European legislative experience is weak, rarely leading to top political positions, whereas European executive experience is relatively prized, as top national civil servants and politicians find posts in European institutions. Politics has become increasingly dependent on European decision-making, but its capacity to structure domestic politics has not grown (Katz and Wessels 1999, 245).

While these structural transformations condition career patterns, individuals do shape outcomes. Some, who are likely to have had unconventional political careers, invest more than others in the European Parliament, but this investment is at the same time an investment at the national, regional and local levels. These do not exclude one another, because politicians use their assets to further their careers on all levels, their national careers being dependent in some cases on their local mandates.

Conclusions

Like Weber (Lassman 2000, 83–98) and authors such as Michels (1962) and Marx, Bourdieu assimilates political action to the continuous struggle for power. In this he follows the Macchiavellian tradition. The task of social science is to unmask and demystify the mechanisms of power. Because he sees the mechanisms of domination as universal, Bourdieu does not attempt to theorise a specific kind of democratic legitimacy that would take the form of a democratic political field based partly on public debate, deliberation and the public sphere and partly on specific mechanisms of power struggle which would contrast with Weber's vision of charismatic, legal and traditional rule. Instead, Bourdieu is concerned with demystifying the political game, showing how delegation leads to alienation and usurpation, and how the dominated reproduce their own domination. Politics as the noble activity of organisation and regulation of human communities turns into domination. Bourdieu sees politics neither in terms of the institutional construction of a public sphere and public instruments that aim at promoting the general interest and preventing the private use of physical violence to settle accounts, nor as a process of adjustment to social pressures (Lipset 1962, 32). In this respect his theory of politics is very much tied to France and its political structures.

Following Max Weber's analysis of spheres of life, Bourdieu analyses politics like any other area of social activity such as the economy, religion or education. Bourdieu's concept of field refers to a relatively autonomous sector of activity that could also be called an organisational field (Powell and DiMaggio 1991) or a game (Bailey 1969). Each field has its specific capital, or resources. Concepts that come close to capital are legitimacy, recognition or status. Political capital as a scarce symbolic resource is what agents endowed with varying amounts of power fight for in the political field.

Each field has its dominant habitus, a culture or internalised set of principles of action, preference and evaluation that regulates resource accumulation and what is acceptable and what isn't. This specific, internalised culture or set of 'internalised institutions' constrains and empowers individuals, assigning them roles and providing guidelines for legitimate behaviour. There is no empowerment without constraints. Far from value-free or power-neutral, this culture and its institutional supports are constructed in order to protect the value of certain resources and to institutionalise their access and usage. The board is tilted in favour of those with the most capital. The field is composed of positions that depend on the capital structures of the individuals and groups occupying these positions. Adapted from structuralist research, homology or structural isomorphism is the tool with which structural constructivists draw qualitative parallels between position and policy stance and between different fields. The idea of structural isomorphism, or an interpretation of it, has been successfully applied by some organisation theorists like Powell and DiMaggio (1991), and sociological institutionalists/social constructivists more generally.

Binary logic organises the political field as a whole. From political parties and other political organisations, where it is expressed in the distinction between progressive and conservative wings and the dominant and the dominated, all the way down to the habitus of an individual who might have evolved from a radical youth into a conservative party official. Consideration of this structuralist binary logic differentiates the structural constructivist theory of politics from most forms of social constructivism, which analyse structures as regularities in social interaction, as partially organised along binary lines, or as culture (see for instance Wendt 1992, 391–425 and 1999; Jepperson, Wendt and Katzenstein 1996; Fligstein 2001; Fligstein and Stone Sweet 2002, 1206–44).

The institutional location of an agent, for instance in the European bureaucracy, is both the result of resource accumulation and a condition for the accumulation of resources. By being appointed to the Commission, a national civil servant is transformed into a European civil servant, the carrier of collective European symbolic capital, which enables him to acquire even more of this type of resource. In a structural constructivist framework, similarity in political behaviour and cooperation can be attributed to structural location, habitus (certain experiences, for instance) or a mixture of the two. Indeed, some of the most interesting research questions relative to the European Union have to do with identity formation: Have the structural transformations of domestic political fields and the processes of homogenisation of these fields led to the construction of a European political habitus? What mechanisms regulate the political value of this habitus?

Studying the European Union, most scholars commit themselves to outdated theories and concepts. Adapting Bourdieu's structural constructivist political theory to the study of European integration provides scholars with a point of view that focuses on power relations in the constitution of a European polity as a single structure. Who gets what, when and how? Structural constructivism aims at analysing how individuals and groups institute structured power relations by mobilising resources and regularising certain types of interactions and values at the expense of others. This approach has several advantages compared to social constructivism and more traditional approaches such as intergovernmentalism.

First, it presents a holistic approach to political processes that binds together behaviour into a unified framework, emphasising cultural and organisational aspects of politics (Bulmer and Bruch 2000) without committing itself to either a national- or Commission-centric point of view. In contrast to most variations of social constructivism, it offers a formal framework for the study of political behaviour. Individuals and groups act in a structured environment in a goal-oriented manner to acquire political resources. The nation-state is not a unitary agent, as Moravcsik (1983) and even some social constructivists assume, but a structured political space where different interests fight over the right to speak in the name of the state at the supranational level. In the case of the European Union, the European Commission and the Council of Ministers are not unitary political institutions. Some representatives of national governments might share with some representatives of the Commission a federalist conception of the European Union's future, while others might disagree and promote a more intergovernmentalist vision. Partly, this division is tied to the resources available to these agents – resources based on nationality (large versus small member-states), on political ideology (left-right), on careers (pro-European politicians might envision European careers for themselves), and so on. The structural constructivist framework enables an analysis of the structuration of a European political order, composed of both a supranational/intergovernmental level (which resembles a confederal consociation, see Tsinisizelis and Chryssochoou 1998 and Chryssochoou 2001) and more established national constitutional orders and regional units, public and private actors, forming a single structure that constrains and enables political action (Corbey 1995, 262). However, nation-states are not Weberian or Westphalian states. Rather, they are fragmented, disjointed, connected to the European level through various networks and unofficial authority structures, such as that provided by *École nationale d'administration* (ENA) alumni in the French case (Mangenot 1998, 7–32). National political fields have become more fragmented just as supranational political stratification has proceeded. As European integration has advanced, especially through the introduction of the euro, the significance of this European symbolic and social space as the structured context of European political action has increased. National transformations are structurally linked to this supranational space and the system dynamic it provides. As political value is always context-bound, transformations at the national level have to be examined as elements of a broader supranational political field that is becoming more structured. These transformations also include transformations in political strategies. Guided in their actions more by policy and political survival than by loss of national sovereignty, national politicians might have political reasons for not disclosing the full effect of the European Union on their own political actions.

Second, like social constructivism, structural constructivism does not consider culture, norms or institutions to be power-neutral (Checkel 1999, 545–60). However, in contrast to social constructivism's ideational conception of culture, structural constructivist scholars analyse culture 'materially' in terms of power resources which are linked to variables such as political experience, class, education, gender, nationality, and so on. Analysis is not restricted to class, as is often the case in Bourdieu's framework, as national origin, for instance, is a key factor when evaluating a political agent's 'weight' on specific issues. There is no European social field behind or at the basis of the European political field that would match Bourdieu's interpretation of the political field. Nor is analysis limited to a national context such as the French one, as was the case in Bourdieu's own empirical studies, or to discussing the general mechanisms of political representation. Following political theorists like Michels, Mosca and Pareto, structural constructivist scholars' critical approach is sensitive to the power struggles that attempt to define the common good and the structural biases that favour some at the expense of others. For structural constructivism, the European Union is a political system that is not limited to the supranational or transnational level (Scharpf 1999) but that includes four levels of political activity (local, regional, national and supranational). This conceptualisation allows one to see how the European Union transforms some particular interests into European interests and stigmatises others as 'narrow-minded' and un-European.

Third, a developed structural constructivist framework that is more Weberian than Saussurean enables a refined analysis of political action. As the European Union is an emerging political field, the properties of agents are, in certain cases, as important in explaining political strategies as are changing rules and institutional arrangements. The specificity of political resources as a type of symbolic capital can be examined only through an analysis of situated action (see especially Chapter 6). As political capital is to a certain extent valuable only if used, and is acquired only through political action, its analysis has to concentrate on political encounters and political action as the locus of the reproduction/transformation of the structures of the political field. Generally, in structured encounters certain resources are bracketed, while emergent properties provide some agents with additional resources.

In order to account for political action, a developed structural constructivist approach to European regional integration has to address the temporal, polycentric and multilevelled character of the European Union. History is present when political agents adapt to the sometimes rapidly changing European political field. Following their internalised political habitus, they legitimise their actions by referring to cultural models based, for instance, on more or less unquestioned national traditions. Temporality also takes other forms – such as the twenty-five national election cycles which create a complex internal dynamic. Fragmentation is not temporal but also spatial. The European Union's multilevel character requires that the multipositionalities of agents be taken into account. Multilevelled political games are more complicated than the two-levelled games scholars such as Schneider and Cederman, inspired by Robert Putnam's work, have studied (Schneider and Cederman 1994, 633–62). In contrast to Bourdieu's interpretation of structural positions where individuals occupy one position at a time, in a context like the evolving European political field, positions are always overdetermined as individuals occupying them belong to several different relational entities. This multipositionality provides agents with valuable resources. For instance, national ministers, as representatives not only of their member states in Brussels but also of the European Union in their domestic arenas, can use the information they have to further policies at lower levels. The power of institutions to influence preferences and agents depends on the structuration level (i.e. the degree to which behaviour is controlled and practices regulated) of the area under scrutiny. Behavioural uncertainty can be linked to weak structuration, as in the case of the European Parliament. In this case, individual choice is not necessarily institutionally set, which prevents an organisational analysis of choice (Egeberg 2001). Institutional structures constrain and empower to varying degrees.

The challenge scholars working in the same theoretical vain as Bourdieu are faced with, consists of adapting and developing some of Bourdieu's intellectual tools to the study of supranational politics in the context of the European Union. The structural constructivist framework enables an analysis of the structuration of a European political field, composed of both a supranational/intergovernmental level and the more established national constitutional orders and regional units and public and private actors, forming a single structure that constrains and enables political action. By linking political strategies to broader structural transformations of an evolving European political field, structural constructivists can enlighten processes such as the restructuration of national political fields, as will be demonstrated in later chapters for the cases of Finland and France.

On the executive pole of the evolving European political field, structuration is not only institutional but above all symbolic. The analysis of French foreign policy discourse in the next chapter shows how little it has changed since de Gaulle's times, despite important transformations in the European political field.

Notes

1 In Chapter 7, I will discuss Bourdieu's political practices.

3 France's European policy

> On the whole, the French have not seemed determined to jump suddenly from great-power status to minor-power resignation, from the world scene to the hermitage. (Hoffmann et al. 1963, 75)

While France has been involved as a major player in the process of building Europe from the beginning, France's relationship with Europe is paradoxical. On the one hand European integration challenges France's traditional political values and on the other hand it presents France with a unique opportunity to wield global influence. However, French ambitions of creating Europe in France's image have not materialised. On the contrary, as a result of five decades of European integration, France itself has changed in many unforeseen ways.

After the creation of the euro and common economic policies, one of the next items on the agenda of European integration has been the increasing integration of national security discourses. European solidarity has led to the coordination of policies and attempts to formulate explicit policy aims, the latest being the fusion of armaments industries. However, these transformations are conditioned by the structures of national political fields and their specific historical traditions. In this chapter, I will examine the relationship between French political traditions and the construction of a European security structure. This will be approached from the point of view of identity politics and the French post-imperialist syndrome (Kortunov 2001), by investigating a complex set of symptoms arising from the discrepancy between French ambition and reality. National and European identities are intertwined with institutions that frame political action and ideas about what politicians believe they represent are an integral part of their power in the European Union (political mimesis). For many French politicians, Europe is a means of regaining lost power. In contrast, politicians in smaller member-states like Finland, dominated in the emerging European political field, adopt a more adaptive strategy toward European integration, seeking to find their place rather than attempting to mould the whole according to their own image.

The requirements of the French Grand Strategy

> Everything also depends on Europe, that is, first of all, on France.
> (De Gaulle 1970, 88)

> France is our fatherland, Europe is our future. (François Mitterrand, quoted in Delors 1988, 269)

The fragile dynamic between nationalism and supranationalism discussed in Chapter 1 is both the source of and a major impediment to further European political and economic integration. For France, whose political executives have constantly wavered between de Gaulle's minimalism (a Europe of nation-states) and Mitterrand's maximalism (a Commission with more power in certain areas), 'Europe' has always been an important issue of domestic politics and a means of achieving national political objectives (Maclean 1992, 30; Sidjanski 1992, 107). After World War Two, 'Europe was the most logical and almost the only available avenue of leadership' (Hoffmann et al. 1963, 80). It is through Europe that the presidents of the Fifth Republic, de Gaulle, Pompidou, Giscard d'Estaing, Mitterrand and Chirac envisioned a global political and economic role for France. For this global role, France was too small. 'In international negotiations, what is France compared to the US?'(Delors 1988, 60). Fortunately for France, 'none of the Community countries has renounced ... playing a role in the world, keeping its rank' (Delors 1988, 41).

For all, from the euro-romanticism of the federalists Schuman and Monnet, to the euro-scepticism of de Gaulle and Couve de Murville, to the euro-realism of Giscard d'Estaing, Mitterrand and Chirac, 'Europe' was to enable France to regain lost grandeur (for a historical view of this self-image, see Dietler 1994, 596). Delors too, echoed this ambition: 'Europe ... is one of our best chances to guarantee the progress of our economy and French influence' (Delors 1988, 13). Delors agreed with Valéry Giscard d'Estaing's statement that 'France is a medium strength nation' (quoted in Delors 1988, 261). Thus for France (and some other member-states), Europe became the political instrument for 'exercising influence beyond its economic standing' (*The Economist* 1995, 5) and for a long-term strategy aimed at re-taking a global political, economic and military role. For this reason Europe has been and still is being 'built in secret' (Goldsmith 1994, 68). The late historian Fernand Braudel was one of the top intellectuals also to have taken note of France's diminished role in world affairs, and the possibilities Europe presented for regaining lost glory: '[France] has become tiny, not because its genius has shrunk, but because of the speed of modern transportation. To the extent that, having become tiny she seeks to stretch out, to grab hold of neighbouring regions, she has a duty: to build Europe' (Braudel 1985, 7).

De Gaulle's vision for Europe consisted of a confederation of independent states centred on Paris and orchestrated by the French president himself (Lacouture 1990, 313). Only France could be the centre of Europe; the UK and Italy were considered peripheral, Germany was divided and Spain marginal. The only solution was a partnership between France and Germany, with France playing the leading role. In de Gaulle's vision, France had to construct a European Europe, not an American Europe centred on NATO. Europe should not become a dominated element within a larger Atlantic community comprised of Europe and the US, and placed under American tutelage. For de Gaulle, building Europe was not an end in itself as it was for European federalists. Rather, Europe was 'the means of a foreign policy devoted to putting France back in its "normal" place as a world power' (Hayward 1995, 23). The Fouchet Plan of 1961 crystallised de Gaulle's vision of Europe. It was going to be a cooperation organised by states, comprising common policies in military and foreign policy areas. The aim was to supersede the existing European institutions, an aim which caused the other five states of the European Communities to reject de Gaulle's plans.

As a result of his talks with German Chancellor Konrad Adenauer in 1958, de Gaulle understood that an institutionalisation of the bilateral interaction between France and Germany was a necessity. After the failure to construct a political union of the Six in 1962, de Gaulle realised that the future of Europe would depend on Germany's fate: cooperation between France and Germany had to be at the centre of a new Europe, and Germany had to choose between a European Europe and an American Europe. During de Gaulle's visit to Germany in 1962, the press characterised his visit as the consecration of a European emperor.

The chances Europe presented, and still presents for France in terms of politics, economics, and culture, are widely recognised among French elites. To use Delors's terms, Europe presents 'a unique opportunity' (Delors 1988, 261). However, these new opportunities have not translated into dramatic changes in terms of French political culture and discourse. In this sense, there is a gap between the political significance of Europe in the practices of the French political class and the official pro-European rhetoric. A closer examination (see Chapter 4) will reveal that European Union institutions are *de facto* situated at the margins of the French political field. For this reason, they do not represent first-rate positions for French politicians in their career-paths. Furthermore, France's role in the Union has been weakening as more and more members have joined, and Germany has undoubtedly become the most powerful European nation, aggravating the French post-imperialist syndrome.

For foreign observers, the predominance of political interests over economic interests in France's European policy has been clear from the beginning:

> It is widely acknowledged that monetary union has been promoted by advocates like Jacques Delors primarily on political grounds, as a mechanism for stimulating further political integration. (Whiteley 1994, 302)

The complementarity of European and French goals was reiterated by the former French president of the Republic François Mitterrand in his last New

Year's speech: 'Never separate France's grandeur from Europe's construction ... while serving one, we serve the other' (Mitterrand 1994). This objective emphasises France's thirst for a global political, economic, cultural and military role, lost with Napoleon's defeat, two World Wars and decolonisation. France's precocious position in Europe was further weakened by Germany's unification, an event François Mitterrand tried to prevent by attempting to convince the Soviet leader Mikhail Gorbatshov of the dangers of German unification.

France's weakening position has, however, not led to a re-examination of its ambitions with respect to Europe. The obsession with French grandeur, developed for centuries in the form of French cultural and political imperialism, and prevalent still today in all aspects of French education, is a vicious circle which might become a handicap in a multicultural and multiethnic Europe (Duverger 1994, 2). Sporadic Europeanism has developed on the background of a quasi-religious chauvinism. In the French collective psyche, losing the share of power to Germany is balanced by an impulse to exercise power outside of France's borders.

In France's Grand Strategy for Europe, French hegemony in the European Union was to be achieved by maintaining a dominant position in the French-German duo and by modelling European institutions on French administrative structures and their culture. This goal united politicians from de Gaulle and Monnet onward (Riemenschneider 1992, 145). According to an American observer, 'previous French pride in the universality of France could be diverted toward, and grafted on, the making of Europe' (Hoffmann et al. 1963, 80). If Delors claimed that 'France will grow with Europe' (Delors 1988, 263), the implications for Europe of this ambition did not go unnoticed by other political decision-makers. According to former German Chancellor Helmut Kohl, 'In the EEC, France directs everything' (Attali 1993, 814).

Numerous studies show that European integration is most effective when it is concordant with vital national interests (see for instance Morse 1973; George 1991). But some national interests are more vital than others. Because Paris has been one of the most important actors in European construction in Brussels since the very beginning, there has been and still is a close affinity between French and Community (and Union) policies. This symbiotic relationship, nevertheless, is increasingly being challenged by changes in the Union itself, notably through its enlargement. The rules of European integration have to a large extent been set by French politicians and civil servants (see Monnet 1976). Accordingly, policies which satisfy both the goals of the European Commission, that is the protection of the *acquis communautaire* (tied to the Treaties and their implementation, Coombes 1970, 1; Swann 1990, 178), and those of powerful political actors responsible for policies relative to the European Union (such as the French president and the German chancellor), are more likely to succeed than those which only further the interests of a single country ('nationalism') or those of the European Community ('Communitarianism'). Likewise, for instance Sweden and Finland succeeded in establishing the institution of the Ombudsman and of pushing for more transparency in the European bureaucracy. The history of European integration has been a succession of balancing acts between these often contradictory sets of requirements, which have been subjected to larger political and economic changes such as the breakdown of the Soviet Union (Murgazina 1992, 5–9; Kozyrev 1995). For member-states, the key question is how to transform national interests into Union interests. Sometimes single countries are left standing alone. France's 'empty chair policy' in 1965 when General de Gaulle withdrew his ministers from Council meetings in response to then President of the European Economic Community Walter Hallstein's attempts to define a common *nécéssité objective,* is a good example of the breakdown in the delicate balance between national and supranational goals (see Morse 1973, 72; Tiersky 1994).

As the European Union has acquired more power, its position in the national politics of the member-states has strengthened. Take the French presidential elections in the spring of 1995, in which a struggle for the value of Europeanism took place. The Socialist Party and centrist parties like the CDS (*Centre des Démocrates Sociaux*) promoted and developed two issues, which they presented as being neglected by the right-wing parties and their representatives, Prime Minister Edouard Baladur and Jacques Chirac: unemployment and Europe (Mitterrand 1994; Rocard 1994; Stasi 1994). In effect, Europe became already in 1995 one of the two most important issues in French domestic politics: some would even say, the most important. In 2001, both main presidential candidates Jacques Chirac and Lionel Jospin had developed their own visions of Europe and of France in Europe.

A clear example of the shifting political meaning of European institutions was the attempt by the Socialist Party to present Jacques Delors as a candidate for the French presidency in the spring of 1995. Before going to Brussels, Delors had been a finance minister in the government of Pierre Mauroy. After having spent ten years as president of the European Commission, a return to Paris might have lead Delors to the presidency had he not refused to become the Socialist Party's candidate. Delors's example demonstrates that executive European experience can function as a source of domestic political power – as is represented in denominations such as 'international statesman' or better, 'European statesman' – that situate politicians above national party politics (O. Duhamel 1994; Jakobson 1995, B2; Safran 1995, 102). Some elected politicians like the late Sir James Goldsmith, political science professor Maurice Duverger and Finnish rally driver Ari Vatanen have also developed new career paths that overcome national borders and the national varieties of political resources. The late Goldsmith was a French MEP but was also going to run for Parliament in the UK as the leader of the Referendum Party. The Socialist Duverger, although French, was chosen to the European Parliament in 1994 on the lists of the Italian Communist Party from the Umbria region in Italy. The Conservative Ari Vatanen was listed second in the French *Union pour la majorité présidentielle* (UMP) list in the European Parliament elections of 2004. So one can see that democratically elected officials such as MEPs and high civil servants working for the Union have developed various strategies to transform purely national political projects into more legitimate European political projects. This symbolic transformation is dependent on the frequency of political situations in which European expertise is seen as credible and acceptable and on the availability of influential networks and circles.

European security and French identity

> Originally conceived as an extension of French power, the European Union has, from the beginning, bathed in an administrative and political culture inherited from Paris. (Denetz 1999, 69)

General Wesley Clark, Commander of the NATO forces in formerYugoslavia during the Kosovo war, declared at NATO's fiftieth anniversary in Washington on 23 April 1999 that 'we are going to win', but that to win required patience. At the same time French President Jacques Chirac was celebrating noisily in front of TV-cameras 'the victory of French diplomacy' (Emptaz 1999, 1). According to Chirac, it was thanks to France's efforts that NATO's new strategy was submitted to the authority of the UN's Security Council. The confused Americans, who had not heard of this 'new strategy' before, refused to comment. They were probably used to statements of this type from the French president.

Chirac's statement illustrates the larger question of France's position in Europe and in the world at large. At this time, France was engaged in a war, and for the first time the war was explained to the French on TV from Washington or Brussels in 'Anglo-American'. Decisions were being made beyond the control of Paris. The purpose of Chirac's showmanship was to send a message to the world, showing that France – just like the US – had a leading role to play in Kosovo. Furthermore, he wanted to make sure that his popularity, which soared to new heights during NATO's meeting according to public opinion polls, would stay there until the European Parliament elections, which were to be held on 13 June 1999.

Neither public opinion outside France nor experts in France believe in France's superpower position. According to the French weekly *L'Express*, for instance, in February 1991 only 25 per cent of Germans considered France to be a superpower. The French international relations scholar Pascal Boniface has stated that France's position is one of a medium-size power (Boniface 1998, 12). For many Frenchmen, this statement is synonymous with treason.

Losing its colonies in Africa and Indochina in the 1950s were the last historical events in a long sequence signifying the waning of French power, of which the most memorable were Napoleon's defeat at Waterloo, the knock-out of French troops by Bismarck's military machine in Sedan and the military humiliations incurred by Germany in the World Wars One and Two. During the Cold War, France was not in the same league as the United States and the Soviet Union. And today France can not compete with the US, the number one in world politics.

France's official history, however, is composed of both bitter defeats and rejoicing victories. After the World War Two, France's leaders have seen in Europe the possibility to salvage lost grandeur. Already General de Gaulle, the liberator of France in 1944 and French president from 1958 to 1969, saw in European integration or cooperation a strategic opportunity to win back France's lost superpower status. De Gaulle's reading of French history was tinted by a superpower scenario in which France was the unlucky and temporarily powerless superpower, with the US, Great Britain and the Soviet Union as its allies, and Germany its arch-enemy.

According to this scenario, it was above all thanks to the French themselves that France was liberated from Hitler's forces. The Americans and the others were in important, supporting roles. Dwight Eisenhower, supreme commander of the Allied troops, wanted to legitimise this patriotic interpretation for political reasons, in order to guarantee that cooperation with de Gaulle would continue. Eisenhower gave the French the opportunity to liberate Paris in style. Winston Churchill also reinforced this interpretation. He saw the satisfaction of the French sense of honour as a way to bind the humiliated de Gaulle to the reconstruction of the continent.

Team play was not the General's forte. In his mind, post-war France had to create a new Europe composed of nation-states from the Atlantic to the Urals, now assisted by Germans and other Europeans. France's quitting NATO in 1966 was designed to reinforce the impression that it was the only alternative to American security dominance (Olivi 1998; de la Gorce 1999). De Gaulle did not succeed in convincing other Europeans, however. France's return to NATO under President Jacques Chirac's leadership thirty years later demonstrated how unrealistic that goal was. Despite this and other setbacks, the current neo-Gaullist president, Chirac – like his predecessors, the Gaullist Georges Pompidou, the centrist Valéry Giscard d'Estaing and the Socialist François Mitterrand – sees in European unification an opportunity to build Europe through French leadership. Rhetorical continuity, however, hides existential uncertainty.

The more Europe has become integrated, the more France's goal of constructing Europe in its image has become unrealistic. The Union's centre of gravity has moved to the East, and as new countries have joined the Union – most recently Austria, Finland and Sweden in 1995 and ten eastern European states in 2004 – France's role has been diminished. Although French civil servants such as Jean Monnet and Emile Noël have influenced European Union institutions, the Edith Cresson affair in 1999 demonstrated that the rules of the game have changed. A French journalist stated that Cresson's quitting the European Commission in 1999 was the sign of the end of a French Europe (Denetz 1999, 69). Evidence of this abounds.

The English language has become Europe's *de facto* lingua franca. France's political strategy in the area of language is to make sure that French will be the Union's second language and German its third language. Some have even demanded that French become a compulsory language in Europe. But Germany has for a long time functioned as Europe's economic engine and German unification has ousted France from the first seat to a shared first seat or even a secondary role in Europe's political architecture. Even the consulting firm Arthur Andersen sees Berlin as being Europe's capital in the future (Kahn 1999, iv). In Europe's security landscape the Americans dominate, at least for the moment, as the Kosovo war has shown.

Due to a mixture of changed visions of reality and an inferiority complex Chirac's rhetoric has become sharpen and not milder, as his statement in Washington demonstrates. In this way President Chirac hopes to save face and maintain his position. The reasons for this sharpening rhetoric are found in internal politics, where the French president's greatest symbolic weapon since Mitterrand's terms of office (1981–88, 1988–95) has been the construction of Europe. In his attempt to gather the right behind him for the presidential elections of 2002, Jacques Chirac systematically played the Europe-card and declared that France's, that is, his, main political goal was to construct Europe. For this reason France's official European policy swings from Europhilia to patriotism.

The competition between Chirac and Jospin, the main presidential candidates of the right and left of the 2002 presidential election, raged since the soccer world championships 1998 in which France became world champion. This political situation led Chirac to a series of spectacular political moves through which he attempted to direct the direction of political development. The dissolution of the National Assembly in the summer of 1997 was one of these moves. Chirac calculated that this way he would get the backing of his own troops. The gamble failed. The left won the elections and formed a new government with

Jospin as prime minister. Chirac's statement in Washington about 'French diplomatic victory' was mostly a move in internal politics, in which he tried to keep together a dispersed right before the elections to the European Parliament on the 13th of June 1999. Some politicians had very cynical views of Chirac's tactics. In the middle of the Kosovo war in April 1999 Chirac's former right-hand Philippe Séguin estimated that Chirac could make a separate deal with Slobodan Milosevic anytime without informing American president Bill Clinton or even his prime minister Lionel Jospin (*Le canard enchainé* 1999a, 2). In this way he might stay in the history books as a peacemaker and not the squire of the Americans.

How European is Chirac in reality? He learned his fluent English working in a hamburger restaurant while studying in the US. In his free time he reads Pushkin – in the original. This compares favourably with other French politicians, who barely know any foreign languages. In the French political game, Chirac's Europeanism is most easily seen in the symbolism of presidential power. Following the example of then US president Bill Clinton, Chirac took up the habit of speaking directly to the French people to inform them of the development of the war in the Balkans. While Chirac gave these world–political speeches addressed to a worldwide audience the audience could see both the European and the French flags behind him. President Mitterrand had started this practice – a real political *tour de force*. The flags symbolising France and Europe told the French viewers that Chirac talked not only in the name of France but also in the name of Europe, which in its turn reinforced the credibility of Chirac's rhetoric about France's influence in the world.

In many milieus, economic and military mostly, a very different vision of France's position dominates. It is a vision that proposes a cure to the French post-imperialist syndrome. This vision puts into question France's national self-sufficiency and, tied to it, the inferiority complex towards the US (Kessler 1999, 481–91). If wisdom starts with the acceptance of facts, many experts think, there is only one way out of foreign policy blunders: France needs a more realistic foreign and European policy (see, for instance, Boniface 1998). France should draw all the conclusions from its changed situation. Still, France is an influential global actor along with half a dozen other countries like Great Britain, Russia, Germany, Japan, China and India. In order to continue playing a constructive role in Europe France should revise its centuries-old habits of cultural and political imperialism. The problem is that the leader of French foreign policy, the president, must be transformed from a whimsical monarch (Duverger 1974) into a reliable team player. This would require, however, a deeper change in the political culture of the Fifth Republic, where power is personified in the President, who was ironically referred to during Mitterrand's time as 'God'. God is condemned to play God's role, whether he wants it or not. Already de Gaulle understood that he had to play the game of France's grandeur, although political reality might have indicated otherwise (Vaïsse 1998).

Because of France's internal politics and national political culture, the credibility of French foreign policy is regularly questioned. Let us mention François Mitterrand's surprising attempt to prevent German unification in 1989 so that French influence in Europe would not be diminished – an attempt that will surely be remembered in Berlin (Olivi 1998, 439). At Nice, the requirement to increase the number of German Members of the European Parliament from 87 to 99, in proportion to the German population, raised a wave of protest in the French political class, whose whole world view is still today dominated by a fear of Germany and France's loss of its leadership position. Concerning European Union institutions, France has stubbornly insisted that the European Parliament continues holding its monthly plenary sessions in Strasbourg instead of Brussels. The other institutions of the Union are in Brussels and Luxembourg. The onerous necessity of constant travel in the triangle formed by Brussels, Strasbourg and Luxembourg has sharpened the tensions between France and other member-states and decreased France's credibility in their eyes. More generally, the struggle over the seat of the European Union's institutions has led to an extravagant waste of resources that has influenced the political credibility of European Union institutions through, among other things, a negative public image.

Agricultural policy is another example which has aggravated the relations between France and other European Union countries. France has for a long time succeeded in bending the European Union's agricultural policy to serve the dominant interests of its own agricultural policy. France's nuclear tests in Muroroa in 1995 were for many the last straw, finally proving that France was a too unpredictable solo-player to be the European Union's leader in defence matters. Shortly after the tests, the European parliamentarians in Strasbourg booed Chirac's speech at the closing of France's presidency of the European Union. The outraged comments of representatives of other Union countries have led to questionable reactions on France's side, such as when Chirac cancelled lunch with Finnish Prime Minister Paavo Lipponen (among others) because of the criticism France received of its nuclear tests. Chirac's Washington-statement above is in line with this policy. One of the problems is that the French president does not interpret critique from the rest of the world as being a sufficient reason to change French foreign policy. And why should he, at a time when the UK's press claims that rival France has lost out to the UK in NATO's decision structure as its most important link to the US!

If France needs a new European policy, the decisive question remains how this is to be accomplished and *what* it will be: Chances for change are small, largely because of the strength of the institution of the presidency, and the commitment of the political class to these powers as well as their political culture. According to some classical definitions the president of the Fifth Republic is a monarchical president (Duverger 1974; Mény 1996, 14). In the constitution of the Fifth Republic, founded by de Gaulle in 1958, foreign policy, which includes European policy, is the *domaine reservé* of the president. In internal politics his position is nearly dictatorial, especially when he and the prime minister's government belong to the same political party. The president can prevent the development of alternative foreign policy visions. The constitution grants the president important powers, such as dissolving the National Assembly and thus setting the political calendar, the appointment of ministers and military leadership. As a result, it is rare that he is challenged. Paradoxically, a progressive European policy is in nobody's interest in the internal politics of one of the European Union's leading countries.

There are no signs of changes in Chirac's European policy. The defence of France's honour and historic mission are still the main instruments in his foreign and internal policy. Neither he nor any politician in France is willing to give these up. God in Paris can not be a mortal in Brussels or Washington. The only alternative to this political situation would be a new Constitution that would, to a certain extent, come back to the more parliamentarian Fourth Republic (1946–58). But nobody in France discusses the option of a Sixth Republic. One of the dangers might be an even greater splitting of Europe-policy and its turning into an even more contentious internal issue.

Everything seems to indicate that, seen from Paris, Europe will continue to be French. The common European security and foreign policy can be formulated only when France is the leader – an excellent example of de Gaulle's famous 'dissuasion tactics' that prevents further integration if France does not lead the Union! In Jacques Chirac's vision, he is the architect of a new Europe, Gerhard Schröder and Tony Blair are cast in assisting roles, George Bush is but a visiting star. In this vision the France–Germany axis will continue to be the engine of European construction. Chirac sees the UK's, the only other European member-state having a seat in the UN's security council and nuclear weapons, growing involvement in European affairs as being a threat to France's privileged relationship with Germany. Some right-wing politicians see the UK's relative exteriority to deepening European integration as presenting a window of opportunity for France to strengthen its position in relation to an increasingly domineering Germany. This would, however, require that France give up some of its political cards (Lamassoure 1999). Why not sacrifice France's nuclear defence for a European nuclear defence? Or offer the European Union France's seat in the Security Council? France could propose this, provided certain compensations were granted that would guarantee its leading role in Europe with

Germany. The logic is analogous to the one applied by the Germans. They sacrificed their Deutschmark for the euro, transferring their culture and control from Germany to Europe. In this way they guaranteed their economic supremacy on the old continent.

For the French political class, constructing Europe is the only significant political project of the beginning of the millennium. However, the pace of European integration is, in many ways, conditioned by internal politics. Chirac's europhilia is dominated by French grandeur, which dictates the terms of European construction. Chirac's nationalistic rhetoric reinforces his internal position and, at least in his own mind, France's position in Europe and in the world. There are no signs that France's foreign policy's main lines will change.

Chirac's plan for Europe

In general terms, President Chirac's vision of France and Europe has been very much in line with de Gaulle's intergovernmentalist vision of the 1950s and 1960s. Europe is to be a confederation of nation-states. In this vision, the prerogatives of the Council of Ministers and the European Council are to be reinforced, because these councils are the only European institutions that draw their legitimacy from the principle of state sovereignty (Chirac 1995, 28–9).

On 4 July 2000, Chirac presented in front of the European deputies the programme of the French presidency of the European Union (Chirac 2000). The presidency would reform the institutions of the European Union, a reform that would respect fundamental values and national and cultural identities, respond to the citizens' needs and combine economic performance with social progress, and affirm the role of Europe as a key player on the international scene. In this spirit, France's objectives were fourfold: prepare the Union to the enlargement to the East, improve Europe's economic growth, employment and social progress, bring the Union closer to its citizens and affirm Europe's place in the world.

In terms of the enlargement to the East, Chirac emphasised the need to introduce the idea of reinforced cooperation (*coopération renforcée*). By this he meant that in certain areas certain member-states could cooperate more, and move faster on the road to integration. While the European Council meeting in Nice in August 2000 was devoted to institutional reform, the one in Biarritz in December 2000 was concerned with the enlargement of the Union to the East in 2004. The second axis of the French presidency was to promote a Europe in the service of economic growth, employment and social progress. Chirac called for a better coordination of economic policies in the eurozone. According to the French president, France had already for quite some time asked that employment be at the centre of the Union's plans. The strategic goal would be full employment with an annual economic growth of 3 per cent. In line with this objective, Chirac received representatives of the European Confederation of Syndicates on the first day of the French presidency. By this the French president wanted to demonstrate that he, a neo-Gaullist president, was at least as interested in social issues as his presidential rival, Socialist Prime Minister Lionel Jospin. Chirac did not forget to mention that he was very attached to the European social model, which was based on social dialogue, on social protection adapted to the times and on the role of the state as the guarantor of social cohesion. He also decided it was time for the European Union to better coordinate its economic policies. The 'Euro 11' had to be transformed into an 'Euro 12', giving it more visibility and flexibility. Chirac called for a more thorough coordination of budgetary policies and a harmonisation of fiscal policies.

In Chirac's vision, Europe was going to become an industrial and technological world leader. This was to be achieved through supporting innovative enterprises, coordinating and promoting Europe-wide training and scientific cooperation, and fighting against cyber-criminality. All European schools should be connected to the internet by the end of 2001. This would prevent technology-related marginality and discrimination. All this was to be done with special attention to peripheral areas, such as the Canary islands and France's overseas departments.

Chirac third point of concern was the famous democratic deficit, the fact that the Union's citizens felt that the European Union was distant and illegitimate. Chirac called for the creation of a Charter of Fundamental Rights, which would help develop civil, political, economic and social values, principles and rights that were at the basis of the Union. Europe had to become a Europe of people (*l'Europe des hommes*), which would be promoted through construction of a Europe of mobility and knowledge geared toward young people. While respecting the competence of member-states in the area of education, the Union had to promote university exchanges and the mobility of scholars. What was at stake here was not only the synergy between European laboratories and firms, but also the dialogue between cultures and different conceptions of European citizenship. In terms of the everyday lives of Europeans, the epidemic of 'mad cow' disease was forcing the Union to set up an independent European food agency. According to Chirac, the French presidency of the European Union would be especially attentive to agriculture in the context of the WTO negotiations, the enlargement to the East and specific problem areas like fruit production.

In environment issues, Chirac mentioned the ecological catastrophe caused by the tanker Erika on the coast of Brittany. Tragedies of this type were to be avoided in the future by enhancing the security of maritime transportation. On the global environmental scene, Chirac renewed his commitment to implement the Kyoto Protocol and to strive to obtain a good treaty at the The Hague conference on the greenhouse effect and climatic change.

In the sector on justice and internal affairs, the French presidency would work on putting together a European policy of asylum and immigration. This will involve granting long-term residence permits, harmonising the conditions of reception and struggling against illegal immigration. Other frauds that Chirac mentioned as needing special attention were drug traffic and financial criminality, especially money laundering. On this point of bringing Europe closer to its citizens, Chirac reasserted that the French presidency was committed to the realisation of a European legal space. Chirac also mentioned the issue of sports. After all, France had won the Euro 2000 soccer tournament. According to Chirac, the Union would in the future take into account the specificity of sports and the social function played by sports.

Chirac's final point concerned the role of Europe on the international scene. One of the French presidency's priorities was to consolidate a Europe of defence and security. The Political and Security Committee (*Comité politique et de sécurité*) that was to replace the Political Committee (*Comité politique*) would become the backbone of the European Union's common security and defence policy (CSDP). The military armament industry would come to back the political ambitions of a European defence. More broadly, the French presidency would do all it can to give Europe the means of its foreign policy. In this area, Chirac mentioned three priorities, the first one being the Balkans. The Union would give to the countries in the Balkan area a clear European perspective in order to encourage them to reform their societies and cooperate on a regional level. The second area was the Mediterranean in which the Union would adopt a charter for peace and stability and reinforce economic and cultural cooperation between the two shores of the Mediterranean (presumably the northern and southern shores). The third area was Asia. Chirac mentioned the third ASEM meeting and the bilateral meetings between Europe and China and Europe and Japan. To finish, Chirac mentioned the French presidency's commitment to renew the treaty between the Union and the countries of Africa, the Caribbean and the Pacific.

In this speech at the European Parliament inaugurating France's term of the rotating European Union presidency, Chirac mentioned several times the role of the Union in the world. Chirac's ambition was to make out of the European Union a world player not only in economic issues but also in military issues. This goal was in line with de Gaulle's European policy of developing European security and military cooperation. In Chirac's speech, there was a total silence over Russia. Curiously, Chirac's strategic plan was profoundly Gaullean in its main tenets: keep Russia out, keep Germany in and keep the Americans in control. This way the French-German duo stays in charge in Europe.

Conclusions

Chirac's speech reveals that he sees France's place in Europe by way of a projection of French political culture and its values onto a European level. The integration of French foreign policy and security discourse translates into a vertical symbolic substitution of France with a European Union led by France with German assistance. In this metonymic vision of France's future, we are still in the traditional framework of realpolitik and the culture of imperial politics, which prevents the construction of a common European security framework (Boniface 1998). According to some scholars, this common security framework would be based on a common European moral agency that would overcome the current lack of European moral governance (Habermas 2001). This moral agency should be based on common, collective security requirements and not the fantasies, however legitimate from its point of view, of one of its members. The power of the French post-imperialist syndrome, to construct Europe in its image when it is no longer possible, has not weakened. On the contrary. It is truly paradoxical that one of the originators of the Europe Union is fundamentally anti-European in its approach to European construction. Its representatives legitimise certain authority relations, the pre-eminence of the executive at the expense of the legislative, elitism instead of democracy, and certain European countries, mostly Germany, at the expense of others. Curiously enough, France's European policy has not altered since the 1950s, although the political environment has changed dramatically. The Nice summit in December 2000 and subsequent actions to create a common European defence demonstrate that the French president, Jacques Chirac, intends to keep to a vision of Europe led by France.

Since de Gaulle, French leaders have seen Europe as providing France with a means to regain a lost global and economical political role. This political vision has structured French European policies, and will continue to do so despite the enlargement of the European Union to the East. The integration of French politics has two sides: the official pro-European rhetoric of the French executive elites and the dominance of French domestic structures over European ones. Officially, French executive leaders like Chirac have recognised that France has no other political option but to further European integration in such a way as not to weaken France's position in the European polity. At the same time, however, as I will show in the following chapters, political agents like MEPs follow and reinforce domestic political structures in their career choices and political strategies, thus *de facto* delegitimising European political careers. By following models of political behaviour and action that are fundamentally national in character, they reinforce the primacy of these values over common European ones. European institutions still today present marginal positions that are not sought by the French political class.

Following this brief discussion of France's European policy, I will examine the integration into European institutions of French politicians and civil servants and the constitutional reforms in Finland and France in the next chapter. What kinds of transformations between groups in French politics has European integration promoted? Can we find, in French politics, a prototype form of *homo politicus europaeus*?

4 Social and constitutional integration in Finland and France

> Brought up in the school of François Mitterrand, [French Commissioner Edith Cresson] considers it normal to surround herself with a clique of close friends. (Denetz et al. 1999, 94)

European integration has numerous effects on key national institutions, national constitutions and national political personnel in all European Union memberstates. As in any other Western society, in France the limits between politics, economics and administration are not always clear. In contrast to most Western societies, however, French politicians are characterised by an astonishing uniformity in class, gender and education (Bourdieu 1966b, Suleiman 1997, 19–47) that reproduces a structure of political domination in the French political field. They are often men of upper middle-class origins that have often been trained in schools like the *École nationale d'administration* (ENA) and the *Instituts d'études politiques* (IEP). More than in other European Union member-states, a collective psychology unites the *crème de la crème* of the various branches of French society. This uniformity in terms of resources is both a strength and a weakness. Effectively orchestrated action – through the active connivance and spontaneous understanding among insiders – makes for advantages. Disadvantages, however, include a lack of diversity and flexibility; the cultivation of an ideology of elitism; and the quasi-impossibility of taking into account other points of view and democratising the power system. The ENA symbolises these features of the French political and bureaucratic elite. With it, the influence on European politics of specific educational and social resources is significant. Indeed, many influential Eurocrats have been trained in the ENA, bringing with them to European institutions patterns of behaviour learned at the ENA.

The *École nationale d'administration (ENA)* and Europe

> Thanks to communication flows, the United States can control a good deal of the circulation of information, whilst the importance and diversity of cultural flows enables it to control the formation of elites in most parts of the world. (Badie and Smouts 1992, 83)

Some sectors of French politics are more open than others. One such relatively new sector is composed of the institutions dealing with the European Union, in which administrative, economic and political questions are combined. The emergence of the European political field has partly accelerated the disappearance of the division between politics and administration. Because of the openness of the European Union institutions, it is not unusual for a highly-placed civil servant who has close connections to former classmates from the ENA to engage for some time in a political career as an aide to a French commissioner in Brussels, and later to switch to private business after retirement, or simply to be on secondment (*détachement*) from the civil service. In 1994, the choice of a European career was made easier for former students of the ENA (known as *énarques*) by a decision of the *Conseil d'état* enabling French civil servants to retain their posts while working in Brussels. As a consequence they did not have to fear losing their job, which reinforced an existing trend in French politics and administration: the combination of political and civil service careers.

As a result of European integration, the incremental and uneven transformations in the French political field have been accompanied by modifications in the institutions that train French politicians and the bureaucratic elites. In response to European integration, the venerated ENA has been partially relocated from Paris to Strasbourg. From 1994 onward, the students of the school spent seven out of twenty-seven months of training in Strasbourg, studying such topics as territorial administration, European Union affairs, comparative European administration and social issues (Rivais 1995, 61). According to some observers, this move was initiated in 1991 by the incumbent minister of European affairs and future French Commissioner Edith Cresson, who was 'suspicious of the male dominated ENA' (Allen-Mills 1995, 24). It was resisted by former *énarques* on the grounds that it would separate the school from national decision-makers (Bellier 1993, 237 8).

Until the 1980s, French high civil servants and their educational institutions – mostly the ENA, but also the *Institut international d'administration publique* (IIAP) – were suspicious of European integration. The ENA's conversion to a pro-European outlook was not the result of a deliberate strategy on the part of the leaders of the institution (Mangenot 1998, 8). Rather, it was the outcome of the activities of two distinct groups: the alumni of the school that became interested in European issues, and the school's foreign students. The alumni pioneered European careers and the foreign students also carried with them, into the wider European arena, the legitimacy which the label 'former student of the ENA' carries.

From 1958 to 1988 about twenty ENA alumni worked in European institutions, two-thirds of them in the Commission. Two circumstances accelerated the recruitment of *énarques* to the Commission: the presidencies of François-Xavier Ortoli (1973–77) and of Jacques Delors (1985–95). Before being appointed president of the Commission at the age of 33, Ortoli had already worked in Brussels, and in Paris, where he had been director of President Georges Pompidou's

Social and constitutional integration   69

cabinet and minister in 1968. Ortoli's own cabinet in Brussels was largely composed of *énarques*. During his presidency, several *énarques* were appointed to high-level positions in the Commission, including Raymond Phan Van Phi as director of Relations with International Organisations and P. Malvé as director of Agriculture in 1975. With the arrival in 1985 of Jacques Delors, a former professor of economics at the ENA, as president of the European Commission, a second wave of French *énarques* was ushered in. Pascal Lamy, *Inspecteur des finances* in Paris and future European Commissioner for trade, became Delors' cabinet director for both of his two terms. Other *énarques* included Jean-Louis Dewost, Jean-Paul Mingasson and Guy Legras. All were subsequently appointed to important positions in the Commission: Dewost became Director General of Legal Services in 1987, Mingasson Director General of the budget in 1989, and Legras Director General of Agriculture in 1985. In the 1990s, the number of *énarques* in European institutions was steadily on the increase: thirty-five in 1990, forty in 1993, and fifty in 1995 (Mangenot 1998, 15–16). Of these, the most visible was the nomination of Jacques Attali to head the European Bank for Reconstruction and Development (EBRD) in 1991.

The foreign students of the ENA also played a central role in the process of orienting the ENA toward Europe. *Énarque* and writer Odon Vallet even declared that the ENA was more important for the education of foreign civil servants than for the education of French civil servants (Vallet 1991). The first foreign students were invited as *auditeurs libres* in 1949. They were almost exclusively from *Union française*-countries. The entry exam to the ENA was reserved for French nationals. Little by little, French-speaking Canadians and Europeans started attending the school. The creation in 1966 of the IIAP modified the composition of the ENA's foreign students. Prompted by a long trip through Latin America, President Charles de Gaulle's decided the IIAP would be in charge of the training of foreign civil servants, whereas the ENA would train French civil servants alone. Having heard of these plans, the German contingent of civil servants that were already studying at the ENA insisted that they stay at the ENA and not be transferred to the IIAP. Appealing to a treaty signed by de Gaulle and German Chancellor Konrad Adenauer, they insisted that the ENA should be their host. Many of these German students later went to work in Brussels. In order to become European bureaucrats they had to broaden their training, and knowledge of the French language and administration helped them get good posts in Brussels. De Gaulle's and Adenauer's motive for keeping the Germans and French together was that the elites of the two largest European states should partly be trained together. The German students' successful lobby resulted in an implicit division of labour between the IIAP and the ENA: the former would host students from the developing countries, the latter from European countries, Japan and North America.

For a long time, foreign students of the ENA did not have the same status as their French classmates. The school does not offer an official diploma; or rather, the label '*énarque*' acts as a diploma instead. The entrance exam (*concours*) and the ranking at the end of the school endow each student with an identity and specific values. To protect the value of their education, the association of former students of the ENA was hostile to the idea of accepting foreign students to the school.

Partly because of the internationalisation of civil service careers and partly because of the political advantages of having foreign students at the school, the ties between French and foreign students were strengthened. But this *rapprochement* was short-lived. Disappointed in the lack of interest of French officials, the foreign students themselves became more active and decided to create their own organisations on the basis of nationality. The Germans were the first to create an association of former students in Bonn in 1983. The Finns followed. The German association quickly became an influential group. According to a French journalist's account:

> This brotherhood is as influential as it is discreet. It counts 250 members, of which 150 are active. The association's yearbook is a real Who's Who of power in Germany. The president Diethart von Preuschen, councillor of the FDP's parliamentary group, is a former member of the Robespierre class. It is true, he admits, our people are everywhere. When one calls somebody in the network, one is certain to feel welcome. (*Le Point*, 15 July 1995, quoted in Mangenot 1998, 23–4).

As a result of these efforts, a diploma intended for foreign students was created in 1990, the *Diplôme international d'administration publique*. The same year, the first meeting of the *Association européenne des anciens élèves de l'ENA* was convened and presided over by Jacques Delors in Brussels. The association set out to develop ties between *énarques*, furthering the idea of Europe and the influence of the ENA through debates, colloquia and meetings. The *énarques* started to form a powerful informal network in European institutions, a distinct epistemic community extending French influence beyond French borders. Today, it constitutes a major force in European politics, creating a real parallel diplomacy across the old continent. The ENA seems to have succeeded in becoming a European school of administration. By contesting American domination, it is a way to extend French influence beyond its national borders and to integrate individuals from various countries into a common mental and cultural framework. The educational and social homogeneity of French civil servants provides a political resource that certain individuals can use in Brussels, influencing the direction and form of European integration, as I will show in the next chapter.

Social and constitutional integration

French Eurocrats: a portrait

For a diplomat in any of the member states, the posting to the position of permanent representative in Brussels is regarded as one of the three or four most important postings in the entire diplomatic service, and in some cases it is considered the most important (Gallagher et al. 1995, 95)

If the percentage of alumni of the *grandes écoles* (French elite schools) is relatively low among French MEPs (see Chapter 5), it is relatively high in the Commission. It reaches the percentages prevalent in the French dominant political classes in the case of Commissioners, and increases still more in the cabinets of French Commissioners, in the administrations of French civil servants working in European institutions such as the Commission, or in related institutions such as the Monetary Committee of the European Union or the European Bank of Investment (EBI). For instance, out of twenty-one French top civil servants having worked or currently working in the Commission, 61.9 per cent (thirteen) combined their studies at the IEP with studies at the ENA. All of these individuals figured in the *Who's Who in France 1993–1994* and all are men. 42.9 per cent (nine) were members of the *grands corps* (elite corporations of the state): seven were former *inspecteurs des finances*, two members of the *Cours des comptes* and one a member of the *Conseil d'état*. In terms of educational assets, French politicians and civil servants working in the European Commission clearly belong to France's executive elite (*Who's Who in France 1993–1994*).

The American sociologist George Ross, in his study of Delors's staff at the European Commision, provides an interesting portrait of his chief of cabinet, Pascal Lamy. Lamy is a former student of the ENA, where he was the classmate of Delors's daughter, Martine Aubry. From the position of Finance Inspector in Delors's cabinet at the French Ministry of Finance and Economics in 1981, he moved quickly to the cabinet of Prime Minister Pierre Mauroy in 1983 and then on to Delors's cabinet in Brussels in 1985. Lamy, along with François Lamoureux and Jean-Pierre Jouyet (the number-twos in Delors's European cabinet), exemplify how a certain group composed almost exclusively male *énarques* have made careers in ministerial cabinets ('the executive avenue'). Ross describes Lamy as being highly efficient and competent:

> Pascal, who confessed to being a St. Simonian, radiated the self-containment of someone who believes that superior effort and lucidity can engineer positive changes. His asceticism and discipline are extraordinary ... The way he ate was another demonstration: carefully planned, nothing rich, nothing extravagant, everything designed to pack in the power ... His eyes gave away delight in games of power. (Ross 1995, 62)

Another facet of this French-style Socialist militantism was an air of superiority and even contempt for other Eurocrats, 'everybody else' who was just 'out to get us'. This mindset of 'us against them' is particularly transparent in a description of the negotiation techniques of the Delors's cabinet given by Jean-Charles Leygues, another cabinet member:

> When we're strapped it often works to call a meeting, say, late Friday afternoon ... Then as things get along towards the moment when most people normally go home or out to eat dinner, we start to gain our advantage. When their attention begins to wander, they daydream about the drink they'd like to have or the people they'd like to see, we then turn up the heat. The longer we keep at it, the likely we are to win. By midnight we're a length ahead of them. (Ross 1995, 278)

These techniques also included setting meetings during holidays, and raising the costs of resisting Delors's positions by implying, for instance, that if a civil servant was against Delors's proposal, then this was against the Commission *tout court*. A member of the British cabinet characterised Delors's cabinet as practising 'Rottweiler politics' (Ross 1995, 51), a characterisation that is almost too mild.

Parachutage from Paris into Brussels developed especially during the Delors years (de la Guérivière 1992, 9). George Ross confirms this impression:

> Over the years, Delors, with Pascal [Lamy]'s advice, had very carefully replaced a considerable number of high Commission officials, directors general and divisions heads, in critical areas. Needless to say, the criteria of choice had been competence plus agreement with the Delorist strategy. These people had power bases and ideas of their own, of course, but they were also indebted to Delors and Pascal and this made them particularly amenable to Pascal's concerns. (Ross 1995, 67)

Most, although not all, of these high civil servants were French, guaranteeing a certain 'natural' affinity, a common cultural framework between them and the Delors cabinet. This shared cultural framework was transformed, through struggles in the Commission with other cabinets, into a political affinity. The ties between these Eurocrats and French political, economic and social interests were very complicated. It is, for instance, very difficult to trace the flow of information and influence between French decision-makers and the European Union bureaucracy. Because French Eurocrats were most often on *détachement* in Brussels, it was natural for them to be in touch with the French government and various interest groups on a regular basis. For instance, when negotiations about the nature of the European Monetary Union (EMU) were underway, the French proposal to consider the EMU-process as 'irreversible' might have been influenced by Lamoureux, former 'number two' in Delors's European cabinet,

Social and constitutional integration 73

who had become then-Prime Minister Edith Cresson's 'number two' in Paris (see Ross 1995, 299 n.87). Delors's cabinet's dependency on French institutions was reflected in the ways other Eurocrats and members of other cabinets tried to find out what was going on in Delors's cabinet. One European Union-official put it bluntly: 'Check out Lamy's friends, his classmates at the ENA, see what Elisabeth Guigou [France's Minister of European Affairs] is up to' (quoted in Ross 1995, 279 n.28).

Indeed, one way for the Commission to indirectly further a member-state's interests is to have this country send a representative to Brussels as an 'expert' for elaborating papers and programmes. This is exactly what happened in the case of Jean-Luc Demarty. Recruited into Brussels by Delors from the agricultural forecasting unit of the French Ministry for Agriculture (Ross 1995, 59), Demarty combined excellent knowledge of the Community's Common Agricultural Policy (CAP) with intimate knowledge of French concerns. He worked closely on reforming the CAP alongside Lamy and several top civil servants who were also largely of French nationality (among others, Guy Legras, Michel Jacquot and Jerôme Vignon) in the Commission's General Directorate for Agriculture. In fact, it is difficult to separate French and Community interests from one another in Demarty's activities. It would be too simple to state that Demarty was an agent of the French government, or that Lamoureux, who was first Delors's and then French Prime Minister Edith Cresson's adviser, was a representative of France in Brussels. There is no doubt the Commission has its own programme. But nevertheless, it is not far from the truth to say that while elaborating policies for the European Community as a whole, Demarty – even involuntarily because of his knowledge, competence and connections with his countrymen in Brussels and in Paris – always had one eye on the Parisian scene and the reactions of French civil servants and politicians. And often that is all that is needed. Because of the dangers of being seen to favour one country's national interests to the detriment of others, a whole array of manoeuvres were necessary in the elaboration of texts. The European Union's policies could not be similar to Paris policies, but could be in accordance with them. For instance, a thorough knowledge of the position of French farmers in questions of CAP-reform might lead a member of Delors's cabinet to an even involuntary or unconscious effort to meet these requirements to the detriment of others, or simply to leave certain burning issues out of the proposal.

As the language used at this time in the Commission was French, and the procedures French, it is not surprising that French civil servants were capable of mastering the ins and outs of the system more effectively than many other nationals (see Labrie 1993, 111–16 for a discussion of language politics in the Commission). Not surprisingly the adjectives 'competent' and 'highly qualified' were often used to describe Delors's cabinet.

The effects of French cultural domination on the power structure in European Union institutions and on the policies implemented by the Union were multiple. In fact, the greatest source of power for the Delors cabinet was its capacity to formulate proposals and thus set the tone and limits to debates. Delors set the political agenda like a European prime minister would. His power to initiate and frame debates, problems and questions, and to elaborate draft proposals was combined with the privileged position of his cabinet members in networks uniting French decision-makers and the Brussels bureaucracy. These conditions enabled the insertion, in more or less subtle forms, of French interests into draft proposals. The fact that these proposals had to be written in French guaranteed the mobilisation of cultural and intellectual resources that anticipated potential criticism. Keywords could be used. Invisible connections could be inserted. These would later legitimise further propositions. François Lamoureux served as an 'all-purpose quick writer of texts'. It was he who wrote the Commission's 'energy' text, for instance. One way to control the Brussels Directorates-General – all the 'others', that is – was to change the schedule of events in the calendar. Before Delors's cabinet, the Directorates-General proposed the Commission's Annual Programme to the Commission's President. Since Delors took office, the President and his cabinet dictated this programme.

Appointing French civil servants to the Commission was only one of Delors's strategies as President of the Commission. Another was the highly efficient and effective coordination and control of administrative procedures inside the Commission. In Ross's words, this meant 'coordinating, arguing and insisting upon ideas, generating proposals, monitoring the work of others, obliging institutional "flexibility", and simply pressuring to get its way' (Ross 1995, 158). Without doubt, this degree of pressure and control would not have been possible without the numerous political assets French civil servants had. The tactics of pressure and control were inherited from France, where ministerial cabinets were created to serve one individual, the minister, and protect him or her against the departments of the ministry, which were often formed in the course of earlier political and administrative regimes (Thuillier 1982, 17). For instance, the Socialists taking office in France in 1981 meant a division between the Prime Minister's cabinet and the departments of the ministries which was sharper than ever before. The militant character of Delors's cabinet was based on the French presidential-style cabinet system, transposed from Paris to Brussels. Delors's cabinet can be compared in many ways to the prime minister's cabinet in France, which supervises the other ministerial cabinets in the same way Delors's supervised, or attempted to supervise, the other Commissioners' cabinets.

In the Commission, additional factors played a significant role. For instance, there were national, intellectual, social and educational differences between

Delors's French, largely ENA-trained cabinet, and the 'others'. The 'others' could not participate in the cabinet's communication structure, as its only foreign member quickly found out:

> Lodewijk was uneasy. He had had some problems with Pascal and François over positions to take on important cases of state aid to industry – French cases in particular (over large fines on Renault and Pechiney, among others). Commission competition policy was part jurisprudence and part political realism. (Ross 1995, 57)

Although Delors's cabinet members officially depicted the cabinet as being an 'egalitarian college', the power structure in it was in tune with the 'monarchistic instincts and on hero-worshipping tendencies of French people' (Safran 1995, 62). Commands flowed from top to bottom, from the general to the foot soldiers. A civil servant in Brussels characterised the Delors cabinet as representing 'centralised Bonapartism'. Delors's Socialist 'French model' combined a French prime-ministerial cabinet structure with the militant ideology of Socialist political groups. This unique blend set Delors's cabinet apart from other cabinets in the Commission, some of which applied more egalitarian approaches to decision-making. The success of Delors's cabinet cannot be, however, explained solely on the basis of this administrative model and its charismatic administrative politics, although it is certain that this was of advantage in terms of effectiveness of action. Ross's interpretation of Delors's cabinet's success boils down to the following: 'Knowing what they wanted, having complete personal commitment to achieving it, knowing how to argue for it, and knowing how to use the "house" to tease out agreement with it: these were the cabinet's real resources' (Ross 1995, 71–2).

After the end of Delors's term as President of the European Commission, many of his cabinet's civil servants migrated either to the Directorates-General in Brussels or to ministerial cabinets in Paris, that is to other positions on the executive avenue. For many, promotion in the Commission was the reward for faithful service. Joly Dixon, Jean-Charles Leygues and François Lamoureux became the directors of DG II, DG XVI and DG III respectively. Lamy returned to France and was for some time a candidate for head of the treasury (Ross 1995, 294), but became a director at the bank Crédit Lyonnais instead (*Le Figaro* 1995, 16). In 1999, he became French Commissioner in Brussels along with the centre-right, neo-Gaullist *Rassemblement pour la République* (RPR) Senator, former Minister for European affairs, and President of the General Council of the region of Savoie, Michel Barnier.

After having examined Delors's cabinet in relation to the pressures of domestic and European politics, and the collective educational and social resources it successfully mobilised in the Commission, I will next briefly discuss

Delors as a member of the more restricted group of French Commissioners in the Brussels bureaucracy.

French Commissioners

> Whatever the value of [European Commissioners], they cannot be really politically responsible. (Couve de Murville, 1971, 294)

Founded on intergovernmental cooperation with the assistance of a 'supranational' bureaucracy, the Commission's legitimacy is grounded more in constitutional law than in democratic politics. To guarantee the national control of European Union institutions, numerous posts in the Commission are distributed according to nationality, although, officially, all but the Commissioners' positions are filled by merit. Thus individual, nationally nominated Commissioners represent both their government and the Community, although the Treaty of Rome, elaborated in the language of what might be called euro-romanticism, emphasises only the second aspect. According to Article 157 of the European Economic Community (EEC), Commissioners are chosen for their 'general competence'. A commissioner is to give an oath of independence from national governments, serve as a driving force of the Community and guardians of its Treaties, as well as being an 'honest broker' (Hallstein 1972, 58). Practice has shown, however, that what is needed to further Community interests is a balance between national and Community interests (Coombes 1970, 86). Thus, the basic dynamism of European integration lies at the heart of the Commission's recruitment policies, namely the interaction of external and internal processes to European Union institutions. Disproportionate internal recruitment would lead to suspicion from the member-states, and insufficient internal recruitment would lead to charges of partiality. Likewise, excessive government pressure has to be counterbalanced by concessions to the *intérêt communautaire* (see Coombes 1970, 283 on the technique of package dealing or *engrenage* designed to comply with these political requirements). Thus, the individual Commissioner's task is one of an 'acrobatic exercise without a net' (de Donat 1979, 138). Pulled by partly contradictory requirements, a commissioner plays on two boards simultaneously: that of the European Union, and that of domestic politics.

The political dependency of Commissioners on national politics guarantees national political control. The French Commissioner Claude Cheysson felt this control in 1973, when the then French Minister of Agriculture Jacques Chirac publicly attacked him in *Le Monde* and denounced him as 'knowingly ignoring the interests of the country' (de Donat 1979, 139). *The Economist* could write in 1992 about Jacques Delors's relationship with Mitterrand,

Social and constitutional integration

revealing the dependency of Commissioners on domestic decision-makers: 'If the French socialists take a drubbing in local elections in March, Mr Mitterrand might call Mr Delors home to be prime minister. The offer would not thrill him' (*The Economist* 1992, 46).

Individual Commissioners like Delors, although nominated by common agreement by European governments, draw most of their political weight in the Commission from national politics.

Compared to the European Parliament, still representing a weak form of pan-European legislative power, the European Commission is closer to French national power centres, especially the French president and government. Already in 1953, a French law professor declared triumphantly that the legislation of the European Coal and Steel Community, which was transposed later to the EEC and to EURATOM, was a 'conquest of French administrative law' (Chevallier 1975, 459; Cassese 1987, 12). French administrative law and especially the *Conseil d'état* had been its model (see Kovar and Wendling 1975, 455–71; Cartou 1983, 220).

As we have seen above, because of political and administrative proximity between the Commission and French bureaucracy (see also Willis 1983, 9–15) the structural conditions for ascending the national-European Union career ladder have been prepared in advance. These conditions are bureaucratic and political. A French civil servant like former Commissioner Yves-Thibault de Silguy is always welcome to return after *détachement* in Brussels to his initial ministry (see also Suleiman 1978, 259–60). Political conditions are not that automatic. The price of a politician's successful career as a commissioner lies in a more or less subtle political dependency on national political actors. In the French case it is above all the president who wields this influence, but there are also French interests more broadly. As George Ross expresses it in his study of Delors's staff,

> Other Commissioners and their staffs, including the Delors team, had to try to protect their 'national interests' (represent the positions of the member states of their origin) against [Sir Leon] Brittan's [the British Commissioner in charge of competition law] efforts. Jobs and political positions were at stake in such matters. (Ross 1995, 57–8)

Needless to say, psychological, political and social proximity to Paris easily translates into a special sensitivity for questions important for France. These touchy issues might require special treatment in the Commission. For non-French members of the cabinets of French Commissioners, insensitivity to French concerns easily became a handicap. As we have seen in the case of Delors's cabinet, these members were often ill at ease, and could not find an appropriate place in Delors's staff which was engaged in protecting national interests, for instance in matters of competition policy (Ross 1995, 130). The Dutch member of Delors's cabinet Lodewijk Briet resigned because communication with his colleagues deteriorated so badly. Geneviève Pons, an *énarque*, replaced him. Ross seems to suggest Briet wasn't sensitive enough to French concerns: 'Commonality of culture between Geneviève and the leadership made communication easier'. (Ross 1995, 131)

For some French civil servants like Raymond Barre, Jean-François Deniau, Claude Cheysson, Christiane Scrivener, Yves-Thibault de Silguy and Pascal Lamy, entering the Commission has constituted a way to switch from the French to European civil service. For others, like Ortoli, the Commission functioned as a springboard for jumping (*pantoufler*) from the public to the private sector.

Compared to other French Commissioners, Delors was in a unique political situation, as he was backed by an ambitious French president and a German chancellor who were ready to push forward major integration policies. This, combined with Delors's competent, motivated and hierarchical cabinet, made him into a kind of *de facto* European prime minister, who reproduced French political manoeuvres and reflexes on the level of the European Commission.

European integration and the structuration of a European political field have not only led to the integration of national civil servants and politicians into the European Commission, they have also led to a process of constitutional integration that takes two forms. On the one hand, a European constitution is in the works; on the other, national constitutional orders have been transformed. I will now discuss this second effect in the cases of France and Finland.

Referendum Gallicus

According to article 11 of the French constitution, the President of the Republic can consult the French people on social issues that he deems of importance. In October 2000, President Jacques Chirac decided to submit to the people a misleadingly simple question: 'Do you think that the term of the President of the Republic should be shortened from seven to five years?' The majority said yes, and the constitution of the Fifth Republic created in 1958 was radically renovated. The reform was not just quantitative, but also qualitative. As the relationships between political institutions changed – especially the Elysée Palace and the National Assembly, that is, the presidency and the lower chamber of parliament – the effects of the constitutional reform was seen in all aspects of French politics, including its policies concerning the European Union.

In France the word referendum raises mixed feelings. General de Gaulle liked the possibilities offered by this political instrument to bypass the quarrelling political class. This led to his political destruction. De Gaulle had to resign from the presidency in 1969, when a majority did not back him in a referendum on reforming the Senate. President François Mitterrand (1981–95) was also struck by this tenacious sickness, the *referendum gallicus*. Intoxicated by power, he decided to let the people ratify the Maastricht Treaty in 1992. But Mitterrand was lucky: the people accepted the Treaty by the slightest majority of 51.05 per cent. This same disease struck President Chirac in the summer of 2000.

Why did President Chirac voluntarily expose himself and his neo-Gaullist party RPR to the dangers of a referendum? This was a timely moment for Chirac to take a political risk, and to attempt to reaffirm the political resources invested in him. According to Chirac's conception of political heroism, which he shared with de Gaulle and Mitterrand, this was an occasion to be written into the history books, himself starring as the moderniser of France and Europe, and as a hero of democracy. This status was to be attained only by taking risks, and big risks. The political momentum was there. At the beginning of July 2000, Chirac gave a speech at the German Bundestag defending a European constitution, which later became perhaps the most visible result of the French presidency of the European Union in the second half of 2000. In domestic politics, Chirac decided to campaign for a shortening of the president's term, partly because of the fierce competition presented by Lionel Jospin, Socialist Prime Minister and Chirac's main rival for the presidency in 2002. The prime minister and president represented different political ideologies, Jospin the left and Chirac the right (implying a so-called 'cohabitation').

The French president is called the monarchical president, the republican king or the 'king elect' (Duverger 1974). The president's powers are broad. De Gaulle had tailored them to suit his needs, to lead France in grand style without resorting to politicking. The president appoints the prime minister and government, can dissolve the National Assembly, and leads defence and foreign policy. The presidents of the Fifth Republic had exercised these constitutional prerogatives with varying success. To a great extent, this has depended on personal chemistry and political power relations, especially with the prime minister who to some degree shares the spotlight.

Not surprisingly, this ninth referendum of the Fifth Republic became an object of contention between left and right in a public debate. Chirac and Jospin were in open competition, although they both supported the reduction of the president's term. The next presidential elections would be held in 2002, and both were determined to win. Jospin presented himself as the moderniser of French political life since 1995. The length of the president's term was not the only issue on the Socialists' agenda. Other terms needed shortening too: Senators held office for nine years and municipal councillors for six. And why should the president's term be shortened to five and not four years, as it is in the US? French politicians also held too many elected posts, which prevented them from concentrating on a single one of them (see Chapter 5 for the case of MEPs). As to the powers of the National Assembly, they were to be increased if the Socialists had their way.

In October 2000, just before the referendum, Jospin's political credit was at its lowest, thanks to nation-wide demonstrations against rises in the price of fuel. Chirac had avoided any major catastrophes. By feeding the public with one political initiative after another, Chirac was trying to stay ahead of Jospin, and present himself as being above politicking, as a European statesman. From the mid-1980s on, French political life had been in this state of permanent political campaigning. Cooperation between Chirac and Jospin was not smooth, and democratic principles were devalued in the chronic state of competition, with all sorts of blows going about. This state of cohabitation had led French democracy to a dead end. All players wanted to fix the problem. What were the alternatives to this cul-de-sac? One was an English-style parliamentarism, in which the powers of the prime minister are increased and those of the president trimmed. The problem is that this reminded everybody of the Fourth Republic (1946–58), when the contentious National Assembly paralysed democracy. A second alternative, chosen by Chirac with this referendum, was paradoxically to reinforce the position of the president by shortening his term. How was this to work? If the president and the parliamentarians are both in office for five years, and the elections of both are held the same year (the first time in 2002), the cooperation between the Elysée and the National Assembly would probably deepen. If both president and prime minister came from the same party or ideological group, the president, not the prime minister, would be the undisputed leader, a leader who would add to a presidential majority a parliamentary majority. According to some experts, this would imply an American-style presidential political system.

To repeat, Chirac's motives for shortening the president's term were clear: to present himself as the moderniser of French democracy and the only serious contender in the presidential elections of 2002. It was not clear whether either hope would be realised. Nobody had a crystal ball to read the future. In agreement with Chirac's reasoning, many thought that if the president's term was shortened the president's power would increase in relation to his toughest rival, the prime minister. The reform would mean a strengthening of the president's prerogatives through a qualitative displacement of power. This would happen if president and prime minister represented the same party or ideological group. The president would become a 'super-prime-minister' and the prime minister an American-style vice-president, the second in command. Undoubtedly, democracy would work better as the president would be backed by a parliamentary majority, that is to say, that parliamentary and presidential majorities would fuse. France would see fewer elections and the media would find it easier to concentrate on the substance of politics. In reality, France would be declared the Sixth Republic. But if president and prime minister did not represent the same ideological group, the tug of war between them would continue as before: bye-bye reform.

In 2000, Jospin's position as prime minister was precarious as he was under threat of losing his office after the presidential elections in 2002. Chirac, whose term was to end in 2002, wanted to make Jospin's position as awkward as possible. As an old gambler, Chirac took the initiative. He enjoyed taking risks and did not see himself as merely a political manager. The referendum on the length of the presidency was only one in a series of *coup de main*. His previous, and unsuccessful, gamble had been the dissolution of the National Assembly in 1997. Chirac calculated that new elections would silence the discordant notes on the right, from Charles Pasqua to Philippe de Villiers. This did not happen. The Socialists won the elections and formed the government with other leftist parties. However, in the case of the referendum Chirac had something called 'common sense' on his side. Common sense said that it was self-evident that the president's term was too long, at least in comparison with other countries. By shortening it, dictatorship would be prevented. Common sense said, shortening the term means strengthening democracy. Common sense won. 73 per cent of the votes approved a reduction of the presidential term from seven to five years.

The importance of this referendum, however, might be elsewhere. 69 per cent of the electorate abstained from voting, an unprecedented abstention rate in the history of the Fifth Republic. 16 per cent of those who voted left their ballot paper blank or spoiled. The referendum was thus as much about the people backing Chirac's efforts, as about a vote of non-confidence to Chirac's opportunism and cynicism. Chirac was at the same time implicated in the Méry-scandal, in which he and his followers were accused of rigging municipal elections in Paris.

If the French constitutional reform seems to have reinforced the position of the president vis-à-vis the prime minister and as the decision-maker in French European policy, in the Finnish case discussed in the next section, a constitutional reform led to the strengthening of the prime minister and the government vis-à-vis the president and of their position as the setters of Finnish European policy.

The Finnish constitutional counter-coup d'état: institutional isomorphism and the constitutional reform of 2000

If in France constitutional reform led to a shortening of the president's term in office, in Finland constitutional reform had more far-reaching effects. The pressures of European integration on national decision-making structures led to significant constitutional transformations in Finland (Jyränki 2000; Uimonen 2001), which was until then the only other semi-presidential political system in the European Union alongside France (Sartori 1994). The Finnish reform changed the relationships between central political institutions, the presidency, the government and parliament – empowering government and parliament and disempowering the president. European integration was the catalyst that enabled the political elite to push through and legitimise political reform and political system change that had been in the works since at least the 1980s.

In terms of European Union affairs, and as a result of a process of imitative institutional isomorphism (Powell and DiMaggio 1991), the Finnish reform led to the abandoning of a dual-authority structure in which both president and the prime minister represented Finland, and transformation to a simple authority structure in which the prime minister is in charge of Finnish European Union policies. This is in contrast with France, where political power over European Union policies is still shared between the president and the prime minister.

In 1772, Gustav III, King of Sweden (and Finland, its eastern province) became an absolute monarch through a *coup d'état*. 228 years later, in the year 2000, a Finnish counter- *coup d'état* took place through the inauguration of constitutional reforms stripping the successor to the absolute monarch, the Finnish president, of substantive powers. The main goal of this constitutional reform was the parliamentarisation of the president's powers – that is, the transfer of the president's powers to parliament and government, and the transformation of the semi-presidential political system into a semi-parliamentary or even parliamentary system (Nousiainen 2001). The European Union has been one of the catalysts for this reform, with the most common domestic political systems of the European Union – parliamentary systems – representing a 'normal' state of democracy.

National sovereignty is not what it used to be before 1995, when Finland joined the European Union. Because of the growing significance of the European Union in Finnish politics, certain constitutional jurists, like Antero Jyränki (Jyränki 2000), speak of divided sovereignty between national institutions and European institutions when talking about the contemporary Finnish constitutional order.

Traditionally, the Finnish political system has been a textbook example of a semi-presidential political system (Duverger 1974; Sartori 1994). According to Maurice Duverger, Fifth Republic France, Finland, Portugal and Weimar Germany are examples of semi-presidential political systems (Duverger 1974). In typologies of political systems, these countries have formed a system apart, distinct from typical political systems, the parliamentary system and the presidential system. Until 2000, the exceptions were Finland and France. In these

Social and constitutional integration

political systems, the electors choose parliament, and the winning party or coalition forms the government. In contrast, in the presidential system, the prototype of which is the American system, electors choose the president who functions as a counter-power to the Senate and the House of Representatives (upper and lower houses of parliament).

The Finnish semi-presidential system before 2000 combined elements of parliamentary and presidential regimes. Executive power was divided between president and government. The president was independent of parliament, but ruled with the consent of the government that had the parliament's backing. The government was of parliamentary type, whereas the president was of presidential type (Duverger 1974, 18). According to Sartori (1994, 131–2), a semi-presidential political system has to fulfil the following conditions:

1 The head of state is elected directly or indirectly for fixed term.
2 The head of state shares executive power with the prime minister, forming a dual-authority structure that has three characteristics.
   (a) The president is independent of parliament, but cannot rule alone or directly and thus his will has to be transmitted to the government.
   (b) The prime minister and the government are independent of the president but dependent on parliament. They need the support of a parliamentary majority and are subject to parliamentary votes of confidence or non-confidence.
   (c) The dual-authority structure enables different equilibriums and displacements of executive power, on the condition that the 'autonomy potential' of each unit is safeguarded.

Before the constitutional reform of 2000, parliament and the president played significant roles in the formation of a government. The president invited political leaders to discuss potential candidates for ministerial portfolios. As in France, the Finnish president was in charge of foreign policy. In Finland, the semi-presidential system led to both strong and weak presidencies. That of Urho Kekkonen (president from 1958 to 1987) was a strong one. He created a parallel system of friends and networks he used to lead the country in spite of opposition, both parliamentary and extra-parliamentary. Against Kekkonen, several influential political groups, many connected to the Social Democratic Party, began the process of reducing presidential powers in the name of democracy and parliamentarism.

Throughout the 1990s, the Finnish parliament worked for a reform of the constitution (Tiitinen 2000). The goal of this political activity was the reinforcement of the parliament as a political institution through the 'parliamentarisation' of the president's powers. The first government of Social Democratic

Prime Minister Paavo Lipponen (1995–99) initiated the 'Constitution 2000' project, which resulted in parliament giving its sanction to the new constitution in 1999. According to some experts and civil servants involved in the Constitution 2000 project (Tiitinen 2000; Nousiainen 2001), the juridical goal was to unify the country's 'constitutional order', which included four distinct texts. Politically, the project involved a direct empowerment of parliament and an indirect empowerment of the government and the prime minister vis-à-vis the president. The new constitution, adopted on 1 March 2001, meant a reduction in the president's substantive power vis-à-vis the government and its leader, the prime minister. This reduction of powers is clear in four areas: (1) foreign relations; (2) government formation; (3) legislative initiative; and (4) nomination to high public functions.

(1) In the old semi-presidential system, the president decided on Finnish foreign relations, or more precisely, 'determined Finnish relations with foreign countries'. According to Section 93 of the new constitution, 'Finnish foreign policy is directed by the President of the Republic in cooperation with the Government. Concerning the European Union what is crucial, however, is that the government is in charge of the national preparation of European Union decisions. European issues belong to the jurisdiction of the prime minister and the government. *De facto* then, the prime minister directs a large section of foreign policy and European affairs as a whole.

(2) In the old semi-presidential system, the president played a key role in government formation after parliamentary elections. In the new political order, parliament plays the key role while the president now has a secondary role. It is the task of parliamentary groups to negotiate the governmental programme between themselves, and decide on the composition of the government. In reality, the ministries and their civil servants formulate the so-called governmental programme – perhaps the most significant political document in Finnish domestic politics. Formally speaking, the president communicates to parliament the name of the prime ministerial candidate on the basis of a decision made by parliamentary groups. The candidate that gets the majority of votes in parliament is designated prime minister. Following Section 61 of the new constitution, the president nominates the government on the basis of the prime minister's proposition.

(3) In contrast to the old constitution, according to which the president could prevent a law from being passed, the government has becomes the main actor in legislative matters, too. The government drafts laws that are submitted to parliament for approval. If the president and the government do not see eye-to-eye and the president refuses to sanction the law in question, parliament can sanction the law without asking for presidential approval. Parliament has the last word and can enact a law in face of a president's opposition or resistance.

(4) The power of the president to nominate individuals to high positions has been reduced. As a general rule, the power of such nominations is now in the hands of the government and the ministries. For instance, universities nominate their professors, which in the past was a presidential prerogative. However, despite this clear transfer of power, the president still can influence the nomination process to state posts.

In 1994, the president was chosen by direct popular vote for the first time. From the point of view of the distribution of power, this meant that both the president and parliament received their mandates directly from the people. This reinforced the public legitimacy of the presidency. As seen above, the constitutional reform parliamentarised the president's powers, and reinforced the position of the prime minister in the government. But the direct election of the presidency was not abolished. As a result, the basis of presidential power moved from the political organisations and elites to the people. Before the constitutional reform the president was structurally tied to central political processes: government formation and foreign policy. In fact, the president was the main player in both areas. To these was added direct popular election in 1991. After the constitutional reform of 2000 the president was marginalised in both government formation and foreign policy. But today, the post is still elected by popular vote. The political resources that the president can mobilise are found in his/her relationship to the electorate. He/she can be an opinion leader, represent the people above and beyond politics, and engage at the opportune moment in symbolic acts. But the president's position in policy-making has been drastically reduced. Structurally speaking the president is being cut off from political elites and organisations, becoming a 'constitutional president', the same way monarchs have become constitutional monarchs.

From 1919 when the Finnish Constitution was created until 1987, presidential elections were indirect, the electorate choosing an electoral college of 300 persons who elected the new president. In 1987 a new mode of elections was instituted, according to which the electorate chose at the same time a person from a list of official candidates and an electoral college of 301 members. If no candidate receives over half of the votes, the Electoral College chose the new president by majority voting. In 1988, Mauno Koivisto did not succeed in winning over 50 per cent of the votes. Consequently, he was elected by the Electoral College. The current mode of election, the direct vote, was used for the first time in 1994 when Martti Ahtisaari was elected president of the republic. According to political scientist Jaakko Nousiainen, this reform of the presidential election procedure signifies a transformation of the power base of the presidency in the Finnish political field and a monopolization of political resources by the prime minister (Nousiainen 2001). The importance of this reform for the argument of this book is that it 'regularised' the position of Finland as a member-state of the European Union in the sense that the prime minister and his government are now in charge of Finnish European Union policies. European integration has been an important element in this transfer of power in the sense that the example of other European Union member-states and the decision-making procedures in European institutions have legitimised this reform.

Conclusions

As I have shown in this chapter, the emergence of a European political field has directly and indirectly led to the strengthening of the executive at the expense of the legislative pole in the national political fields. In this uneven process, the French president, the Finnish prime minister and his or her government, have been reinforced.

In this chapter, I have examined the integration of Finnish and French elites into the European bureaucracy, which is one side of a dual process, corresponding to two forms of integration, executive and legislative. I also studied the issue of constitutional integration, or the relationship between the Union as a political order and national constitutions. It was seen how the French executive elite is comprised of a group from predominantly elite schools such as the *Instituts d'études politiques* (IEP) and the *École nationale d'administration* (ENA). Since the 1950s, the graduates of these schools have been integrated into the European bureaucracy, forming since the 1980s an unofficial network of ENA alumni that extends French influence into the Commission. Top positions in the Commission have been, since Jacques Delors, ministerial-level positions sought by ambitious politicians, who reproduce a specific structure of political domination. In Finland, politicians have enacted the same scenario: the European Commission is of prime importance, the European Parliament less so.

Both in Finland and in France – the only semi-presidential political regimes in Western Europe – political elites undertook to implement constitutional reforms in 2000. In France the position of the president seems to have strengthened. In Finland, partly through a process of adaptive isomorphism, a move toward the normal state of European democracies – parliamentarism – took place. Political pressures to engage in constitutional reforms to reinforce democracy led to reforms of different types. In Finland, a large consensus and an eagerness to join Europe led to far-reaching reforms that *de jure* transformed the Finnish semi-presidential political system into a semi-parliamentary one, reinforcing the prime minister's position and political resources. In France, President Chirac decided it was time for him to use his presidential prerogatives and submit the reduction of the president's term of office to a popular referendum. Paradoxically, however, instead of clearly parliamentarising the system,

Social and constitutional integration

the reform backed by the population seems to have reinforced the president's position as the country's political leader, leading to a presidential monopolization of political resources.

In the next chapter, I will examine more closely the effects of this uneven structuration of the European political field on some parts of the legislative pole. How are these processes reflected in the political status of MEPs and the role of civil society in European democracy?

5 French Members of the European Parliament

A sociography of the French Members of the European Parliament

> My area of activity is Europe, my constituency is France. (French MEP quoted in Abélès 1992, 184)

As the above epigram demonstrates, an MEP is a diplomat representing France and a parliamentarian representing his or her electors. While there is an evident contradiction in the role of the MEP and more broadly the European Parliament, some observers have been arguing for some time that, among European Union institutions, the power of the Parliament is likely to grow during the years to come (Jacobs et al. 1990; Abélès 1992, 363; H. Wallace 2000, 21). German Chancellor Gerhard Schröder's vision of Europe implies a dramatic increase in the European Parliament's powers (Schröder 2001). Although French top politicians are, as a rule and as we have seen in Chapter 3, lukewarm to the idea of increasing the power of the European Parliament (see for instance Chirac 2000; Jospin 2001), concrete changes have taken place since the Intergovernmental Conference of 1996. The European Parliament's powers have accrued over time in many policy areas, and it has become, unlike the elitist Commission, the voice of European peoples more than that of European governments (Nugent 2003).

The European Parliament is a dominated element in the evolving European political field (see Chapter 1). The European Parliament is integrated into national political fields following the two modalities exemplified by the Finnish and French cases: annexation that extends political parties' power into European elections and differentiation that applies a different political logic to national and European elections (see Chapter 6 for a more thorough analysis). Party politics rule in France in European elections, whereas in Finland broader cultural factors play an important role. National political cultures still to a large extent determine the political value of experience in the European Parliament. The significance of the European Parliament in national politics in a unifying Europe might turn out to be that it provides a forum for the partial inversion of a multitude of nationally determined political values and hierarchies. In France, for instance, it may be those that determine the sexual division of political labour, in Finland those that determine the criteria of European representation.

In the European Parliament, the electoral law works according to the d'Hondt system, a method for allocating seats in party-list proportional representation

French Members of the European Parliament

systems. Political influence is distributed among political groups in proportion to their party's representation. Representation is translated into points: the more points a party holds, the more important the issues and areas it controls. This means that large parties such as the Social Democrats and the Christian Democrats from large member-states like Germany or France monopolise top positions, such as the presidencies of important parliamentary committees. All smaller member-states like Denmark or Finland can hope for is a vice-presidency in a less prominent committee.

From 1979 to 1999, French electors have been choosing their representatives to the European Parliament directly and by proportional vote, with a 5 per cent threshold rule. Despite the *anti-cumul* laws, double mandates (i.e. politicians holding both national positions and European positions) were not forbidden for a long time in France, but for practical reasons they remained rare (6.9 per cent in 1994). Other double-mandate configurations were more frequent, however. In 1994, for instance, 20.6 per cent of French MEPs were also mayors of provincial cities (data compiled from *Who's Who in France 1993–1994*). In 2001, the situation was somewhat different as double mandates had become illegal.

Table 5.1 Abstention percentages in French European Parliament elections

1979	1984	1989	1994	1999
39.29	43.27	51.11	46.55	52.98

Sources: *Le Monde* 1994, 2; *Le Monde* 1999g, 1.

Ever since the first direct elections to the European Parliament in 1979, for French political parties that control the nomination process, the stakes in European Parliament elections have been lower than in national elections. Voter turnout has traditionally been modest and the abstention level has been rising (see Table 5.1). Partly, this level of abstentions is due to the public image of European elections as elections of a second order. But the high abstention level in European Parliament elections is also the result of ignorance on the part of the electorate. In the opinion of former prime minister Michel Rocard, half of the French do not know that, in contrast to presidential elections that often have two rounds, European Parliament elections are decided in one round (Rocard 1999). As there is no parliamentary majority in the European Parliament and no government to form and control (the Commission is of course appointed separately), the European Parliament does not fit the image citizens have of politics. In 1989, the level of abstentions in European elections was 51.1 per cent, compared to 21.6 per cent in regional elections in 1986, 31.3 per cent in regional elections in 1992 and 29.8 per cent in municipal elections in 1992 (Safran 1995, 100). Paradoxically, the abstention rate has been going up as the powers of the European Parliament have increased. The Parliament has more power but fewer links with the citizens. Despite the relatively high level of abstention, European elections are now an integral part of French national politics, at least for politicians and the media. The media-hype during the 1994 European Parliament elections, with intellectuals (e.g. Bernard-Henri Lévy) and populist rightist politicians (e.g., Philippe de Villiers) taking the front stage, prevented the abstention level from rising too much. In 1999, however, when there were no charismatic public figures in the race, the abstention rate skyrocketed.

As a result of low interest from citizens and politicians alike, France has, until now, sent only low-profile delegates to Strasbourg (Abélès 1992, 46). This has not been the case for Germany, for instance. German MEPs have been more eager to become professionals of European politics than French MEPs. Domestic voting systems are in part the cause of this. They have multiple effects on European politics. To give one example: as French MEPs do not have a geographical constituency to nurse as do their British counterparts, sectoral (or functional) and regional questions can develop more freely in their political agendas.

Table 5.2 Seats in the European Parliament (number of seats followed by percentage of votes)

	1979	1984	1989	1994	1999
RPF	–	–	–	–	13(13.1)
FN	–	10(12.3)	10(12.3)	11(12.6)	5(5.7)
L'autre Europe	–	–	–	13(14.9)	–
CNPT	–	–	–	–	6(6.8)
RPR	–	–	–	–	12(12.7)
UDF-RPR	15(18.3)	41(50.6)	26(32.1)	28(32.2)	–
UDF	–	–	–	–	9(9.3)
Centre	25(30.9)	–	7(8.6)	–	–
Énergie radicale	–	–	–	13(14.9)	–
Socialists	22(27.2)	20(24.6)	22(27.2)	15(17.2)	22(22.0)
Greens	–	–	9(11.1)	–	9(9.7)
PCF	19(23.5)	10(12.3)	7(8.6)	7(8)	6(6.8)
LO-LCR	–	–	–	–	5(5.2)
	N=81	N=81	N=81	N=87	N=87

Sources: Jacobs et al. 1990; *Le Monde* 1994, *Le Monde* 1999g.

Table 5.2 presents the evolution of the seats of French political parties, or rather of the French electoral lists, in the European Parliament since 1979. The 1994 elections were a victory for two political movements, which succeeded in splitting the centre of the political spectrum: the anti-Maastricht list *L'autre Europe* of Philippe de Villiers's (UDF), and the pro-Maastricht list *Énergie radicale* led by millionaire Bernard Tapie. There was a relative weakening of the Socialist Party and the PCF (*Parti Communiste Français*) (including the other leftist parties), while the extreme-right party FN (*Front National*) remained steady in the polls. Symptomatic of the French anti-European mood in 1994 was that only 54 per cent of lists favoured Maastricht (*Le Monde* 1994, 2).

The 1999 contingent of French MEPs fits by and large the profile of their predecessors. The European Parliament witnesses the meeting of French political activists (from trade unions, agricultural unions, ecological groups, and so on), regional politicians (mayors of provincial cities, regional and municipal counsellors, members of regional political organisations, etc.) and top-level politicians (former ministers, for instance). Although for some time strongly represented in the European Parliament, top French politicians such as Jacques Chirac, Laurent Fabius and Valéry Giscard d'Estaing have not been active in the European Parliament (see Jacobs et al. 1990, 45). Usually, chief candidates give up their seat in the European Parliament after having been elected. Undoubtedly, this indicates a weak level of involvement and investment in European affairs, though French politicians have nonetheless made sure that sectors vital to French interests, such as agriculture and development aid, are controlled by French representatives. Traditionally the most important positions in this respect for the French are the Presidencies of the Commissions of Agriculture and Development Aid in the European Parliament (Kovar and Wendling 1975, 433).

In order to present a general picture of French MEPs in relation to national politics, it is useful to divide them into three groups: those who combine their European mandate with their careers in both regional and national politics; those who combine it with national politics alone; and those who combine it with regional politics alone. A comparison between the delegates elected in 1989 and 1994 suggests that the per centage of those combining all three has been steady: 41 per cent in 1989, 40 per cent in 1994 (*Who's Who in France 1993–1994*; *Le Monde* 1994). Top politicians are in this first group. The relationship of regional and national politics to European politics has changed dramatically at the end of the 1980s and the first half of the 1990s: in 1989, 19 per cent of French MEPs were regional politicians compared with 29 per cent in 1994, whereas in 1989 40 per cent of MEPs were also national politicians compared to 28 per cent in 1994. Thus, in 1994 a relative strengthening of French regional representation in the European Parliament against a weakening of central political institutions may be observed. On the other hand, as the European Parliament has been institutionalised into French politics, internal recruitment has steadily risen as MEPs have been re-elected to the Parliament.

Table 5.3 Political experience of French MEPs (percentages, 1989–94)[1]

	National politics			Regional politics	
	Ministers	Deputies	National organisations	Mayors	Regional organisations
1989	24.7	34.6	40.7	17.3	56.8
N=81	(20)	(28)	(33)	(14)	(46)
1994	16.1	31.0	42.5	20.6	62.1
N=87	(14)	(32)	(37)	(18)	(54)

Sources: Information compiled from *Who's Who in France 1993–1994*; *Le Monde* 1994.

Table 5.3 demonstrates in another form this same fundamental transformation that took place in the first half of the 1990s, between the regions, the national political centre and the European Parliament. As these numbers indicate, in 1994 there was a net increase of MEPs having previously represented or concurrently representing regional interests as either municipal or regional counsellors, advisers to mayors or regional assemblies, or mayors of provincial cities. In 1994, over half of the MEPs were or had been regional politicians. On the other hand, the per centage of politicians tied to national political institutions – that is, institutions forming the central French political market (for this term, see Gaxie and Otterlé 1985, 113) – had decreased. In contrast, in 1993, 35 per cent (202/577) of French national parliamentarians were mayors, 2.4 per cent (14/577) regional councillors and only 1.7 per cent (24/577) departmental councillors (Safran 1995, 226). The increase in the proportion of regional politicians among MEPs seems to indicate that the grip of central political institutions on the European Parliament has weakened, thus leaving space for the autonomisation of a subgroup of Euro-regional politicians, removed from national politics and unknown to the general public.[2] Often these European politicians have a specific competence relative to socio-professional organisations and economic and social issues (Abélès 1992, 94–5). Not surprisingly, political, military and diplomatic questions have been left to national authorities, following the implicit division of labour tied to the form European integration has taken over the years.

This transformation in the composition of the European Parliament has been accompanied by other changes. The Parliament has become more than before a self-recruiting institution as the share of former MEPs has risen, while the percentage of individuals with national parliamentary experience has declined and the per centage of those having international experience has increased, as table 5.4 indicates. Apart from the strong presence of regional politicians, there are other signs of the relative distance between the French central political market and the European Parliament. Compared to other national political groups such as deputies, senators, cabinet members and ministers, two characteristics of the French MEPs stand out. On the one hand, there is a relative absence of businessmen, and on the other, a relative lack of members of the *Corps* (*grands corps de l'état*, literally, 'large corporations of the state') and of elite-school alumni (*grandes écoles*, literally, 'large schools').

In terms of socioprofessional groups, the absence of businessmen confirms the distance between European institutions and the French business world. In the 1950s, the *Centre National du Patronat Français* (CNPF, the National Confederation of French Employers) campaigned against the EEC, the predecessor of the European Union, but was overruled by French state executives (see George 1991, 156). In 1989–94 and 1994–99 respectively, only 6.3 per cent and 6.9 per cent of MEP delegates declared themselves to be businessmen or industrialists by profession (Jacobs et al. 1990; *Who's Who in France 1993–1994*; *Le Monde* 1994).

However, what is in this case striking about the educational background of French MEPs is the near absence of elite schools alumni, and more so, the even fewer members from the French state's administrative branches. Only 12.7 per cent of the 1989 contingent were former IEP-students, 9.5 per cent *énarques* and 7.9 per cent were former 'X', that is alumni of the *École polytechnique*. Only 6.3 per cent originated from the *Corps*: the *Conseil d'état* was represented by 1.6 per cent, the *Inspection des finances* by 1.6 per cent, and the *Cours des comptes* by 3.2 per cent (*Who's Who in France 1993–1994*). Of all French MEPs since 1979, 12.6 per cent (26/206) went through the *grandes écoles* and only 3.9 per cent (8/206)

Table 5.4 European, national and international (including ministerial) experience of MEPs (in percentages)

	MEP experience	National parliamentary experience	International political experience
1979 N=81	12.3	45.7	38.3
1982 N=81	11.1	41.2	29.6
1989 N=81	31.8	27.3	53.3
1994 N=87	35.6	46.1	60.0

Source: Information compiled from *Who's Who in France 1979–1994*.

were in the *grands corps*. Table 5.5 shows the relative absence of both groups quite clearly.

Table 5.5 Alumni of *grandes écoles* and members of *grands corps* in the European Parliament (in percentages)

Grandes écoles	IEP	ENA	Polytechnique	ENS	Total (individuals)
1981	17.7	–	2.2	–	45
1985	27.4	11.3	1.6	3.2	62
1989	22.7	7.5	7.5	3.0	66
1994	26.4	11.3	1.9	–	53

Grands corps	Cours des comptes	Inspection des finances	Conseil d'état	Total (individuals)
1981	–	–	–	45
1985	–	–	–	62
1989	1.5	1.5	1.5	66
1994	3.8	1.9	–	59

Source: Information compiled from *Who's Who in France 1993–1994*.

This weakness translates on a more general level into an opposition between national political elites and MEPs. As table 5.6 shows, the elitism of the European Parliament is not as pronounced as that of the National Assembly. The social representation indexes demonstrate that the European Parliament mirrors better than the National Assembly the social and gender composition of the French population. For the upper classes, the representation index of the European Parliament is 670, whereas that of the Assembly is 1078; for the middle classes, the European Parliament is 58, whereas the National Assembly is 7. For the working classes and the farmers the differences are slight.

A closer comparison of MEPs as a social group compared to the French dominant classes (mostly the upper middle class and the middle classes) is revealing. Of the French dominant classes, 22.2 per cent were alumni of the *École polytechnique* while 18.5 per cent were students of the IEP (Bourdieu 1989, 461). The contrast between MEPs and top businessmen is even more striking: 94.7 per cent of the CEOs of the 100 biggest French firms were alumni of the *École polytechnique* and all of them had gone through the IEP! 33.3 per cent (5/15) of Chirac's first government (1974), 28.6 per cent (12/42) of his second government (1986) and 18.4 per cent (9/49) of Rocard's first

French Members of the European Parliament

Table 5.6. Social representation indexes of deputies and MEPs

Social origins of deputies and MEPs 1978–1979	1978 Deputies Σ=71	1979 MEPs Σ=59	1978 of active population	Deputies repres. index	MEPs repres. index
Industrialists, big business	9.9	20.3	1.1	900	1845
Liberal professions	29.6	10.2	0.8	3700	1275
Managers (private)	14.1	5.1	2.8	504	182
Managers (public)	21.1	8.5	1.4	1507	607
Professors	7.0	3.4	1.1	636	309
Intellectual professions	5.6	6.8	0.9	622	755
Total upper classes	*87.3*	*54.3*	*8.1*	*1078*	*670*
Artisans, small business	1.4	1.7	6.7	21	25
Medium-level managers	–	8.5	10.2	0	83
Teachers	1.4	3.4	2.5	56	136
Employees	–	5.1	19.2	0	26
Total middle classes	*2.8*	*18.7*	*38.6*	*7*	*58*
Workers	–	18.6	37.7	0	49
Agricultural workers	–	1.7	1.7	0	100
Service personnel	–	1.7	5.7	0	29
Total working classes	–	*22.0*	*45.1*	*0*	*48*
Farmers	9.9	3.4	7.6	130	44
Other	–	–	0.5	0	0

Sources: Birnbaum 1985; *Who's Who in France 1993–1994*.
The social representation indexes are calculated using the following formula:
percentage of deputies or MEPs divided by percentage of active population x 100.

government (1980) were *énarques*. These educational characteristics emphasise the peripheral position of the European Parliament in the French 'neo-Colbertist' (Duverger 1994, 2) field of power, the top positions of which are colonised by elite schools and *Corps* (Birnbaum 1985). Therefore, the absence of senior administrative branches in the European Parliament confirms that this democratically elected institution is a modest source of institutional power in the French political field. This implies more generally that the roles of the executive and of the administration are given priority over the legislative. This built-in structure of political domination is structurally similar to the one in place in the evolving European political field.

The European Parliament's political marginality in the French political field manifests itself in yet another, more general form – that of structural instability. The overall turnover of the French MEPs is very high, making the development of a stable political image and the institutionalisation of political practices difficult. In 1989, 57.1 per cent of French MEPs were first timers (*Who's Who in France 1993–1994*). In 1994, the figure rose to a record 65.5 per cent (*Le Monde* 1994, 2). In 1989, the average length of service of French MEPs was very low, 2.5 years, compared to 5.5 years for British MEPs (Jacobs et al. 1990, 44). In part, the European Parliament's weak pulling-power is tied to its reputation as being 'the wild area' of French politics, to use Alain Duhamel's characterisation (O. Duhamel 1994, 2). European Parliament elections see new lists created all the time, focused on Sarajevo or the hunting of pigeons today and on nuclear waste tomorrow. As the mechanisms of social control are loose, at least in contrast to national parliamentary elections, *ad hoc* mini-parties are formed and disappear every five years. In 1994, new lists included Philippe de Villiers's *L'autre Europe*, Bernard Tapie's *Énergie radicale*, which both won seats at the expense of established political parties, as well as Bernard-Henri Lévy and Léon Swartzenberg's Sarajevo list, which succeeded in attracting media attention without winning any seats. Other movements included Jean-Pierre Chevènement's leftist anti-Maastricht list *L'autre politique* and an 'anti-capitalist' *Pour l'Europe des travailleurs et la démocratie*. In 1999, the same scenario was repeated. The hunters created the *Chasse-Pêche-Nature-Tradition* list (CNPT) and former minister of interior Charles Pasqua the *Rassemblement pour la France* list (RPF).

In addition to the overall high turnover rate, and the obstacles this presents for the institutionalisation of political practices, and indeed of a European political identity among MEPs, it is of interest to note that this rate varies dramatically from one political group to another. Not surprisingly, only 7.6 per cent of the politicians in the anti-Maastricht list *L'autre Europe* were second timers. In contrast, 71.4 per cent of the Communist list and 63.6 per cent of the extreme-right anti-Maastricht list led by Le Pen had previously been members of the European Parliament (*Le Monde* 1994). These figures might indicate that the European Parliament is a channel for alternative, young and radical political movements, such as Villiers's list, the intellectuals' Sarajevo list or the hunters' list, which are on the margins of the central political market. As we have also seen above, it is also part of the political circuits of small political parties like the *Parti Communiste Français* and the extreme-right (*Front National*), both anti-European movements; as well as of the right-wing UDF-RPR list (*Union de la Démocratie Française-Rassemblement pour la République*) (in 1994, 42.8 per cent had been previously MEPs), which is partly Europeanist in outlook. From the point of view of political power within political parties, the meaning of the European Parliament in career mobility thus varies depending on the time-frame and the political party in question.

Evidence seems to show that politicians in small parties most effectively combine European experience and national political status. In the *Parti Communiste Français* (PCF) and the *Front National* (FN), practically all MEPs (6 out of 7 in the Communist group, all 11 for the FN) were also members of the parties' central committees! Membership in the European Parliament, an ersatz of power for these political movements, guarantees after all a very generous fixed income, if nothing else. In 1999, a French MEP's salary was approximately 470,000FF. In contrast, in 1993 the average salary of a national parliamentarians was about 360,000 FF (or $75.000), half of which was subject to tax (Safran 1995, 225). In 1992, the salary of a French Commissioner was about 1 million FF (about $200,000) a year (de la Guérivière 1992b, 61) (for the economics of European representation, see Wickham and Coignaud 1986, 192–3). But despite differences in subjective factors, the financial benefits and the perception of the desirability of European integration, the unintended consequence of integration into the European Parliament of European 'federalists' and 'nationalist' (or 'sovereignist') politicians alike reinforces the legitimacy of European democratic representation in the European Parliament.

In conclusion, the European Parliament seems to be a mixed bag of top, medium-level and novice politicians, without any unifying characteristics. French MEPs combine new and old political styles and follow drifting domestic and European currents. The structural looseness and general instability of the European Parliament has been the condition for the emergence of new political cleavages and *ad hoc* inter-groups tied to regionalism and sectoralism, parallel to the strengthening of regional loyalties. Regions have become parts of the European polity (Zeller 1999) and national political jurisdictions have become regional entities (see Streeck and Schmitter 1991, 153). This looseness is partly due to the lack of uniform voting procedures within the parliament. According to rule 2–2 of the European Parliament, MEPs 'shall vote on an individual and personal basis' (Jacobs et al. 1990, 47). Another factor is that in 1989 one third of the French delegation of MEPs was under 45 years old. The members of this generation have proven to be more open to other European countries and more eager to become professionals of Europe than previous contingents have.

The European Parliament is situated in a less codified sector of the French political field than institutions such as the Senate or the National Assembly. While its members are part of the core group of the evolving European political field, they are often mid-level politicians on the national scene, often unknown to the public. European legislative experience is not easily put to use in other sectors of national politics. Not necessarily an asset, European legislative experience contrasts with European executive experience in the European Commission. In normal circumstances, a commissioner is a ministerial level politician. In exceptional circumstances, such as during Jacques Delors's terms of office, a commissioner could become a European statesman of the highest calibre, leading the Commission like a national prime minister leads his government.

The role of women politicians in the history of the European Parliament has also been central to shaping the institution and offering women politicians new career opportunities. But as in the case of MEPs in general and in accordance with the structural position of the European Parliament in the evolving European political field, old and new trends are fused in the characteristics of this social group, as the next section will show.

French women politicians in the European Parliament

What is the political significance for the careers of women – a social majority but political minority – of this particular European institution? From the point of view of traditional political and social science, including Bourdieu's political sociology, the question of gender is a minor one. However, the promotion of women politicians is one of the most important forms of the Europeanisation of French politics. The issue of gender touches directly on the forms of political domination individuals construct through more or less established political practices.

The level of women's representation in the European Parliament varies from one European Union country to another (see European Database 1999). Based on data from 1994 (Jenson and Sineau 1995), three types of relationships between lower houses of national parliaments and the European Parliament have been detected. In the first type, women were well represented in both the lower house of the national parliament and the European Parliament (Denmark, Finland, Germany, the Netherlands and Sweden). In the second, women were modestly represented in both institutions (Italy and Portugal). In these two cases, the representation indexes of women in both institutions were very close to one another, reflecting the position of women in these societies. The majority of European countries fell into a more interesting third type, in which women were far better represented in the European Parliament than in the lower house of the national parliament (Austria, Belgium, France, Greece, Ireland, Luxembourg, Spain, and the UK). Although this higher representation in the European Parliament compared to national parliaments has been noted by numerous researchers (see Kohn 1981, 210–20; McRae 1990; Mossuz-Lavau 1992, 1–8), its political significance has been unaccounted for. In other words, what is the political significance of women representatives in the European Parliament? In this section, I will examine this issue through a case study of French women MEPs.

Women in French politics

In the minds of many citizens, a politician is always a man, and posts of responsibility and prestigious offices are still reserved for men. The familiar French expression homme politique is telling in this connection. (Yvette Roudy quoted in United Nations, 1992, 32)

The poor representation of women in France's power elite has long been the subject of complaint, both in France and abroad (Sineau 1988; Janova and Sineau 1992, 115–28; Henry 1995, 177–80; Beauvallet and Michon 2004). French politics is no exception. French women politicians perceive male domination as a fact of life. Real power is where the men are. For this reason, politics is seen as being beyond the bounds of possibility. 'The political world is the last stronghold ... it is the unimaginable' (Florence d'Harcourt quoted in Sineau 1988, 25). Not surprisingly, it is in the domain of electoral politics that masculine domination is perceived as being the greatest. This perception is not unfounded.

For instance, between 1981 and 1991 only 5.5 per cent of French deputies were women (Jenson and Sineau 1995, 5). In 1994, the figure had dropped to 5 per cent, while the European Union average was 17 per cent (*The Economist* 1995, 51). After the elections of 1999, around 10 per cent of French European deputies were women. From 1981 to 1991, a mere 2.8 per cent of Senators (members of the French national upper house) were women. In 1995, in local government women accounted for 6 per cent of mayors and 12 per cent of regional councillors (*The Economist* 1995, 51).

In terms of women's political representation in elected bodies, France is closer to Southern European countries than to Central and Northern European countries. For instance, between 1981 and 1991, 34.4 per cent of Norwegian parliamentarians were women. Germany had three times more women in its Bundestag than France did in its national parliament. The public demand for more equal representation in France has been partly met in the composition of Lionel Jospin's 1998 government: 29.6 per cent (8/27) were women. However, the increase in women in parliament has not been steady (Jenson and Sineau 1995, 351–2). If French female representation today has somewhat improved in ministerial cabinets, for instance, it is still quite low on the whole (on the order of 10 per cent). The subordination of electoral politics to executive politics in Fifth Republic France partly accounts for this under-representation. Is it true that 'politics ... provides the last bastion of masculinity', as has been suggested by some scholars? (Janova and Sineau 1992, 118)? It does, but with nuances. Former Prime Minister Lionel Jospin tried to permanently change this state of affairs. Dominique Gillot, Secretary of State for

Health and *rapporteuse* of the *Observatoire de la parité*, proposed in 1999 to ensure that 40 per cent of candidates in the municipal elections of 2001 would be women, rising to 50 per cent in 2007. Jospin wanted 50 per cent everywhere: for municipal elections (in municipalities with more than 3500 inhabitants in 2001), and in regional, European and Senate elections. He also wanted respect for parity to be linked into public subventions directed at political parties: public subventions were to be frozen if parity was breached (*Le Monde* 1999b, 6).

According to some observers (see for instance Bashevkin 1984, 75–96), the European Parliament is an exception to overwhelming male domination. Indeed, female representation in the French contingent of the European Parliament stands in stark contrast to other sectors of the French political field.

Between 1979 and 1994, 21.2 per cent (59 of 278) French MEPs were women. For the first time in 1999, the per centage of women rose to 30 per cent (26/87). The lowest figure had been 19.7 per cent in 1979, in the first direct elections to the European Parliament. In 2002, the group of French delegates to the European Parliament is composed of more women than that of many other countries. For instance, a mere 12.6 per cent (11/87) of Italian MEPs are women. The similarities and differences between French female and male MEPs might provide a partial answer to this question. Both generally enjoy a low level of state recognition and political experience. The level of state recognition can be assessed by measuring the frequency with which individuals have attended select schools such as the *Institut d'Études Politiques*, IEP, the *École nationale d'administration*, ENA, and more generally the elite graduate and professional schools known as the *grandes écoles*. The status of former ENA-students or *énarques* and former students of the IEP is revealing in this respect. Nearly half (48 per cent, 13/27) of the members of Lionel Jospin's 1998 government were former students of the IEP and had passed through the *grandes écoles*. One third (33 per cent, 9/27) of Jospin's government had studied at the ENA. In 1998 about 30 per cent of the members of ministerial cabinets were énarques (*École nationale d'administration*, 1999). In contrast, only 5.9 per cent of deputies and until 1994 6.3 per cent (13/206) of MEPs were *énarques* (*Who's Who in France 1979–1994*). Elected institutions like the National Assembly and the European Parliament do not do well in terms of per centage of students from these elite institutions.

The difference between men and women MEPs in terms of educational resources is clear. Although 12.6 per cent (26/206) of all MEPs passing through Brussels from 1979 to 1994 studied at the *grandes écoles*, just 7.7 per cent (2/26) of these were women. Of the MEPs from 1989 to 1994, 12.7 per cent were former IEP students, while only 16.7 per cent (6/36) of these IEP graduates were women. A mere 12.5 per cent (1/8) of MEPs that were members of the *grands corps* were women (for details see Bellier 1993, 40–5 and also Suleiman 1978). In short, these facts indicate that in terms of their education, French MEPs do not have the diplomas that correlate with political power, and women score even worse than men.

Of the 1999–2004 contingent, about one-quarter of MEPs holding doctorates were women. Only one sixth of those not having passed the baccalaureate were women. Thus, on average, women MEPs were better educated than their male counterparts. The crucial difference is in the type of formal education they have received. In France, a good education cannot be converted into political influence whereas an elite education in an institution such as the ENA or another *grande école* eventually can.

Another index of proximity to the national political centre is the per centage of MEPs that figure in the *Who's Who in France*. Although French national deputies figure in it automatically, 25.4 per cent of French MEPs were excluded from it in 1993. The exclusion per centage increased from 21 per cent in 1979 to 43.7 per cent in 1994. In 1989, nearly half (46.7 per cent) of women MEPs were absent from the *Who's Who in France* (*Who's Who in France* 1979–1994). More generally, those excluded from the *Who's Who in France* are more likely to be women than men, younger than older, and with a lower rather than a higher level of political experience. They are also more likely to be members of smaller rather than larger political parties (see European Parliament 1996; *Who's Who in France 1993–1994*).

These indexes of proximity to the national political centre in terms both of educational characteristics and of mention in the *Who's Who in France* indicate that, as a group, French European deputies cannot be considered part of the French top political leadership, and that on the average, women MEPs are even worse off than men in terms of the probability of acceding to positions of executive political power.

Access of men and women to the European Parliament

Eligibility for the European Parliament is an entirely national and not a European matter (Bibes et al. 1979, 998; Abélès 1992, 93). Political loyalty and the degree of access to collective political resources, not merit in European affairs or European competence, are the criteria for selection. In this sense, European legislative experience is not easily transformed into domestic political resources. In France, entrance to the European Parliament is regulated by political party leadership that decides on the composition and order of election lists. Until 2004, European election lists followed proportional principles and France constituted one district. Candidate lists reflected power relations between currents inside political parties. Fluctuations in these power relations sometimes explained why a successful Euro-politician may suddenly find him- or herself unfavourably placed on a list, and possibly fail to be re-elected for this reason.

Gisèle Charzat's example is particularly illuminating in this respect. After Charzat served for ten years (1979–89) in the European Parliament, the Socialist Party decided not to place her high on its list in 1989. She was not elected, despite her devotion to work in the European Parliament. However, she was duly compensated with an important position in the central political market, at the *Conseil d'état*. In this sense, for a politician, access to collective political resources tied to leading politicians in parties by far outweighs personal political resources (Gallagher et al. 1995, 53). Gaining access to collective political resources depends on a politician's relationships with leading politicians in the respective party. For instance, Marie-Noëlle Lienemann was placed on the Socialist list because she was the leader of one of its major currents and because she had the party leadership backed her (Sineau 1988, 128–9). Martine Buron, a noted female MEP, confirms this state of affairs: 'I navigated in the party machinery before becoming a European deputy' (quoted in Abélès 1992, 74).

In France, party service thus provides the basis for female (and male) political careers in the European Parliament. For access to European politics, affiliation with a hereditary political fief that provides influence and relations is in some cases more important than valued school diplomas are. For instance, MEP Jacqueline Thome-Patenôtre's husband was ex-minister Raymond Patenôtre. Her father was the former deputy André Thome. In another case, the father of former European deputy and former president of the RPR Michèle Alliot-Marie was Bernard Marie, the former mayor of Biarritz and deputy to the National Assembly. MEP Martine Buron (mentioned above) was the daughter of Robert Buron.

The 1984 elections stand out as a turning point in the study of French women politicians in European Parliament elections. 30 per cent of Socialist candidates and 50 per cent of Green candidates were women. Women made their presence felt in all Socialist currents, as Martine Buron testifies: 'We saw it in the European elections. In order to assure decent places for women candidates, we all had to find ourselves in the party's currents' (Martine Buron quoted in Sineau 1988, 156). Ten years later, Michel Rocard led a Socialist list consisting of an equal amount of men and women candidates. However, this Socialist strategy found no echo in public sentiment, with only 41 per cent of French voters approving of it. A mere 38 per cent of French women supported lists where men and women candidates alternated (*The Economist* 1995, 51).

In 1999, practically all lists followed the parity-principle, which had entered official political morals. The Green list led by Daniel Cohn-Bendit had 44 women candidates and 43 men candidates. On the conservative side, parity was a must, too. However, conservative parties like the RPR were faced with the problem of where to find female candidates. This search for candidates turned into a comedy, as they tended to be found amongst the wives of mentors or fellow politicians.

The European Parliament as a political resource

Women constituted 21.2 per cent of the French European Parliament delegation during the 1989–94 term. During this time, 23.5 per cent of top French MEPs and 20 per cent of veteran MEPs were women. Top MEPs include the presidents and vice-presidents of the parliament, as well as the leaders of political groups and of committees. They constitute 7.1 per cent of the entire delegation. Veteran MEPs are the ones that have been in the post for three successive terms or more. They constituted 6.2 per cent of French MEPs during the 1989–94 term. These figures indicate that, compared to the National Assembly, where women compose 5 per cent (1/21) of the conférence des présidents (Assemblée nationale 1999), relatively many women occupy high-profile positions in the European Parliament. Leading examples are Simone Veil, a former president of the parliament and of its juridical committee, and Pascale Fontaine, likewise a former president of the parliament.

Some scholars have argued that the forced specialisation of women on social and cultural questions does not apply in the case of the European Parliament or the European Commission (Vallance and Davies 1986, 71). The French women Commissioners, Christiane Scrivener and Edith Cresson, were nominated to such 'unfeminine' portfolios – budget and science, and technology, respectively. In some sense, European institutions seem to provide fora for the partial overturning of national political hierarchies and divisions of labour.

However, the traditional sexual division of political labour is far from absent from the European Parliament. For instance, in terms of committee work, women have been over-represented in traditionally feminine areas such as social affairs and culture, and under-represented in committees such as transport (European Parliament 1996). More precisely, the committees on which French women had more than two seats and on which their number exceeded those of French men, included the Committee on Social Affairs and Employment, the Committee on Culture, Youth, Education and the Media, the Committee on Civil Liberties and Internal Affairs, the Committee on Women's Rights and the Committee on Petitions. Conversely, French women MEPs were totally absent from the Committee on Research, Technological Development and Energy, the Committee on the Rules of Procedure, the Verification of Credentials and Immunities, the Subcommittee on Human Rights, the Subcommittee on Monetary Affairs and the Temporary Committee of Inquiry into the Community

Transit System. On the other hand, only one male MEP was represented on the forty-member Committee for Women's Rights!

How can the coexistence in the European Parliament of two sets of contradictory criteria – those of non-traditional political roles for women and those of traditional sexual division of political labour – be explained?

First, the marginal position of the European Parliament in French politics will not entice upwardly mobile male politicians to seek a mandate in European affairs. This is confirmed by Marie-Jane Pruvot, a French MEP: 'In France there is a very ambivalent feeling about Europe – to such an extent, that my male colleagues were less interested, and so left more room for women' (quoted in Vallance and Davies 1986, 71).

Secondly, the political practices developed in these marginal areas might indirectly promote the exploration of new political dimensions, including in those involving the sexual division of political labour. The political style of many women politicians appears to be more in tune with the style prevalent in European Union institutions than with the style dominant in the national political centre, Paris. Some statements reinforce this impression. 'Women don't like confrontation as much as men – that's the only real difference between them. Women prefer to find agreement, to discuss and find practical solutions' (Christiane Scrivener quoted in Vallance and Davies 1986, 8). Some scholars have echoed this sentiment by stating that 'the processes and arrangements of the European Parliament itself are an encouragement to greater female participation' (Vallance and Davies 1986, 8). Because women often perceive politics differently than men do, an affinity can be detected between the alternative political competence accumulated in European institutions that many women are eager to promote (Sineau 1988, 199) and the specific political practices in use in European Union institutions. European multicultural negotiations favour the search for compromise, and thus favour those qualities that traditionally have been labelled as feminine. This might explain why many women feel more comfortable in Brussels than in Paris. Nor can the example for women of politicians like Simone Veil be neglected when assessing the reasons for the relative success of women politicians in the European Parliament (see Vallance and Davies 1986, 36).

The political value of European Union institutions varies greatly depending on gender and the political calendar, especially the election cycle. For instance, a seat in the European Parliament has been a stepping stone to a national political career for 15.1 per cent (25/166) of all French male MEPs from 1979 to 1989. For women representatives the figure was slightly higher (8/40, or 20 per cent). Following a career as an MEP, 10.2 per cent (17/166) of male MEPs and 10 per cent (4/40) of female MEPs acceded to a position in the

National Assembly. Here, no significant differences can be detected between women and men.

If one examines access to electoral politics, men and women differ in relation to the significance of a post in the European Parliament. For only 3.6 per cent (6/166) of men MEPs was a seat in the European Parliament their first political post outside the party structure. In contrast, 25 per cent (10/40) of women MEPs found their first political post outside party organisations in the European Parliament. Thus, for one-quarter of women MEPs a seat in the European Parliament was their first electoral office. For women, the European Parliament is clearly a significant entry point to national politics.

An additional factor that might explain the success of women politicians in partly overturning the traditional sexual division of political labour is the zeal and competence of many women MEPs. The 'existential' situation of women politicians in French politics must also be considered. They have a constant need to prove they are worthy of the trust given by electors and peers alike. This frame of mind is evident in the self-perception of some women MEPs, such as the following:

> Besides, we saw that the women elected to the European Parliament in '79 ... were the best, the best on paper, the best in many ways. I am thinking of Gisèle Charzat, Nicole Pery, Marie-Claude Vayssade, well ... they have been the most assiduous. They really took ... things seriously when for many it was ... well, a means to earn a living. I think it has been an important and interesting example ... of effectiveness and ... seriousness. You know, they often are more serious because they know they are being watched. (Sineau 1988, 187)

Despite the clear difference in political value for male and female political careers of the European Parliament, the majority of French men and women MEPs alike consider the European Parliament as complementary to a national mandate. Institutional and symbolic structuration has its limits. If forced to choose between Paris and Brussels, most would prefer to drop the seat in the European Parliament and continue their careers in national forums (Abélès 1992, 87–8), although sometimes women are considered to be 'more European than men' (Sineau 1988, 202). The reason for this might be that political mobility is subordinated to national political values internalised by men and women politicians alike. Though the opportunities available to women politicians may have altered, partly thanks to European institutions, French political culture and the mechanisms for accumulating political power have – until now – changed very slowly.

Apart from the political strategies of parties such as the Socialist Party and the Greens for attracting female votes, and the proportional lists used in European elections that enable women to figure as viable candidates, defeat in national elections is another cause of political interest in the European Parliament. Above all else, a position in the European Parliament enables many top politicians as well as politicians in small political parties such as the Communist Party to maintain a political position and acquire a salary when nothing else is available. The European Parliament is a safe haven in times of political turmoil. A politician in dire straits can wait here for a change of season, as the example of millionaire and political stunt man Bernard Tapie demonstrates. A seat in the European hemicycle also enables politicians to cultivate new social networks for possible use later on. Evidence seems to indicate that politicians do not invest in the long term in a post in the European Parliament, as members of the National Assembly might for their posts. Contrary to deputies, most MEPs have acquired their political experience in political organisations, at the national or local level, as I mentioned earlier. Compared to politicians trained at the *grandes écoles* and with experience in ministerial cabinets, MEPs lack power and influence.

The changing position of women in the French power elite

Beginning in the 1980s, women's positions and opportunities in French politics have certainly changed for the better. As Dorothy McBride Stetson has remarked, 'for those who seek it, there are opportunities for experience and visibility' (McBride Stetson 1987, 45). Partly, these opportunities are due to the electoral calculations of politicians like François Mitterrand and Michel Rocard. Women candidates on the parties' lists have attracted some types of women in the electorate. Further, it would have been strange if, for instance, the female members of President Mitterrand's cabinets had not moved into other spheres of French politics. In 1989, 38 per cent of Mitterrand's cabinet was composed of women, while only 24 per cent of ministerial cabinet members were women at that time (United Nations 1992, 83–4). Edith Cresson, a member of Mitterrand's cabinet, became prime minister in 1991 and French European Commissioner in 1994 (from which, however, she was forced to resign in 1999 for having hired friends as paid employees to work for her). In this way, Mitterrand encouraged women to engage in politics. In sum, the synchronisation of top politicians' strategies, of changes in the perceptions and evaluations on the part of the electorate and of the creation of new posts in the European institutions have enabled women candidates to figure on election lists to the European Parliament since the first part of the 1980s.

Entering national electoral politics through the back door (so to speak) provided by the European Parliament since 1979, women politicians have created further pressures in the central political market to open up even more and higher positions. Not surprisingly, politics has become one of the areas in which changes in the men–women ratio have been noticeable. As is well known, women are more numerous in lower than in higher positions in party hierarchies. For instance, in 1990, 21.3 per cent of the members of the Socialist Party's directing committee, 18.5 per cent of the members of its executive bureau and 7.7 per cent of the members of its national secretariat were women (Jenson and Sineau 1995, 359). In 1995, 5 per cent of the nation's 100 most powerful *énarques* were women (*Le Figaro* 1995, 16), despite the fact that since the 1970s each graduating class from the ENA has consisted of about 20 per cent women. These 100 most powerful *énarques* were distributed among four areas: politics, administration, prefects and enterprises. Surprisingly, the only category in which women were present, forming 16.7 per cent (5/30) of those composing it, was politics. Women were absent in the other categories. Contrary to popular belief, politics does not seem to be, then, 'the last bastion'. Generational differences might explain the absence of women in some categories. For instance, while the average age of men in the list of *énarques* was 55 years, that of women was considerably lower at 43.8 years. This list of the 100 most powerful *énarques* as defined by the journalists of *Le Figaro* indicates that while women are absent from most of the French power elite, quantitative transformations are occurring, specifically in French national politics. In 2004, the last bastions of male domination might be found less in politics than in the top positions of public and private enterprise, or in sectors of administration such as the prefecture or the diplomatic service.

Having examined above French MEPs, I will link in the next part the analysis of social resources held by French MEPs and Commissioners to the analysis of the institutional structuration of European institutions in the French political field.

Social resources and the structuration of the French political field

Ever since the first direct elections in 1979, French women MEPs have continued to strengthen their presence in the European Parliament. Up until 1979, only 11 out of 198 delegates (5.5 per cent) were women (Vallance and Davies 1986, 6). In 1995, 29.8 per cent (26/87) of them were women, while only 5 per cent of French national deputies were women. This disproportion in the number of women in the respective parliaments seems to be accounted for by the marginal position of the European Parliament in French politics. Because French politicians, men and women alike, perceive the European Parliament as a modest source of political power, space has been left for women to gain posts. The political significance of the unusually high representation of women politicians in the European Parliament is twofold.

First, because of its structural position the European Parliament is a revolutionary site that enables women and other dominated political groups to partly overturn traditional political hierarchies and challenge an established political culture. Although the traditional sexual division of political labour that assigns men to economic affairs and women to social and cultural affairs, is not reproduced as such in the European Parliament, it is not entirely absent from it either. Nevertheless, women have access to positions of power and may work in traditionally male areas like economics and finance. This has permitted women to acquire political experience in areas traditionally closed to them. Secondly, the European Parliament provides women politicians with a point of access to national electoral politics. As an alternative to the National Assembly, the European Parliament has provided some French women politicians with an opportunity for collective conversion from party politics to electoral politics, and from local to national and European politics. The European Parliament is also used by politicians to accumulate political experience and to transcend national symbolic boundaries.

Despite the broadening of the powers of the European Parliament in terms of co-decision and budget control, the number of French men politicians compared to French women politicians in the European Parliament has not increased in correlation. On the contrary, the expansion of the European Parliament's power has developed in parallel to the strengthening of women's representation. Traditional political and social theories relate an increase in women representation with a decrease in social status and/or salary. However, this study of European integration indicates that as the number of women politicians multiplies, the pressures on social conventions regulating access to mid-level and top positions intensify, and the likelihood of women's presence at these levels increases. The entrance in 1999 of the idea of gender parity into French political morals testifies to this. Male politicians previously unscrupulously used women to further their political goals. Former Socialist minister and MEP Bernard Tapie had the nerve to say what many thought, when he stated, 'with her [the Guyanese politician Christiane Taubira-Delanon], I will certainly make the cover of *Paris-Match*' (quoted in Grosjean 1999). In 1999, male politicians understood that parity was becoming something serious and even dangerous for them. Rosalyne Bachelot, the neo-Gaullist deputy and *rapporteuse* of the *Observatoire pour la parité*, declared that, 'It is encouraging, the buddies are terrorised, they understand that parity is not only words, but that it means: leave your seat' (quoted in Grosjean 1999a). The left has traditionally been more successful in recruiting female candidates because many of its militants have professional competence. This started worrying the right in 1998. François Hostelier, sixth on the RPR-DI list for the European Parliament in 1999, even asked for an audience with a Socialist politician in order to find out exactly how the Socialist Party got so many women on their list.

French Members of the European Parliament

In relation to national politics, the European institutions present an alternative political market, which until the 1980s was still insufficiently developed and whose revenues were modest (Wickham and Coignard 1986, 127). As we have seen in the above, in the 1990s in France, their political weight has unevenly increased in relation to the French central political market. Europe, Thomas Hardy's 'prone and emaciated figure', has become, for some, a powerful image that triggers images of global political and economic power. The development of supranationally institutionalised political resources has been uneven. The Commissioner's post has become a ministerial, executive-level position, which has enabled politicians occupying it to accumulate both personal and collective ('European politician') political resources. For numerous civil servants appointed to a vacancy in the Commission, such as Raymond Barre, Jean-François Deniau, Claude Cheysson, Christiane Scrivener or Yves-Thibault de Silguy, service in Brussels has enabled a climbing of the social ladder and a conversion from public service to executive politics (see Brigouleix 1986). For some other top civil servants having worked in Brussels, individuals such as Commissioner Ortoli or chief of cabinets Gauthier-Sauvagnac and Lamy, the Commission has been a sidestep in an ascending career which has led from civil service to the private sector. Ortoli was appointed to the petrol company Total and Lamy to the bank Crédit Lyonnais after his nomination as Director General to the DG I (Foreign Economic Affairs) was vetoed by Sir Leon Brittan (Ross 1994, 509), and later back to the Commission as a Commissioner. Gauthier-Sauvagnac slipped into a private bank, Kleinwort Benson. In other words, these individuals have succeeded in prolonging their political resources from their initial posts in Brussels to positions in France and, in some cases, to return to Brussels later.

The European Parliament, in contrast, which is situated in a lowly codified and socially less regulated sector compared to French central political markets, does not offer the promise of central positions sought after by high-level politicians, such as ministerial positions. Today in France, European legislative experience seems to be merely a positive accessory to a political curriculum vitae. The status of accessory is evident: only 7.1 per cent (3/42) of Alain Juppé's 1995 government were former MEPs. Many of Juppé's government's members were experts in economic affairs, not in European affairs. The variability of the value of European parliamentary experience is exemplified by the fact that only 4 per cent (4/100) of the most powerful *énarques* had been or were members of the European Parliament (*Le Figaro* 1995, 16). Even women politicians like Alliot-Marie or Lienemann, whose careers have greatly benefited from European legislative experience, consider the European Parliament to be a secondary institution (see Sineau 1988, 211–24). This marginality is reflected in the political careers of political heavyweights. For instance, Laurent Fabius, one of the youngest auditors in the *Conseil d'état* and one of the youngest ministers ever, entered the European Parliament in 1989, only to exit a few years later to take the position of First Secretary of the Socialist Party. Likewise, Valéry Giscard d'Estaing, former President of the Republic, known for his fervent Europeanism and ambition to become the first real 'President of Europe', joined the European Parliament in 1989, but did not seek re-election in 1994. In 1999, he was hoping to be elected one of the Sages that would have renovated the institutions of the European Union, which he did: he became the president of the Constitutional Convention.

Positions held by French politicians in European institutions are reflected in the average age of politicians reaching given posts. The average age (counting from 1967 onwards) of Commissioners on taking up their posts was fifty-four years, whereas the average for the 1989–94 contingent of MEPs was forty-six years. Of the 1989–94 contingent of French MEPs, 13.5 per cent were in ascending trajectories, 67.8 per cent in stable trajectories, and 18.6 per cent in descending trajectories. In ascending trajectories the entrance point into Parliament is lower than the exit point, a ministerial *cabinet* or ministerial level position, in stable trajectories the entrance and exit points are roughly equivalent, and in descending trajectories the entrance point into Parliament is higher than the exit point. For the Commission, the figures were 20 per cent for ascending trajectories (e.g. leaving for a senior ministerial position), 45 per cent for stable trajectories, and 35 per cent for descending trajectories. The high percentages of stable trajectories in both cases might indicate that entry to these levels takes place mostly in other, close positions (such as that of deputy, regional representative, or member of ministerial cabinet) and that it is difficult to capitalise on the kind of political resources available in European institutions. The high per centage of descending trajectories for Commissioners can be explained by the post's elevated status in national political hierarchies, often leading to retirement.

These positions correlate with the frequency of attendance in elite schools and the *grand corps*, a central factor in career mobility. As a rule, women rarely pass through the ENA. However, for men and women alike, a diploma from the ENA is almost the *sine qua non* for insertion into the French executive structures of European political integration. For instance, the per centage of French Commissioners who have been members of the *grand corps* (which includes the *Inspection des finances*, the *Conseil d'état*, but not the *Cours des comptes*, which is more closely linked to more traditional institutions) and who have passed through elite institutions such as the ENA and IEP is close to the average found throughout the French dominant classes (compare to Bourdieu 1989). As we have seen, in contrast, the per centage of MEPs who have the required educational characteristics (and the probable career patterns that are associated with them) to access to and retain top political positions in the French central political market was below the average registered by Bourdieu for the French dominant classes once again taken as a whole. This relative social distance to the political centre enables these MEPs to integrate into cross-national and regional political groups at the medium-level of national political hierarchies. As the renewal rates have shown, MEPs have become increasingly self-regulating, seeking to protect the value of the alternative resources they have access to.

However, these resources are dominated in the domestic political value hierarchies. For instance, for obvious reasons, the training of national and European political elites is controlled by national institutions. In France, training at the ENA emphasises the capacity to examine various problems on a general political level (see Stevens 1981, 137–8). The emphasis placed by the ENA's programme (oral expression, use of literary language, general education ...) has been duplicated at the level of the entrance exam into the overall European bureaucracy (Willis 1983, 19). However, in contrast to these criteria the regional and sectoral character of the European polity and the very technical competence necessary in the European Parliament requires from MEPs expertise in one or more sectors (agriculture, telecommunications, and so on), in one or more regions, and a capacity to communicate with individuals from other cultures in other languages than in one's native tongue. In other words, a discrepancy exists between the criteria used in the selection of candidates and those applied inside European institutions.

Sectoral and regionalism are the main elements of the specific type of collective and personal political resources accumulated by Commissioners and MEPs alike. By sectoralism I mean competence and power tied to sectors of political, economic and social activities (such as telecommunications, energy and agriculture) which spread across national borders. Experience in local government is unequally distributed among national delegations. In the European Parliament of 1989, for instance, France had, after Italy, the strongest regional representation, in contrast to the Dutch, Danish and British delegations, which had very little local political experience (Jacobs et al. 1990, 46). Decision-making in European institutions, which bridge simple political, occupational and national divisions and which apply technical knowledge to regional issues, challenges the largely national variety of political decision-making based on divisions such as left/right, parliament/government, and so on, dominant in national political fields. The institutional forms of this alternative variety of European political resources in the European Parliament include the Crocodile Club, the Kangaroo Club, the inter-group of local and regional representatives, and the Animal Welfare Group. The obvious weakness of this type of resource is that it is situated at the lower end of national political value hierarchies, distinct from the dominant political values with their traditional logic of representative government and conceptions of political legitimacy. Speaking on a more abstract level, one could say today, that three political spheres are clashing into one another within

```
French political field          European Union
                                ────> Commission
National politics               ─────────────────

                                ────> Parliament
                                      Top parliamentary positions
─────────────────────────
Regional politics               ────> Rank and file MEPs
```

Figure 5.1 The French political field and European institutions

the European political field: the national and statist (for France, see Badie and Birnbaum 1979), the 'neo-feudal' (subnational or regional) and sectoral, and the supranational (Streeck and Schmitter 1991, 151). The European political field can be best described as a hybrid of these three sectors.

While MEPs and Commissioners represent different types of resources and structural positions, in terms of the interaction of executive and legislative poles, the interaction between French Commissioners and MEPs has been on the increase since the end of the 1970s (see also De Clerq and Verhoef 1990, 153–4). Since then, five Commissioners were MEPs before going to Brussels and one became an MEP after having been a Commissioner. Until now, most top politicians have become members of the European Parliament in order to add this experience to their political portfolios, but without committing themselves to Europe. Some have done the reverse, however. Delors, Pisani and Scrivener held important positions in the Parliament before going to the Commission: Delors and Pisani were Presidents of the Commission's economic and monetary committee, and Scrivener, Vice-President of the Kangaroo Club (a federalist club in the European Parliament). The complex relationship between these institutions in the French political field are summarised in Figure 5.1. Not surprisingly, top positions in both the Commission and the Parliament have been occupied by top national politicians from large parties, while the more modest positions have been left to middle-level and novice politicians from national or regional politics.

The cultural resources of French MEPs and Commissioners do not differ in many respects from those of the rest of the French political class. To take an example, only 5 per cent of Commissioners and 1.7 per cent of MEPs have studied abroad. Apart from working in European institutions, only a single Commissioner had worked abroad. Few spoke foreign languages, and the prevalence of French in Union institutions does not entice them to study other languages. The middle position of the European Parliament in French domestic political hierarchies prevents French politicians from developing predispositions and policies that reinforce a European perspective on political issues (e.g. knowledge of issues in other countries, language skills, and so on). For better or worse, political attitudes and career constraints reinforce one another.

In order to succeed politically in European institutions, a politician's contacts are essential. She or he must be inserted in various horizontal networks based on such criteria as technical competence (membership in an epistemic community) or nationality. For instance, a well-connected French MEP has easy access to other French members of the Commission and the European Union bureaucracy. This enables him or her to create new political projects. One of these new projects is the Atlantic group, which unites representatives from the costal regions of the Atlantic who are creating inter-regional projects (for instance, the GEANT, *Grands espaces d'aménagement naturels du territoire*), and organising seminars with high-level civil servants from the European Union bureaucracy. By inviting the President of the European Union and the French Minister of European Affairs to a conference devoted to the Atlantic area, the French MEP Jean-Pierre Raffarin, for instance, succeeded in mobilising support for his own projects for his region, Poitou-Charentes. He successfully mustered a 161 million FF grant for his region from the ERDF (European Regional Development Fund) (Abélès 1992, 318–19). In Raffarin's own words, 'Sophisticated lobbying helped me see new possibilities. We invited experts to intervene in the Commission of regional policy and in the framework of the Atlantic Group' (quoted in Abélès 1992, 320). In many ways, the 40 to 50 inter-groups that operate in the European Parliament, ranging from industry, to tourism, to foreign policy, are the real decision-makers in the European Parliament. French Socialist MEPs, headed by Catherine Trautman, Minister of Culture in Jospin's 1997 government, helped develop the Eurocity network, which regularly organised international conferences. Alain Lamassoure, UDF Minister for European Affairs in Edouard Balladur's 1993–95 government, mayor of Anglet and MEP (1999–2004), has been a vocal Vice-President of the Federalist inter-group for the European Union, the Crocodile Club.

Evidence seems to indicate that the simple reason why French politicians are unlikely to support rectifying the European democratic deficit has more to do with the division within the domestic political fields and the political trajectories of individuals in them, than with the European institutions themselves, as most observers have claimed (for an example of this, see Featherstone 1994, 149–70). European institutions can develop only to the extent that domestic practices 'give in'. Simply put, by becoming a European Federalist and working in Strasbourg, no politician would ever get (re)elected on the national level. The danger of too eager Europeanism is evident: alienation from domestic politics and possible failure to renew a national mandate. Not enough Europeanism, for its part, prevents access to important positions in European institutions. In the European Parliament, the top positions are the President and Vice-President, the committee chairs and vice-chairs, the committee coordinators, and finally the *rapporteurs* of prestigious or controversial cases (Jacobs et al. 1990, 51). The values promoted by national politicians follow the broad constraints of a too eager federalism or nationalism. Thus, it becomes the burden of the political parties that control the nomination process to update their practices in order for European integration to develop.

As the career patterns sketched above show, the conditions for the development of democratically elected and European-minded supranational political elites are not particularly favourable. The European institutions have developed to the detriment of electoral politics. If there has been an increase of European institutions as sources of power, this increase has not led to the point where these institutions would radically restructure the political careers of politicians still tied to national political structures.

Some scholars have argued that the institutional solutions leading to political harmonisation would be to gradually strengthen the position of the European Parliament (Duverger 1994, 2) and the interaction between national and European parliaments, on the one hand, and to create a uniform European electoral system on the other (Jacobs et al. 1990, 11). The popular will for European supranationalism is assumed here, and the constraints imposed by national politics sketched for the French case above are neglected. Rather than developing into a united supranational empire, it seems more likely that the European polity will take the form of an American-style 'disjointed pluralism' (Streeck and Schmitter 1991, 159). Needless to say, the process of European multicultural and multilingual nation-building involves incremental, multi-levelled and uneven transformations in national political cultures.

These are transformations which will certainly take decades, perhaps even centuries to materialise. The nature of this European state-building process can easily be misunderstood. From a legal point of view, a European state exists already today, although a European nation does not. European institutions and legislation are the product of national public law, not international law, as in the case of the United Nations. The model of European institutions has largely been the French *Conseil d'état* (Chevallier 1975, 459). Both the European institutions and the *Conseil d'état* are based on the argument of the continuity of the state as a source of law.[3]

As has been said above, European affairs have been classified as belonging in the same group as any other political affairs, following the prevalent 'latent' national conception of political competence. According to this conception, a good politician will learn to do the job, independently of its nature, on the spot. This conception is challenged by the specific competence required for the efficient working of European Union institutions. As the European Union is not a nation with a government and an opposition, this binary logic of opposition minority/governing majority does not work. Instead, politicians have to able to compromise between various, often contradictory points of views which are difficult to understand and accept. This alternative conception of political competence and of the resources that are tied to it finds its echo in regional politics, as Jean-Pierre Raffarin, President of the regional council of Poitou-Charentes, states: 'The elected members have to be experts. The time of the *notables* is over. What counts more and more for a president of a region is to have European expertise' (quoted in Abélès 1992, 321). The synergy between subnational regions and a supranational Europe has become a means to counterbalance the power strategies of state centralism (Abélès 1992, 320–1). According to politicians like Adrien Zeller, President of the Alsace regional council: 'All those in favour of the regions are for Europe' (Zeller 1999).

Conclusions

The European Parliament is a key element in the process of institutional, processual and symbolic structuration of the French and European political fields. The modalities of European political integration are dependent on the main divisions in domestic political fields. In France, integration has not led to the development of a Euro-elite, an integrated group with a clear common interest and identity. Identification to Europe has occurred only in those cases where occupying a European post for a sustained period of time was more the result of bad luck or necessity than choice. In terms of career patterns, experience in European Union institutions proceeds along one of two paths. On the one hand, there is the position of Commissioner, which in French political hierarchies is of ministerial level (highest level); on the other hand, there is that of an MEP, whose role is akin to that of a national deputy or top-level regional representative (medium high level). These two modes of integration into a larger evolving European political field correspond to the duality of French politics, which is divided into executive and the electoral domains – corresponding to the royal road to top positions and the proletarian path to middle-level posts. On this macro-level, the structuration of a European political field has reinforced the split between the executive and the electoral domains, and the dominance of the former over the latter. This process has both worsened the 'democratic deficit' and connected executive politicians to new European Union-level formal and informal networks.

Not only has European political integration provided marginal groups in France with access to national politics through European Parliament elections, but it has also supplied the French government and the presidency with new resources, connecting them to trans-European circles and networks that are

116 Democracy, social resources and political power in the European Union

developing their own political culture. The success of neoliberal economic doctrines in the European Union may be partially linked to these networks. We have seen that national ministers spend half of their time wrestling with European affairs in the Council of Ministers of the European Union or and in transnational party structures, developing a common European culture and outlook on politics and economics. The main ingredients for this neoliberal *Weltanschauung* are well known: electoral cycles should not interfere with economic policy, and unemployment figures should not have priority over other monetary indices in the evaluation of economic and political success.

In the next chapter, I will examine the European Parliament campaigns and elections of 1999 in view of the transformations in political discourses and the symbolic structurations of French and Finnish political fields. Among these transformations are the insertion of elements of civil society, social movements and intellectuals into campaigns politics. The elections are a prime occasion for traditionally non-political organisations to take part in public debate, and bring to the fore topical issues tied to Europe, thus leading to a transformation of national political culture. By promoting women in the elections to the European Parliament, French political leaders indirectly have created pressures for augmenting the representation of women in other sectors of French politics. The recently passed parity law demonstrates that fundamental transformations are taking place in French politics.

Notes

1 By national politics is meant politics relative to national organizations, such as the two houses, government, ministerial cabinets, national organizations of political parties, and so on. By regional politics, I mean institutions such as regional, municipal or communal councils, pressure groups, local and city assemblies, and so on. The distance of individual politicians to national political centres can be assessed by the degree of state recognition (for instance, if individuals have been awarded the *Légion d'honneur*) and informal proximity (for instance, membership in prestigious clubs like *Echanges et projets*, created by Jacques Delors).
2 This hypothesis and its significance for the eventual formation of regional, cross-national European elites tied to the 'four motors' (that is, Baden-Württemberg, Rhône-Alpes, Cataluña and Lombardy, see Harvie 1994, 4) and, more generally to a 'neo-feudal' or federal European political structure (see Sidjanski 1992), needs to be explored more in detail. The study has to be extended to the European bureaucracy having regional loyalties (see de la Guérivière 1992a, 133–4).
3 The state, then, is not so much the result of actions by European institutions or the *Conseil d'état*, but is rather based on the presupposition of its own existence. Paradoxically, then, a European state has existed from the beginning. It is constantly strengthened by the retroactive reinforcement of the Treaty and the *acquis communautaire*.

6 European Parliament elections in Finland and France in 1999

> The existence and legitimacy of the European Parliament has not yet become accepted in national political life. (Socialist politician Pervenche Berés, quoted in Beauvallet 1998, 93)

The establishment of elections to the European Parliament, a supranational political institution integrated into domestic political fields of member-states, has contributed to the political mobilisation of traditionally voiceless groups (such as the unemployed) and to the introduction of new issues tied to 'Europe' into public discussion. This brings with it a transformation of political culture and the relationship between national politics and multinational bargaining (Keohane and Hoffmann 1990, 295). These transformations have not only affected the party system, but also some sectors of civil society. The argument of this chapter is that while European Parliament campaigns provide an opportunity for politicians and civil activists to engage in a dialogue that has multiple effects in the French political field, political agents reproduce national political culture and its in-built power relations. The symbolic structuration of the political meaning of European elections cannot be separated from the institutional structuration of national political fields and the evolving European political field.

Although considered to be weak in international comparison, French civil society has been revitalised by European integration. French intellectuals too have seen in the European Parliament elections an occasion to influence political decision-making and to put pressure on political parties. Some intellectuals, such as Pierre Bourdieu, have used these elections as a means to defend a strong French, Jacobin state and the republican values on which it is based. In his view, globalisation and European integration have called into question the role of the state as a provider of welfare (*état-providence*) and economic security. In Bourdieu's opinion, the withering away of the state has meant a radical transformation of its role in society, a transformation from its position as an authority to that of an arbitrator. In the mind of intellectuals like Pierre Bourdieu, the demise of the state and the threat this poses to the political ethos of the Republic is closely tied to the global triumph of neoliberal economic doctrine.

In Finland, a country that joined the European Union in 1995, the effects of European Parliament elections on domestic politics are significant. Seen from the point of view of politicians, it adds sixteen (after 2004, fourteen) elective posts to the existing 200 seats in the national parliament, and has led to the creation of a new type of politician, the Member of the European Parliament (MEP). An MEP is an elected diplomat, a hybrid between a cultural ambassador and a political representative elected to represent Finland 'out there in Europe'.

Elections to the European Parliament

> After all, it is the first time one speaks of Europe. (former French minister of European affairs Alain Lamassoure on the election campaign in 1999, Lamassoure 1999)

According to numerous studies, the European Parliament is a marginal institution in the political fields of all the fifteen member-states of the European Union. The political values it represents are dominated values on the domestic scale of factors determining political activity and judgment (Reif 1997, 115–24). Consequently, many political scientists consider European Parliament elections as of second-order as compared to presidential or other national elections (Reif and Schmitt 1980, 3–44; Eick and Franklin 1996). However, from the point of view of the emerging European political field, and more specifically, the process of symbolic structuration of this space and the legitimation of structures of political domination, these elections are by no means secondary. Domestic politics have been transformed in many ways (Christiansen 1994; Cowles et al. 2001).

In order to properly evaluate the political status of the European Parliament elections, we must relate them to the long-term strategies of individual politicians as well as various parties and political groups. The 1999 campaign's main factors were the media presence of the candidates (eighty-seven on each list) and the events in Kosovo. The elections presented politicians with an opportunity to first test their strength, but also to challenge their enemies inside and outside their respective parties, either by forcing them to elaborate on their stances on certain issues or simply by discrediting them. The main question for the chief candidates was whether they could present themselves as legitimate contenders for presidential office (*présidentiable*).

Because the European Parliament elections are national elections, but less important than the presidential elections, they provide an ideal opportunity to consult the whole population and test the relative support of challengers and minority currents. Precisely for this reason, the leaders of the political parties are not chief candidates in the European Parliament elections. In order to be eligible for the presidency, the grand prize in the French political game, a candidate has to have a sizable base of support and be considered a candidate of the highest calibre, which today more than ever before, means of European calibre.

In 1999 the elections were, as usual, of minor importance in their outcome, but played with high stakes on the national level – a test for all chief candidates. The political challenge for them was to get as many votes as their lists had got in the previous elections in 1994, which set the standard of success and failure.

European Parliament elections function as a social laboratory in which parties, currents and social movements can, by challenging established political practices, test new ideas and present new candidates. Precisely because French politicians take European Parliament elections to be less important than elections to the lower chamber (the National Assembly), they see in them an opportunity to take risks and to experiment – they have a lower price to pay for failure. Because elections to the European Parliament serve as an occasion to innovate, they give us a glimpse of what national politics might be like in the future, revealing social trends that might otherwise remain hidden. Furthermore, elections to European Parliament provide a public space where ideas relative to Europe can be developed.

Structurally speaking, joining the European Union is a significant event for a country simply because it raises the number of elected national officials. In France, for example, the rise in the number of such officials in 1979 was on the order of 10 per cent; in Finland in 1995 it was 8 per cent. Concretely this means that these new five-year posts become objects of struggle between political parties as well as currents inside these parties. Due to the French rules of competition, they also allow for the representation of various protest movements exterior to party politics. Another structural effect of the European Parliament is its position as an extra-territorial institution based in Brussels. It holds meetings once a month in Strasbourg, France, but shuttles between Brussels, Luxemburg and Strasbourg. However, it is an integral part of domestic politics in all European Union member-states.

As a consequence of the integration of national politics into the evolving European political field, issues tied to European political representation have been introduced into national political debates, creating confusion and uncertainty. What should MEPs' role in domestic politics be? Should national political leaders run for office in the European Parliament, or should they restrict their activities to national parliaments? What criteria should parties use to select their candidates for European Parliament elections? Should the candidates be 'Europeans', experts, regional representatives or solely the representatives of political parties?

Elections to the European Parliament exhibit at least two general characteristics. First, in all European Union countries, the post of MEP is less valued than other elected national representatives or deputies. In France, MEPs do not have the educational characteristics that correlate with positions of national political power (see Chapter 5). As the European Parliament is situated in a relatively unstable space of the evolving European political field compared to national institutions such as the National Assembly, the per centage of MEPs resigning from their posts in mid-term is higher than for national posts. For instance, between 1989 and 1994, 36 per cent of French MEPs abandoned their mandates in mid-term. Of the eighty-seven French MEPs elected in 1994, only sixty-nine (80 per cent) were still MEPs in 1999: eighteen of them (20 per cent) had been appointed ministers in Lionel Jospin's Socialist government in 1997 or had switched to local politics. Also, every election to European Parliament has so far resulted in a lower proportion of newly elected MEPs than returning incumbents. In 1994, only 32 per cent of MEPs renewed their positions. In comparison, 48 per cent of national deputies renewed their positions in 1997. French MEP Fabre-Aubespry echoed a general view among French politicians when he said he would have no hesitations about choosing the National Assembly over the European Parliament (Beauvallet 1998, 30).

Second, the level of abstention is much higher in European Parliament elections than in national or local elections. In France, the abstention rate has fluctuated between 39 per cent and 53 per cent. The sociological characteristics of the voters partly explain this lower turnout. Voters interested in European affairs are well-educated and better-off. According to a study conducted by Martine Chadron, Charles Suaud and Yves Tertrais in Nantes, 45 per cent of this French city's inhabitants are already familiar with Europe because of their work. 59 per cent of these are senior managers (*cadres supérieurs*) (Chadron et al. 1991, 34–46). This over-representation of the middle and upper-classes is visible in the European Parliament, although not to the same extent as in the National Assembly (Birnbaum 1985).

In France, national parliamentary deputies are disproportionately drawn from the social and political elite as compared to MEPs. They are also more likely to hold several political positions simultaneously. For instance in 1988, 96 per cent of deputies held local office in addition to their seat in the National Assembly. For MEPs in 1994, the average number of double-mandates was 71 per cent. Differences in the modes of election partly explain this. In parliamentary elections a two-round majority system guarantees that the main political parties get the most votes. In contrast, the proportional system used in the European elections favours smaller parties and various *ad hoc* political constellations, including social movements.

As the European Parliament has gained power in the 1990s and 2000s, the hostility of national deputies toward it has grown. Tensions have developed. For some deputies, MEPs are not real politicians because they do not have a constituency to nurture. They do not have to spend their Sundays at fairs and markets meeting their electors. Because of their extra-territorial status, MEPs suffer from 'collective split personality disorder', and a general sense of inferiority vis-à-vis national politicians. This sense of inferiority is coupled with a reputation in their home countries for being untouchable, unaccountable and irresponsible. While feeling detached from 'real' politics, MEPs have a sense of being part of a great adventure and historical mission, constructing the architecture of the future, a Europe of the twenty-first century (Abélès 1992). This forward-looking outlook legitimises, in their eyes, their present political illegitimacy and hence the perceived stigma of an institution, the European Parliament, in which the relative absence of traditional political partisan divisions enables intra-party cooperation and political discussion.

The rules of political competition

In contrast to other European Union countries that are divided into several regional districts for the elections to the European Parliament, France comprises one national electoral district. As a result, national representation is emphasised over regional or local representation. In a single voting district, the national media plays a decisive role and nationally known individuals have an advantage. Proportional representation channels political competition differently in the elections to the European Parliament than the two-round majority system used in elections to the National Assembly. Proportional representation means that seats are distributed according to the votes a list receives. Moreover, in France, there is no preferential voting system as in countries such as Finland and thus votes go to lists and not to individuals. The political parties, coalitions or movements set the priorities and rank the candidates representing various interests on their lists. For instance, in the 1999 European elections, the *Rassemblement pour la République-Démocratie libérale-Génération écologie* list (RPR-DL-GE) which went under the name 'L'Europe pour la France' and was led by Nicolas Sarkozy and Alain Madelin, included representatives of different wings of these three parties (RPR, DL and GE): from the followers of President Jacques Chirac to supporters of former Speaker of the National Assembly Philippe Séguin, former Prime Minister Alain Juppé, and various public figures, regional representatives, women politicians, and so on.

In France proportional lists have to pass a 5 per cent threshold. If a list does not get 5 per cent of the total of votes, it gets no seats. In preventing the smallest coalitions from being represented, this threshold hinders the excessive splintering of the political spectrum. However, the 5 per cent threshold was not enough for Socialist Prime Minister Lionel Jospin. In 1998, Jospin tried to transform the proportional system into a *de facto* majority system by proposing a 10 per cent threshold for the European elections, and the division of France into several districts instead of a single one (*Le Monde* 1998, 44–5). Surprisingly, neo-Gaullist President Chirac backed Socialist Prime Minister Jospin in these efforts. Both

Jospin and Chirac wanted to eliminate the smaller parties with representation between 5 and 10 per cent, like the French Communist Party and especially the extreme rightist *Front National* (FN) led by Jean-Marie Le Pen. They hoped that as a result of these measures the French party system would be divided into two hegemonic blocks led by Jospin and Chirac. The proposal met fierce resistance not only from the smaller parties but also from the leaders of various currents in the larger parties. Especially vocal in the opposition to any reforms were the small parties on the left, the Greens, the Communists and Jean-Pierre Chevènement's *Mouvement des citoyens* (MDC) (Graham 1998). Because of this resistance, Chirac and Jospin abandoned the reform.

In their attempted reform, Chirac and Jospin were motivated partly by narrow partisan interests in strengthening their positions on the left and the right and partly by national concern over French influence in the European Union. By renegotiating the rules of competition for the European elections, Chirac and Jospin were trying to consolidate their camps, increase their control over the content of political debates, and prepare the ground for the upcoming political battles of the presidential elections of 2002. Jospin's proposal would have cut up the country up into eight super-regions or 'regional baronies' that would have transformed the national campaigns into regional campaigns. The reform would have done away with the possibility of a plurality of posts (*cumul des mandats*), that is, of holding two or more local or national elected offices simultaneously (Mény 1986–87, 230). Indeed, an electoral law restricting plurality of posts was eventually passed. According to Article L46–1 of this law, 'no one can accumulate more than two electoral mandates'. These electoral mandates include those held by French parliamentarians, European parliamentarians, regional and general councillors, and mayors of town of more than twenty thousand inhabitants.

Chirac backed Jospin's reforms because of the results of the 1998 regional elections in which the *Front National* won numerous seats with the assistance of neo-Gaullist politicians, and five Gaullist presidents of regions were elected with the help of *Front National* voters. Jospin's proposal would have eliminated any hopes of small parties gaining representation. For instance, under the reform the Centre district of France was to be allotted six MEPs, and thus any list would need to receive at least 16.66 per cent of the vote (100 divided by six seats) to be represented in this geographical area. *De facto* this would mean that small parties such as the Greens, the *Parti communiste français* (PCF), the *Front National*, or protest movements such as the Trotskyist *Lutte ouvrière* (LO) and *Lutte communiste révolutionnaire* (LCR), would be left without a political voice in the Centre district.

Chirac and Jospin's second motive for transforming the rules of competition was France's influence in the European Union. Because there were so many

French lists (nine lists were represented in 1999), French MEPs were scattered across the European Parliament in a number of small political groups. As a result, their influence was quite modest (Pitette 1998). This influence was further weakened by the system of plurality of posts. Because, as a rule, French MEPs held other national and regional positions, they were often absent when important decisions were made in the European Parliament. An MEP described the effects of this French absenteeism and how political opponents used it to their advantage:

> Friday was the ideal day for passing a resolution in Strasbourg which was unfavourable to France. Half, even three-fourths of the French representatives had already returned to their electoral districts, to make an appearance on market day or give out medals. (Druon 1998)

One of the effects of French absenteeism has been an increase in French MEPs' hostility toward the European Parliament. Because decisions are made to which French MEPs do not contribute and to which they are sometimes opposed, they feel they can criticise the institution they are supposed to represent. Thus, they contribute to the delegitimisation of the Union and its institutions.

Another effect of Jospin's reform would have been tighter executive control over the French debate on Europe. By regionalising campaigns, Jospin and Chirac would have regionalised the debate and reinforced their control over national priorities. Consequently, the grip the two had over the national political agenda would have tightened. The risk the reform presented for Jospin and Chirac was that by promoting a France of German-style *Länder* they might be creating regional baronies or regional super-representatives, who consequently would have real legitimacy in the eyes of their constituencies and hence challenge national decision-makers – currently the real 'electors' of French MEPs from established parties. Chirac revived this reform project a few years later. In 2003, the rightist parliamentary majority passed an electoral law that cut up France into eight regions and reformed the mode of election of MEPs following the Chirac–Jospin plan (*Journal officiel* 2003; *Le Monde* 2004).

The revolt of the underdogs

For political groups that are in the minority or that represent non-party interests, such as various protest movements, the European elections are a unique opportunity to present their message to a national audience and to shape the political agendas of the ruling parties. European elections enable the partial integration into party politics of protest movements which specialise in the 'politics of the street'. In the European elections of 1999 these protest movements included the *Chasse-Pêche-Nature-Tradition* list (CNPT), representing traditional rural values; a movement of minorities and inhabitants of France's overseas territories; a movement of the unemployed; a list composed of candidates from Martinique; and a list demanding lower taxes. Only a few such groups could realistically hope to win any seats. In contrast, for unknown or novice politicians in established political parties the elections offer a way to become national figures. For instance, Dominique Baudis, television journalist and son of Pierre Baudis, mayor of Toulouse, went through a status transformation from media figure to politician. He became a national political figure after being chosen chief candidate of the *Rassemblement pour la République-Union pour la démocratie française* (RPR-UDF) list in 1994. He did not stay in the European Parliament for long, however. In 1997, Baudis was elected to the National Assembly and resigned his seat in the European Parliament.

Some regional politicians have seen in the European Parliament a forum for promoting regional cultural and economic autonomy vis-à-vis national authorities (Zeller 1999). In France, women politicians have been over-represented in the European Parliament as compared to the National Assembly. For women politicians excluded from male-dominated Parisian political cliques, the European Parliament has presented an avenue of political promotion and an alternative to the National Assembly as a gateway of access into national electoral politics. In the 1999 campaign, for the first time in French political history, credible candidates of African descent appeared on television debates, seeking to mobilise the usually non-voting, non-Christian electorates.

Small parties and *ad hoc* lists and movements use the European Parliament elections to apply for public financing for their electoral campaigns. Until 1995, no laws existed in France concerning the public financing of political parties. To clarify the situation and to attempt to control the private financing of parties, the National Assembly passed a new law. According to this law, a party or list not receiving over 5 per cent of the vote will not have its campaign expenses reimbursed from public funds. However, if the party or list gets over 5 per cent of the vote, the following costs will be recovered: the guarantee of FF 100,000 the party or list is obliged to deposit on entering the race; the official campaign expenses, which may include posters, ballot papers, etc., up to a maximum of FF 20 million; as well as 50 per cent of the legal limit (*plafond légal*) of personal funds brought to the campaign by the candidates themselves. In 1999, the legal limit was FF 58.8 million, allowing up to FF 29.4 million to be reimbursed.

As French party structures are weak compared to most European political party structures and European elections are relatively low-risk elections in political terms, they are an ideal occasion for inter-party currents to compete and measure their political legitimacy. Often, list leaders are political players who try to gather followers and shape a team for French presidential elections.

Presidential elections are at the top of the hierarchy of elections in Fifth Republic France, a semi-presidential system where the president is the most powerful political actor (Duverger 1974). Hence European elections can be seen as intermediate elections between big elections like parliamentary or presidential elections. Political underdogs are also provided with an opportunity to increase their visibility.

The example of Socialist politician Michel Rocard illuminates the character of the elections to the European Parliament as a sort of social laboratory. A major contender for the presidency at the beginning of the 1990s, he led the Socialist list in the European elections in 1994. These elections offered Rocard an opportunity to test his national popularity. They ended in a fiasco and, as a result, Rocard lost his credibility as a serious presidential contender (he was no longer considered *présidentiable*). Neo-Gaullist politician Nicolas Sarkozy met the same fate. By the end of the 1990s, as a result of these failures, the only serious Socialist presidential candidate was Prime Minister Lionel Jospin while the only serious neo-Gaullist candidate remained President Jacques Chirac. In this race, European symbolic legitimacy was as necessary as domestic support. Both Chirac and Jospin were eager to present themselves as European statesmen, rather than men merely of national calibre. As a consequence of this transformation of the context of political action from the national to the European level, language skills and contacts with European and world leaders have become political resources. In the French press, Chirac has been praised for his mastery of the English language. In May 1999, during a trip to Italy, Jospin gave his speech in Italian.

For politicians seeking a popular mandate, the political meaning of European parliamentary elections is different in Fifth Republic France than in most other European Union countries. In Finland, for instance, a politician cannot concurrently be an MEP and a mayor, national parliamentarian or regional councillor. In France, holding a plurality of political posts has traditionally been the norm. For politicians concerned about job security, this is an ideal arrangement. And who would not be concerned, given that most political posts are elected posts and as such are subject to changes in voter preference? For a politician, the drawback of being a European representative in Brussels is that it prevents him or her from carrying out in Paris or in the locality he or she represents the many duties a deputy or a local politician has. But local political anchorage guarantees the political survival of an MEP. The MEP Pierre Bernard-Raymond explains:

> If I had not presented myself or if I had been beaten at the second municipal elections for the mayorship of Gap [a small town in the south of France], I would have had trouble convincing François Bayrou [leader of the UDF Party] to put me on his list. (Beauvallet 1998, 65–6)

Local political anchoring is also required for access to high political offices in Paris. In French political culture, a local position is more valuable than a European one. This is why all rising political stars seek local mandates. Even French Commissioner (1994–99) Yves-Thibault de Silguy presented himself as a candidate for mayoral elections in the north of France. European Commission President Jacques Santer had to intervene and prevent de Silguy from running, as local representation was in clear contradiction with European representation. Losing a local mandate can also have disastrous effects on careers. For instance, in 1995 shortly after being nominated to Alain Juppé's government, Elisabeth Hubert lost the municipal elections in 1998 and was thus unable to renew her local mandate. She was not invited to join Juppé's second government.

Apart from the importance of local office, another distinguishing feature of French politics is the unusually high number of civil servants running for public office. In most European Union countries a civil servant has to resign in order to run for parliament, and there is no going back. In France a civil servant can always apply for a temporary leave of absence (*détachement*), and return after holding a political post to the former position in the civil service. As a civil servant, a would-be politician can run a political campaign from his or her office and be paid for it. After failing to be elected in the European elections of 1999, Bruno Mégret and his comrades-in-arms from the alternative extreme right party *Mouvement national* (MN) returned to their ministries to continue their civil service careers. It is no accident that the Fifth Republic has been called the 'civil servants' republic'.

From the point of view of a French career politician who does not have a civil service job on which to fall back, the risk involved in running for the European Parliament is less than in political cultures where holding multiple elected posts is illegal. At the same time, however, multiple posts are a serious obstacle to further structuration of the French political field and to the professionalisation of the role of the Euro-parliamentarian. As the psychological and professional threshold for running for the European Parliament is, relatively speaking, lower than for the National Assembly, the level of investment and seriousness of the campaign is naturally also lower. In general, a French politician's career will not depend only on the level of professionalism she or he develops in an elected post, but also on the existence of a comprehensive social safety net composed of multiple posts, i.e. a network, the social power of which depends on the politician's relations with top politicians representing currents in intraparty factions. This network also undermines the power of political party structures. It is understandable, then, that MEP Jean-Louis Bourlanges would equate electoral sanction and mentor sanction: 'The electorate does not exist for a European parliamentarian. Ten people – Mr. Valéry Giscard d'Estaing, Mr.

Bayrou, Mr. Madelin, and the rest – that's who the electorate is' (Beauvallet 1998, 52). For French politicians, relations with party leaders are fundamental for their prospects in elections.[1] The case of Michèle Barzat exemplifies the structures of domination inside political parties. Elected to the European Parliament on the Socialist list in 1979, she took her work very seriously and specialised in energy questions. In 1989, however, she was placed twenty-fifth on the Socialist list led by Laurent Fabius. Without the backing of a major political figure, she was not re-elected. Continuity requires entertaining good relations with party bosses. Because of the dominance of this executive democracy, in which electors merely confirm a selection made by party leaders, MEPs are not necessarily tied to specific interests but rather drift and improvise, as their role is not yet codified. As MEP Bourlanges put it: 'Well, you're everybody's representative and you're nobody's. You make appearances everywhere. You never know when you should accept an invitation or refuse one, etc. It really doesn't matter if I'm actually in my district or not' (Beauvallet 1998, 52).

The 1999 election programmes and campaigns

Since the referendum of 1992 on the Maastricht treaty, the 'enjeu européen' (the European issue) has split the electorate and become a major political issue in French politics. A sociological study of the referendum found that, of managers and persons holding a university diploma who cast a vote, 70 per cent of the former and 71 per cent of the latter voted in favour of France signing the Maastricht treaty, while 60 per cent of those who voted against it had a diploma lower than the baccalaureate and 58 per cent of these were manual workers (Bidégaray and Emeri 1996, 71). According to the political scientist Pascal Perrineau, the inhabitants of towns voted overwhelmingly in favour, while those living in rural areas overwhelmingly against the treaty (Perrineau 1996, 45–60). This data seems to indicate that the more educated the voter, the more likely he or she is to be pro-European. Another conclusion seems to be that to a large extent, cultural and social criteria determine political opinion.

European integration is a complex process of readjustment of national political structures, not only of French institutional space through institutions such as the European Parliament (institutional structuration), but also of the space of political discourses (symbolic structuration). This was particularly visible during the election campaign in the run-up to the European Parliament elections of 1999. A clear structuration of political discourses split the left and the right into 'federalists' and 'sovereignists', although no politician would publicly have supported the abolition of the nation-state. This split was partly produced and reinforced by the media. For the candidates, media visibility determined success. As the war raged in Kosovo, politicians made trips there to show their support, a gesture that did not go unnoticed by millions of voters glued to their TV sets during the evening news. Nicolas Sarkozy, chief candidate of the RPR-DL list, declared to the press that he was going to invent something new every week, 'in order to stay a fresh product' (*Libération* 1999:2). The press printed photos of him with strongmen Valéry Giscard d'Estaing in Auvergne and Alain Juppé in Aquitaine. Sarkozy's political tour de France was ironically labelled 'the magical Sarkozy tour' on '*La semaine des guignols*' (23 May), a satirical weekly television show on Canal Plus.

To show his backing of François Hollande's Socialist list, Prime Minister Lionel Jospin spent his time travelling to meet other Socialist leaders in Rome and Madrid and hosted a political meeting at the Palais des Sports in Paris with British Prime Minister Tony Blair and German Chancellor Gerhard Schröder. Media coverage of the political events and demonstrations ranged from daily radio-shows like Jean-Pierre Elkabbach's daily interviews of politicians on 'Europe 1' at 8:21 a.m. exactly, to a special political talk-show on Sundays at 6:30 in the evening, conveniently scheduled to come just before the *apéritif* and broadcast on LCI's cable television station and on radio station RTL. Putting in an appearance on these shows was a must for any politician. On the state television Channel 1 (TF1), the programme 'Public' featured a special Sarkozy-Hollande debate. Paul Amar's show 'Direct' on Thursday evenings on France 2, and Christine Ockrent's '*Politique Dimanche*' on Sundays as well as '*France Europe Express*' on Thursdays on France 3, all competed in inviting heavyweight politicians. The media week was crowned on Sundays by the satirical programmes '*Le vrai journal*' and '*Les guignols*' on Canal Plus. During the summer of 1999 Canal Plus also presented a special programme in which every one of the top candidates appeared before the public.

Could Daniel Cohn-Bendit, former student leader of May 1968, deputy mayor of Frankfurt am Main and now chief candidate on the (French) Green list be a player of national importance in French politics? To prove that he could be, he had to get at least 10 per cent of the votes. Could chief Socialist candidate François Hollande build his political career without the explicit backing of Prime Minister Jospin? To prove that he could, he had to attract more than 14.49 per cent of the voters, Rocard's result in the 1994 elections. Would François Bayrou, president of the centrist UDF and chief candidate of the list '*Avec l'Europe, prenons une France d'avance*' and Alain Madelin, second on the list '*L'Union pour l'Europe*' (led by Nicolas Sarkozy), be able to muster enough support for their ideas to present a viable alternative to the dominant party on the right, the RPR led by President Chirac? As a consequence, might the next French President be from the right but not from the neo-Gaullist Party? To demonstrate that this was a real possibility in the spring of 1999 when such a proposition was considered unlikely, both Bayrou and Madelin would have needed at least 10 per cent of the vote each. To achieve this goal, they were faced with a choice: join the RPR or go solo and get the necessary votes by themselves.

On the left, Robert Hue might lose his job as Secretary General of the French Communist Party (PCF) if he did not succeed in getting as many votes for his list as in the previous elections, 6.91 per cent. Could he do this with a separate list or should the Communists join the Socialists? The neonationalist and anti-European MDC, led by Jospin's Minister of the Interior Jean-Pierre Chevènement, which got only 2.3 per cent of the votes in 1994, might try to better its score by forming a coalition with the Socialist Party, with which Chevènement had already started to negotiate in the winter of 1998. Another left-wing movement, the *Parti républicain de gauche* (PRG), which succeeded in winning thirteen seats in 1994 with Bernard Tapie and a different name, *Énergie radicale* (ER), had no alternative but to join forces with the Socialists, although the proportional system used in the elections in fact guaranteed these smaller parties a certain advantage over the larger parties.

Due to the war in Kosovo – and France's role in this war – the architecture of a future Europe, immigration policies, a common European defence and other pan-European issues became, for the first time, major political questions that split the political spectrum and turned the torpid political campaign into a heated, moral one. Table 6.1, which is a simplified table, presents the chief candidates and their positioning vis-à-vis European integration. The two dimensions are left–right and sovereignist–federalist. The federalist-sovereignist dimension cut across the left-right dimension. The leftist federalists were Daniel Cohn-Bendit of the Greens, First Secretary of the Socialist Party François Hollande, and the less openly federalist Communist leader Robert Hue. Dominique Voynet, Minister of Environment in Jospin's government and leader

Table 6.1 Europeanism in the French campaigns to the European Parliament

	Left	Right
Federalist	Daniel Cohn-Bendit, Greens François Hollande, Socialists Robert Hue, Communists Alain Krivine, LCR Arlette Laguiller, LO	François Bayrou, UDF Alain Madelin, DL Nicolas Sarkozy, RPR
Sovereignist	Jean-Pierre Chevènement, MDC	Charles Pasqua Philippe de Villiers, RPF Jean-Marie Le Pen, FN Bruno Mégret, MN Jean Saint-Josse, CNPT

of the Greens, was more critical toward Europe than was Hue. General Secretary of the Communist Party since Georges Marchais's resignation in 1994 and chief candidate of the list '*Bouge l'Europe!*', Hue combined anti- and pro-European elements in his campaign. Rightist federalists included François Bayrou, chief candidate of the '*Union de la France*' list. Slightly less openly federalist was Alain Madelin, leader of DL and number two on the RPR-DL list, led by Nicolas Sarkozy, interim president of the neo-Gaullist Party. In April 1999, Sarkozy, more ambivalent than Bayrou or Madelin toward Europe, replaced Philippe Séguin, speaker of the National Assembly, who had resigned from the presidency of the neo-Gaullist Party as a protest against Jacques Chirac's policies.

Despite this splitting of the political spectrum following the federalist–sovereignist dimension, and in view of Chirac's desire to remain in the presidency for another term, Bernard Pons, president of the association '*Les amis de Jacques Chirac*', tried to create the broadest possible coalition against the left in the European elections of 1999 with the presidential elections of 2002 in view. Chirac's support of Jospin's electoral reform followed this logic. Chirac and Pons wanted to collaborate with rightist politicians Pasqua and de Villiers, who formed a common list '*Rassemblement pour la France et l'indépendance de l'Europe*' (RPF) after Philippe Séguin resigned from the head of the RPR-DL-GE list. Philippe Séguin, at this time still speaker of the National Assembly and president of the neo-Gaullist Party, represented the conservative wing of the RPR. He had serious disagreements with American military dominance in Europe, and would not accept France's minor role in the North Atlantic Treaty Organisation (NATO).[2] A notorious anti-European, Séguin thought it was possible to conduct the European political campaign in 1999 on a purely national programme. Like Pasqua, Séguin wanted to save Gaullism from Chiracism, that is, from its subordination to Chirac's presidential ambitions. Séguin was ready to lead a national list without giving more power to the regions and without collaborating with the hard-right FN and the centrist UDF. In contrast, Chirac's political strategy for re-election in 2002 was to give more power to the regions, to divide and rule and form a broad alliance on the right that could challenge the leftist presidential candidate, which in 1999 looked like it would be Lionel Jospin.

Among the self-proclaimed sovereignists, Jean-Pierre Chevènement, the head of the MDC, represented traditional leftist Republicanism and nationalism, building his campaign on an anti-European integration platform despite being Minister of Interior in Jospin's government. On the far left, Arlette Laguiller, the only female chief candidate, leader of the LO and presidential candidate in 1995, and Alain Krivine, leader of the *Lutte communiste révolutionnaire* (LCR), had inherited an anti-establishment posture from the Communist Party, which had moved toward the centre of the political spectrum in the previous years. On the right among the sovereignists, Charles Pasqua, former Minister of Interior and co-founder with Jacques Chirac of the RPR, and Philippe de Villiers, founder of the '*Mouvement pour la France*' party and deputy from Vendée, headed the RPF list. On the far right, both Jean-Marie Le Pen and Bruno Mégret conducted 'anti-imperialist', 'anti-American' and 'anti-European' campaigns.

Extremist parties such as the FN, LO and LCR resisted European integration in its current form, whereas larger parties closer to the centre of the political spectrum were pro-European. Generally speaking, this same divide – big parties for and small against – was reproduced in other European Union member-states as well, cutting across traditional left/right divisions among others, and restructuring the space of political ideologies. As a result, parties and movements on the extremes of the political spectrum found themselves to have common strategic interests not only symbolically but also pragmatically, at local, national and supranational levels. For instance, Charles Pasqua quit the RPR after it was clear that Jacques Chirac had become its undisputed master. For the European elections of 1999, he created his own list on a sovereignist platform. He saw that Jean-Pierre Chevènement's leftist, anti-European MDC had common interests with his. Apart from Chevènement's anti-Europeanism, one position they shared was overt opposition to France's role in the war in Kosovo and to the bombings there. Despite these common interests, however, Pasqua did not succeed in creating a left–right coalition. Chevènement, who was at this time Minister of the Interior in Jospin's government, probably saw more to gain from a coalition with the smaller PRG and the Socialists in government.

Why, then, are the large French parties pro-European? First, large political organisations aim at forming governments by themselves or in cooperation with other parties. Second, at the moment, dominant economic and political interests in all EU member-states are pro-European to varying degrees. Once in government, party representatives have to collaborate in the context of European Union institutions not only with their equivalents from other European Union member-states in the Council of Ministers and other Union institutions, but also with the administration in Brussels. From a purely pragmatic point of view, expressing anti-European views is impossible in these Europeanised political contexts. However, it is not impossible to be anti-European and hold a ministerial position. But Jean-Pierre Chevènement's activities as Minister of the Interior in Jospin's government and as leader of the anti-European MDC illustrate that the constant contradictions between anti-Europeanism and work in a government that is *by definition* pro-European have in the long run diminished Chevènement's political legitimacy and permanently damaged the MDC's political future.

As a rule of thumb, at the end of the 1990s in the European polity, the higher a political leader is in national political hierarchies the less likely the leader is to be anti-European, at least while in government. This European divide creates tensions for all lists and parties, taking various forms that individual politicians resolve with varying degrees of success.

French Europeans of the left and social movements

The Kosovo war, too, had effects on how the campaigns were run, splitting the political spectrum. Already planned campaigns had to be reorganised, leading to confusion. Henceforth, political meetings could not be too enthusiastic. The Socialists' video clip on the theme 'L'Europe, c'est la paix' had to be cancelled. The Kosovo war also opened the door for intellectual activism that pressured the government into facing certain issues. The threat of an independent list 'to the left of the left' (gauche de gauche) led by sociologist Pierre Bourdieu was real, forcing, among other things, the Communists, the Socialists and the Greens to seek cooperation with certain social movements.

Because of the power of the new European political cleavage between those for and those against Europe, organisations such as Chevènement's MDC and Robert Hue's list *'Bouge l'Europe!'* were caught between contradictory ideological and pragmatic political requirements. Ideologically, the French Communist Party was against market forces and the creation of a common European defence. Pragmatically, as a partner in Jospin's government, it had to back the French war effort in the Balkans. It could not openly question Jospin's moves to forge a common European security structure, to cut public spending or to privatise industry. Hue even declared in the business daily *La Tribune* that 'the Communists are not the adversaries of the market'. He maintained that:

> The Communists have broken with the statist view of things. We are thinking more of a system that will enable us to overcome the division between private and public yet mobilise both, under the auspices of a new kind of social appropriation which does not exclude the private sector. (*Le Monde* 1999a, 7)

Consequently, the Communist Party's strategy for the European elections consisted of being pro-market and pro-European for pragmatic reasons but also critical of the market and of Europe for ideological and historical reasons. These contradictions could not be resolved. For instance, some Communists demanded that Hue resign from the government as a protest against the war. According to Hue, resigning would have only split the left in two, reinforcing the positions of both Jospin on the left and Chirac on the right just before the European elections. Besides, as he put it, 'Why resign when you can be more effective in the government?' (Virot 1999a)

Since Hue's appointment to head the Communist Party in 1994, he has little by little renovated the party's structure and programme. At the beginning of 1999, the party's main newspaper *L'Humanité* eliminated the hammer and the sickle from its front page. This was not just symbolic politics. *L'Humanité* declared that it had found a new way of doing politics. Its director Pierre Zarka stated bluntly that 'L'Huma[nité]-new look' had ceased to be the Communist Party's campaign tool and that it would no longer function as a mouthpiece for the Communist Party. *L'Humanité* and the party had adopted a new conception of the electorate and those elected, tied more to civil society. The party leadership decided to invest heavily in its European campaign as an opportunity to sound out public opinion and test the credibility of its new political line. The party's campaign was the costliest of all the election campaigns of the 1999 European elections: FF 40 million compared to FF 37 million of the Socialists' campaign. It consisted of 1,400 public appearances by politicians in different parts of France. Communist leaders had decided to offer bread and circuses to attract traditionally passive voters:

> Tonight, at the Cirque d'hiver: The ten artists of the list '*Bouge l'Europe!*' invite everyone to the Cirque d'hiver in Paris tonight, admission free of charge. You want the programme? Marko's De Graph' performance; a piece on urban cultures; the Fu(rap) section; Solo jah Gunt (reggae dub faya) … Then, for you jazz-lovers there is Jean-Claude Petit, Mélodica and Jazzcogne. Also, piano solos by André Minvielle and Bernard Lubat. It goes on: Djamel Allam, Farik Berki (hip-hop blues) … Finally, the crucial moment: the 'Citizens' dance-show' … And along with all this, Roger Hanin, Richard Bohringer, appearances by 'surprise' comrades and the whole '*Bouge l'Europe!*' team. The show starts at 7 pm. (*L'Humanité* 1999b, 6)

The Communist campaign for the European elections was, from the very beginning, intended to give a fresh, new image of the party. The campaign was to appeal to various ethnic groups and would be open to social movements, including the diverse activist labour organisations, groups such as the '*sans papiers*' (persons without immigration papers), and the unemployed which had been organising marches and demonstrations in France's largest cities since 1995. The Communist Party no longer wanted to be a militant party. Like the Greens, led by Daniel Cohn-Bendit, the Communist Party tried to attract the young and usually non-voting electorate by minimising traditional politics. In both cases, the campaign for the European Parliament was reduced to pop music, cultural celebrities and buffets. In compiling his list of candidates for the European Parliament, Robert Hue also developed the novel idea of 'double parity'. This meant not only the already popularly accepted parity between men and women, but also parity on the list between Communist and non-Communist, professional and non-professional candidates. To muster support for the Communist list, Hue was forging an alternative to the radical anti-capitalism of Arlette Laguiller and Alain Krivine while responding to the challenge from the Green list by applying the same methods the Greens themselves were using.

The press published the names of a thousand supporters of Hue's list. These included the wife of the former Communist Party Secretary General Georges Marchais; Pierre Bergé, CEO of the fashion firm Yves Saint Laurent; the Kabyle singer Idir; and the novelist Gilles Perrault. The first public meeting of Hue's list *'Bouge l'Europe!'* was held in Saint-Ouen, a working-class suburb of Paris. In organising the meeting, the party contacted intellectuals and activists from various social movements. Theatre director and *'sans papiers'* activist Stanislas Nordley received a phone call and was asked to join the party's list. In spite of the fact that he was, in his own words, 'sensitive' to the issue of harnessing the social movement to the Communist Party, Nordley accepted. Recalling his motives for joining the Communist list, he came to the conclusion that 'a protest vote on the left or the right is not enough' (Nordley 1999). Institutions would have to be changed from the inside, and this would take a long time. Fodé Scylla, former president of the anti-racist organisation *SOS-Racisme*, legitimised his own decision to accept the party's invitation by citing his desire to bridge the gap that separated social reality from the political parties. According to Scylla, the Communist Party gave its candidates total liberty. Personally, he wanted to defend all those 'without' (*'les sans'*) – those without identification papers, those without a home, those without jobs; as well as women, who were victims like the unemployed. 'For me, the European elections are an opportunity to extend my anti-racist struggle' (Scylla 1999a). He was against an 'Anglo-Saxon Europe', and wanted to talk about concrete issues close to the concerns of ordinary people. 'People I meet want to know how they can get dental care' (Scylla 1999b).

The Communist list provided social movements with a platform where militants and human rights activists could meet and forge common goals. The video clip created for the Communist Party's meeting was intended to be an 'interface with society', according to André Campana, a representative of the firm that created it (*L'Humanité* 1999a). Like the Green list, the Communist list also included candidates of colour and Muslim candidates in an attempt to mobilise at least some of the three million French Muslim voters. For Hue, 'this list does not make us less Communist. It makes us Communists of the twenty-first century. If we don't change with society, society will change without us' (Thénard and Virot 1999, 14). For Communist hardliners, however, Hue's activities exemplified sheer opportunism, 'a deviation that will lead to elimination' (Anonymous Communist hardliner 1999).

In their programme for the elections, the Communists wanted to reinforce the European Parliament and weaken the Commission, especially in the areas of competition and commercial policies. They supported the institution of the Tobin Tax on the movements of speculative capital and the elimination of tax paradises sheltering money-laundering outfits and other illegal financial activities. The Communists called for the creation of a social Europe, conversion of all temporary jobs into permanent ones, guarantees of a minimum wage, opposition to the relocation of businesses and the introduction of shorter working hours without cutting salaries. The role of the European Economic and Social Committee was to be strengthened. '*Bouge l'Europe!*' also vowed to develop a common European defence, not in the framework of NATO but rather in one provided by the United Nations (UN) and the Organisation for Security and Cooperation in Europe (OSCE).

On the extreme left, Arlette Laguiller and Alain Krivine represented the unemployed and the workers, labouring for 'rebirth of a force that will renew the revolutionary tradition of the workers' movement' (Bazin 1999, 35). They openly criticised the leftist government for not being on the left and for being lackeys of the bourgeoisie. Commended by some of their supporters for using 'right, simple, natural, and plain words' (Forcari 1999, 18), both candidates of the 'red left' (*la gauche rouge*) demanded the convocation of a representative congress of the European peoples to constitute a New Europe. Like the Communists, they wanted to see more taxation of high incomes and speculative profits. As pacifists, they called for a Europe without wars, ethnic cleansing or intervention by the superpowers. Contrary to Cohn-Bendit's Greens, the LO and LCR were against NATO's bombing campaigns in the former Yugoslavia. They demanded the privatisation of public enterprises be stopped and that new jobs be created in hospitals, public transportation and public education. 'Companies that make profits of billions of francs and then go and fire their workers [...] must be requisitioned' (Fabre 1999, 7). The working week should be reduced from 35 to 30 weeks without cutting salaries.

Laguiller made the statement that, if elected, she would defend in the European Parliament the interests of Europe's 18 million unemployed and 50 million poor people (Laguiller 1999). In a campaign that almost exclusively concentrated on unemployment and social exclusion, Laguiller and Krivine claimed to be not anti-European, but rather against a Europe of the market. As in their previous campaigns, Laguiller and Krivine assumed the symbolic role that the Communist Party had abandoned: the denunciators of those in power. At their public meetings, the International was sung with raised fists, recalling the 'good old days' of the revolutionary movement. A retired manual worker spoke up at one of these meetings about his motives for voting for Laguiller and Krivine, echoing wider sentiments:

Listening to you takes me back to my twenties. With you at least we get down to the essentials. Yes, the bosses are still there. Yes, we have to get rid of capitalism. Yes, exploitation is getting worse. Thank you for bringing up these obvious facts that seem to escape Robert Hue. (Bazin 1999, 35)

Daniel Cohn-Bendit was the most federalist of the main candidates on the left. His ambition was for the Greens to become the strongest party on the left, after the Socialists and before the Communists. In their programme, the Greens promoted qualified majority voting in the Council of Ministers and the elaboration of a European constitution. The European Union also needed a constitutional court, a Senate where the regions and various peoples of the Union would be represented and a stronger European Parliament that would foster links with European civil society. The Greens called for harmonisation of taxes in Europe and the elimination of tax paradises. Taxation should be more just and ecological. As the French ecological party, the Greens also wanted to sponsor a European pollution tax and initiatives of the eco-development type. Like the Communists, LO and LCR, the Greens were in favour of introduction of the Tobin Tax on capital movements between the European Union and the rest of the world, a levy which would finance an 'international public fund for co-development'. The Greens were convinced that unemployment rates could be drastically cut by shortening working hours without diminishing salaries. Ecologically useful activities had to be furthered and a minimum European income equal to the poverty limit had to be instituted. In the long term, a pan-European defence system would replace NATO and the Western European Union (WEU).

Close to Cohn-Bendit in terms of his pro-European sentiment was François Hollande, First Secretary of the Socialist Party which represented the governmental majority and whose slogan was '*Construisons notre Europe*'. According to Hollande the Socialists, who had created a common list with Chevènement's MDC and the PRG for the European elections, wanted a modern Europe that would take into account social, employment and defence issues: 'Our objective is to promote Europe politically through the extension of qualified majority voting, to further the creation of a European defence system, and to jump-start the Europe of citizens and jobs' (Hollande 1999, 13). Because of the anti-Europeanism of Chevènement's MDC, the Socialists replaced the initial formulation in their programme of a 'federation of nation-states' with the more neutral 'a union of nations and peoples freely agreed upon in mutual respect and the interest of all concerned' (*Le Monde* 1999b, 9). The Socialists wanted a European Constitution and the extension of majority voting in the Council of Ministers, increased collegial responsibility of the European Commission and a wider scope for the Parliament's co-decision-making. In conjunction with enlargement of the Union to the East, the Socialist Party called for a renovation of European Union institutions. The party emphasised that the human rights records of the new member-states should be closely monitored. Like the Greens, the Socialists supported the idea of harmonisation of European taxes as well as imposition of a Tobin Tax on capital movement and abolition of financial paradises. The Socialist Party also wanted to see the value added tax (VAT) on manual labour-intensive economic activities cut. In terms of a 'social Europe', the Socialists pushed for a social treaty of the same breadth and scope as the economic and monetary treaties in order to fight social exclusion. In their vision, by 2005 working hours would not exceed 35 per week, a minimum wage would be in force and a mechanism of convergence of real salaries would have been instituted across the European Union.

To demonstrate the seriousness of his commitment to Europe, Hollande declared to the press in March 1999 that he would take his seat in the European Parliament in July after the elections. He wanted to disprove accusations that the Socialists were not taking the elections seriously and that the top candidates would defect from their European seats at the first opportunity, like they had done in the past. Hollande's declaration also surprised Prime Minister Jospin, who responded by saying that Hollande would go to the National Assembly just like all the other first secretaries before him. In the party there was no doubt about priorities, despite the party's pro-federalism: first came the National Assembly, then the European Parliament. Like previous chief candidates Jospin, Fabius and Rocard, Hollande would have to give precedence to the National Assembly. In this way, Jospin confirmed the popular perception that the European Parliament was less important than the National Assembly. He also reinforced a kind of electoral hypocrisy. If the chief candidate preferred Paris to Brussels and thus did not take the elections seriously, why should the electors care about Brussels and vote in the elections? As a consequence of Jospin's pressure, Hollande withdrew his candidature to the European Parliament, but only after the votes had been cast.

Visions of Europe on the split right

On the right, the lists that most fully tapped into the public's anti-European sentiments were Pasqua and de Villiers's RPF and the extreme right lists of Jean-Marie Le Pen and Bruno Mégret, the FN and MN respectively. The RPF, the FN and the MN represented alternatives for the traditional supporters of the RPR, which had turned into a pro-European party after Séguin's resignation from its leadership. Pasqua and de Villiers joined forces after Pasqua failed to form a Republican anti-European coalition with Chevènement's leftist sovereignists. According to opinion polls conducted by the BVA Institute on 2 April 1999, nearly two months before the elections, Pasqua would have won about 4 per cent of the votes by himself, whereas de Villiers would have received just under 5 per cent of the votes. With these scores, neither would have surpassed the threshold of 5 per cent: joining forces was the only alternative.

At the core of the RPF's political message was animosity toward Germany, glorification of the nation-state, anti-Americanism and virulent defence of a neo-Colbertist economic philosophy. Pasqua and de Villiers wanted to reinforce European security by developing a common defence without an integrated European defence system. NATO had to be renovated in order to enable European action to be implemented by the Europeans themselves. In their security system, the WEU would become the pillar of the new European defence. According to a joint communiqué dated 9 April 1999, NATO had become

> Europe's *de facto* diplomatic, defence, and security organisation. We have to change Europe. The European Union, which was devised to guarantee peace and the prosperity of European nations, should not rely on others in the defence of its interests or its political activity. Independence is the condition of Europe's future and world stability. (Saux 1999a, 7)

Pasqua and de Villiers demanded that Europe forge its own defence programme, while condemning the European superstate which prevented economic growth. They demanded a reduction of the European Union's structural spending. In their eyes, the Union had to stay an association of states, and national legislation had to be given the priority over European Union legislation. Consequently, the authority of the Council of Ministers had to be superior to that of the European Commission. The European Parliament's power should be restricted to co-decision, and the powers of the national parliaments should be reinforced. These two institutions, the European Parliament and the national parliament, should form the two legislative chambers of the European Union. Dismayed by the pace of integration, Pasqua noted that 'Treaty after treaty, we create independent institutions to which we grant powers that have taken our states centuries to conquer' (Pasqua 1999, 23). In accordance with the famous Luxemburg compromise, the right of veto of the member-states had to be maintained.

Extreme right leaders Jean-Marie Le Pen and Bruno Mégret had a similar discourse to Pasqua's and de Villiers's. Playing on the general insecurity and fears about immigration, both portrayed Europe as a danger for France. Being pro-European was a crime against France. For Le Pen, for instance, Brussels was a Trojan horse in the service of America and NATO dominance. In terms of defence policy, both Le Pen and Mégret were partisans of a common European defence without the Americans. In economics, national priority had to be reinstated and the taxes of small and medium-sized companies drastically cut. National preference had to be instituted, which would, according to Le Pen, free

France from the fetters of unemployment. Bruno Mégret proposed that the Council of Ministers be replaced by a Council of Nations, which would make decisions in unanimity. In this scheme, the Commission would be replaced by an administrative secretariat, and both the Parliament and the European Court of Justice would become mere consultative bodies.

Nicolas Sarkozy, mayor of Neuilly and chief candidate of the list RPR-DL-GE, was faced with a difficult task. He took over the presidency of the RPR and the common list in mid-March 1999 after the resignation of Philippe Séguin. Séguin, deputy of the Vosges, had been chosen by President Chirac to head the neo-Gaullist Party in an effort to gather a single rightist list behind his presidential programme. Séguin, a noted anti-European, had voted against the Maastricht treaty in 1992. Had the war in Kosovo and the NATO bombings on 24 March 1999 not occurred, France would not have got involved in this war and as a consequence Séguin's European campaign could probably have been run without discussing purely European issues. Philippe Séguin had commented before the bombings that 'In the European elections, talking about Europe is out' (Jarreau 1999, 13). From the beginning of the war, Séguin criticised France's war efforts and its president, leader of French foreign policy and supreme military commander.

Unfortunately for Séguin, the war forced all the lists to take stances on a host of European issues. If Chirac, in appointing Séguin to head the neo-Gaullist list, clearly did not want him to take anti-European stances, Chirac could not expect Séguin to take pro-European stances either. Before the outbreak of the war this understanding remained workable, but it still constrained both Chirac's and Séguin's political activities. Although Séguin might have been able to attract anti-European voters from the extreme right and Pasqua's and Villiers's followers, Séguin's open anti-Europeanism prevented Chirac from attracting pro-European voters who were shifting their support to Bayrou's centrist and pro-European UDF. Had Séguin fully backed French military actions in Kosovo he might have stayed at the head of the neo-Gaullist list. But for Séguin, backing French military action would have meant agreeing to cooperation with NATO and legitimising intra-European military cooperation. He chose not to do so. In these changed political circumstances, the understanding between Chirac and Séguin came under growing pressure and finally broke down.

Sarkozy's political future was totally dependent on how well his list did. A supporter of Edouard Balladur, Chirac's main opponent on the right in the presidential elections of 1995, Sarkozy's political task was to draw the split right together behind a presidential majority. 'My ambition is not to end my days in the European Parliament. The President needs a strong Gaullist movement. That's my mission' (Sauvage 1999, 7). As the architect of Jacques Chirac's European policy, Sarkozy would further Chirac's re-election. Working toward this goal, Sarkozy first attempted to create a common list with Alain Madelin's DL and François Bayrou's UDF. This plan failed, leaving the right in a state of total disarray on the eve of the elections. Sarkozy's pathetic attempt to form a common list with Charles Pasqua was also doomed to failure from the start. For Pasqua, president of the regional council of the Hauts-de-Seine and general councillor of Neuilly, Sarkozy, who was mayor of Neuilly since 1983, was nothing but an opportunist.

Tactically speaking, Sarkozy was trying to bring together the anti- and pro-European supporters of the RPR, the Europeanists of the UDF and the sovereignists of the Pasqua-de Villiers list. The aim of uniting pro- and anti-Europeans was also visible in the president's rhetoric. Pro-European in his public appearances, Chirac was also vehemently nationalistic in his ambition to construct a Europe for France, a French Europe. In order to succeed in this balancing act, Chirac and Sarkozy had to try to incorporate into their programme both Bayrou's openly federalist programme and Pasqua's ultra-nationalism. Indeed, Chirac's main political concern since the 1970s had been to eliminate or at least diminish the power of both the centre-rightist and the conservative wings of the right. Chirac presidential programme went hand in-glove with the RPR's programme.

In its official programme, the RPR stated it was for a Europe of nations and states rather than a federal Europe. Both the RPR and DL wanted to grant more powers to both the Commission and the Council, counterbalanced by an increase in the power of control by national parliaments. They wanted to oppose the independence of the European Central Bank by strengthening the power of the large European Union countries and of the Euro 11, the committee composed of the ministers of finance of the countries in the Euro-zone. In Sarkozy's and Madelin's view, enlargement of the European Union to the East had to be as swift as possible, integrating the new democracies into Europe, a dream of General de Gaulle's. While demanding a reform of social security that would address retirement, unemployment, poverty and exclusion, both politicians were opposed to European taxes and to increases in the European budget. Both Sarkozy and Madelin were also in favour of reinforcing common European defence in the framework of the WEU and NATO and of developing a common European defence industry.

In order to succeed, Sarkozy's operation of uniting the right required the president's full support. The problem was that the president, 'supreme arbiter and above politics' according to the French Fifth Republic Constitution, was solicited by both Sarkozy and Bayrou for support. Publicly Chirac could give his support to neither; although his backing of Sarkozy's neo-Gaullist list was evidenced in subtle ways. For instance, Sarkozy needed the support of other European politicians to challenge the Socialists, who were backed by the

European Socialist Party. Although the RPR was not affiliated in the European Parliament with the European Popular Party (EPP), Chirac convinced Conservative Spanish Prime Minister José Maria Aznar to meet with Sarkozy. Sarkozy had vowed that the RPR would join the ranks of the EPP in the European Parliament. To the great surprise of François Bayrou, president of the UDF, which was part of the EPP, Chirac personally called Aznar and asked him to see Sarkozy 'as a favour' (*Le Canard enchaîné* 1999a, 2), a request which Aznar of course could not refuse.

What interests did the RPR-DL-GE list represent? Sarkozy and Madelin, leader of DL (the former *Parti républicain*, PR), deputy and mayor of Redon, took into account three general criteria in putting together their list of candidates. The first criterion was that no deputies of the National Assembly should run, except for the two chief candidates. Sarkozy and Madelin wanted to prevent the holding of multiple posts from being too widely spread because it would be harmful for their image as modernising parties. The second criterion was that persons having served two terms in the European Parliament should not be candidates. This guaranteed the renewal of French representation in the European Parliament. Of the first thirty candidates on the list, three-fourths were new. The third criterion was gender parity, which had become a political must: half of the first thirty candidates were women, half men. All in all, of the eighty-seven candidates, forty-eight were women and thirty-nine men. Sarkozy was quick to capitalise on this, declaring that his list had more women candidates than Bayrou's or Pasqua's. Clearly the Gaullist chief candidate saw having women candidates as a condition for winning the elections. 'We have gone beyond the requirements of parity. Like this, we can rest easy during the elections' (quoted in Grosjean 1999b, 9). The problem was finding the women, and Sarkozy was forced to list candidates such as Clara Gaymard (twenty-first position), the wife of a former State Secretary of Health.

Apart from these general criteria, Sarkozy and Madelin had to take into account the various currents in their respective parties. By appointing Sarkozy to follow Séguin as chief candidate of the RPR, Chirac secured the passive support of former Prime Minister Edouard Balladur, a potential challenger on the right. Margie Sudre, number three on the list, was a former state secretary of Francophone relations and close to Chirac. Apart from being a woman, Sudre also represented the island of Réunion. Tenth and eighteenth on the list were Christine de Veyrac and Mylène Descanges, former assistants to former president of the UDF, Valéry Giscard d'Estaing. The presence of these candidates on the list in eligible positions attested to Sarkozy's close relations with Giscard and to the former president's willingness to 'play his own game' and give his support to Chirac, instead of backing Bayrou. The followers of Alan Juppé, former prime minister and mayor of Bordeaux, included Hugues Martin (fifteenth position), special adviser to Juppé, Yves Wervaerde (twelfth position), Juppé's former substitute in Paris, and Marie-Thérèse Hermange (nineth position): all had good chances of getting elected. The candidates behind Philippe Séguin, former speaker of the National Assembly, included Serge Karoutchi (eleventh position), deputy and president of the RPR at the regional council of the Île-de-France, and deputy Anne-Marie Schaffner (seventeenth position). One of Sarkozy's candidates was the regional councillor of Auvergne, Brice Hortefeux (thirteenth position). Apart from Alain Madelin, two other candidates were former ministers in Juppé's 1995 government, Eric Raoult of the RPR and François Hostalier of the DL (Saux 1999). DL candidates included, apart from Madelin, MEP Françoise Grossetête (fourth position), MEP Thierry Jean-Pierre (sixth position), MEP Yves Wervaerde (twelfth position), and Anne-Marie Schaffner (seventeenth position). All in all, of the eighty-seven candidates on this list, forty-seven were members of the RPR, twenty-nine of the DL, and three of the GE. Eight of the candidates were regional officials and 'representatives of civil society'.

On the centre-right, the chief candidate of the UDF, François Bayrou, former minister of education in Edouard Balladur's government, was openly federalist, vowing to take his seat in the European Parliament if elected. For a public used to dejection, this was a clear sign of commitment: as noted above, chief candidates usually gave up their seats in the European Parliament shortly after having been elected. Without the war raging in Kosovo, the content of the debate over Europe in the elections would probably have been reduced to abstract internal quarrels over 'political Europe'. As a consequence of the war, a real European agenda became possible. It made perfect sense in this situation for Bayrou to run his own independent UDF list instead of joining forces with other right-wing lists. Sarkozy and Madelin bargained for some time with Bayrou, who demanded fulfilment of three conditions to create a common list: support of a European defence system, a European constitution and a European president.

Since 1998, relations between the UDF and the RPR had been tumultuous. The *Alliance pour la France*, an umbrella organisation created by the parties to further their common interests, had been a disappointment for Bayrou: the larger RPR seemed systematically to get the better deal. The UDF lost the presidency of the Senate in October 1998, confronted the RPR and the DL concerning the succession of Charles Millon to the presidency of the Rhône-Alpes regional council, and was faced with the 'non-negotiable' choice of Philippe Séguin as the head of the list for the European elections. The UDF's campaign slogan was '*Une Europe de la clarté*'. In his programme, Bayrou wanted to see a common European defence on the basis of the WEU, which would be integrated into the European Union. This intervention force would not supplant the national armies. Rather, it would be called in by the Council of Ministers by majority vote. Bayrou called bluntly for a European defence system, a European constitution and the election of a European president who would 'carry as much weight on the world scene as the president of the United States does' (*Le Monde* 1999a, 7). A 'College' composed of national and European parliamentarians would elect the European president. Bayrou also defended a European tax that would replace the national contributions to the European Union budget.

In putting together his list Bayrou had to take into account criteria similar to those Sarkozy-Madelin had to consider when they created the RPR-DL-GE list. On Bayrou's list, forty-five of the eighty-seven candidates were women. Of the first eleven candidates five were women, including such prominent politicians as future president of the European Parliament Nicole Fontaine (second position) and Françoise de Veyrinas, a minister in Alain Juppé's first government (tenth position). Like Sarkozy and Madelin, he also had problems finding women. Bayrou could not avoid listing the wives of political supporters. Jeanne-Françoise Hutin, wife of François Hutin-Desgrées, publisher of *Ouest-France*, the largest French regional newspaper (circulation 800,000), was seventeenth and municipal councillor Janelly Fourton, wife of the CEO of Rhône-Poulenc, was seventh on the UDF list. In response to Hutin's candidature the satirical weekly *Le canard enchaîné* wrote, '*Ouest-France* gives particular attention to the appearances of the UDF list' (*Le canard enchaîné* 1999b, 21). Other well-known candidates included General Philippe Morillon (third position), hero of the Bosnia-Herzegovina war, Alain Lamassoure (fourth position), former Minister for European Affairs in Edouard Balladur's government, and Thierry Cornillet (eighth position), president of *Parti Radical* (PR) and mayor of Montélimar.

In the anti-European camp, the CNPT list led by Jean Saint-Josse, regional councillor of Aquitaine and mayor of Corraze (Pyrénées-Atlantiques), was a clearly rural and regional 'anti-political' list. Its budget was a modest FF 5.5 million compared to the Communist Party's FF 40 million. Many of its candidates were former sportsmen, presidents of hunting associations and individuals involved in the gun industry. Left behind in the wake of economic modernisation, they fought against cultural 'uniformisation' and the power of the European technocrats. Anti-ecologist by constituency, they opposed the policies of Green Minister of the Environment Dominique Voynet, which they thought threatened traditional ways of life connected to hunting and fishing by forbidding, for instance, the night hunting of woodpigeons (*palombes*). According to Saint-Josse, Europe had to stay a Europe of differences, a space 'where regional and national identities are recognised, where elected officials instead of technocrats make decisions' (Garcia 1999, 10).

The election results

The 1999 European parliament elections were held on Sunday, 13 June in all fifteen European Union member-states. In France, the abstention rate reached a record high of 52.98 per cent. As in previous elections, the average French voter was an educated, middle-aged, upper-middle-class man interested in politics. The most attentive to European politics were farmers, managers and members of the liberal professions. The highest rates of abstention were found among the young, women, manual workers and employees (Ysmal 1999, 6). According to Pierre Giacometti of the opinion polling organisation IPSOS, the main reason for the high level of abstentions was the absence of hot issues (Guiral 1999, 8). The electorate felt its vote would not change anything. The results of the elections are shown in Table 6.2.

Apart from the electoral lists of social movements, such as the movement of the unemployed, which did not pass the 5 per cent threshold, the losers in these elections were the extreme right, the Communists and the RPR-DL-GE. The extreme right, once united behind their leader Le Pen, was now divided into two fractions, Le Pen's FN and Mégret's MN. As a result, only Le Pen's party got over five per cent of the votes and succeeded in getting five seats in the European Parliament. The Communists, led by Robert Hue, stayed slightly under their goal of 6.8 per cent with 6.78 per cent of the votes (six seats). Half of these seats went to various civil activists, including the former president of *SOS-Racisme* Fodé Scylla. Chirac's presidential list led by Sarkozy did not succeed in attracting the votes of the more conservative electorate, who turned either to Pasqua's and de

Table 6.2 Results of the French elections to the European Parliament, 1999

List	Percentage of votes	Number of seats
PS-MDC-PRG	21.95	22
RPF	13.05	13
RPR-DL-GE	12.82	12
Greens	9.72	9
UDF	9.28	9
Communists	6.78	6
CPNT	6.77	6
FN	5.69	5
LO-LCR	5.18	5

Sources: Ministère de l'intérieur; *Libération* 15 June 1999.

Villier's RPF or to the extreme right lists. As a result of the electoral failure of the Gaullists, the positions of the Socialists and Jospin were strengthened, whereas that of President Chirac was weakened. The three parties of the traditional right got around thirty-five per cent of the votes. On the left, the parties in government were the winners with about thirty-nine per cent of the votes.

The surprise winners in the elections were Pasqua and de Villiers's RPF, the Greens and the CNPT. The Greens, led by Daniel Cohn-Bendit, succeeded better than the Communists in attracting some of the undecided voters. The hunters' list, led by Jean Saint-Josse, got 6.77 per cent of the votes and six seats in the European Parliament. Not surprisingly, most of its supporters were in the rural areas of southwest France. In some villages, up to thirty per cent of the votes cast went to the hunters.

How can this success be explained? In essence, it was a protest vote against the established parties in elections, who were perceived as being secondary. Many who had previously voted for Bayrou, the president of the general council of the Pyrénées-Atlantique and stronghold of the 'hunters', had had enough of the quarrels between the leaders of the right, and cast their ballot for 'the hunters' as they were familiarly called. Others, feeling that the Green minister of environment, Dominique Voynet, was threatening the traditional rural way of life with the European Nature 2000 legislation, found in Saint-Josse's programme a defence of their rural interests and their heritage. Jean-Claude, the president of a local hunting association in Orion (Pyrénées-Atlantique), justified his choice the following way:

> I voted against the Greens, I blame them for everything. They are anti-hunting, anti-rural, anti-everything. They are against the countryside. There is a general feeling of unease in the countryside, but the politicians don't care, so this is the only way to get heard. (Grosjean 1999b, 9)

For the first time in French political history, lists and parties developed their own visions of Europe and of France's place in it, and made use of the opportunity presented to them.

In Finland, which joined the European Union in 1995, the elections to the European Parliament in 1999 also ushered in many changes. It anchored Finnish electoral politics more firmly in the supranational level.

Delegitimation and European deputation: the case of the Finnish elections to the European Parliament in 1999

> Häkkinen won! (Social Democratic Prime Minister Paavo Lipponen's televised comment concerning the results of the European Parliament elections in 1999)

Why Finland? The Finnish case is interesting because, in contrast to member-states like France, it enables an examination of the effects of European integration on national politics within a limited time-span, from the time Finland joined the European Union in 1995 to the present. It is hardly an exaggeration to say that joining the European Union has profoundly transformed the Finnish political field, the relationships between institutions, citizens and political power, and between foreign and domestic politics (Nousiainen 1992; Murto et al. 1996; Kauppi 1997). The effects of integration are of course not always clear or unequivocal. Certain scholars have talked about an accelerated integration (Murto et al. 1996), an over-Europeanisation induced by historical exteriority to the process of European integration. With this approach, the cases of Finland and Sweden can be separated from those of older European member-states like France or Germany, which were involved in the integration process from the beginning. Accelerated integration is visible especially in the areas of legislation and business, and particularly in terms of privatisations and the triumph of neoliberal economic doctrine.

However, can one assume that the effects of European integration are active only after the country in question joins the European Union? Several economic transformations (connected to admission criteria, for instance) took place prior to 1995, and in preparation and anticipation of the political reality of 1995 (Nousiainen 1992). In fact, the process of joining the European Union officially started in September 1991. The problem is that European integration is a process that affects the Finnish political field as a whole, influencing directly and indirectly multiple discursive and structural transformations that are not restricted to the electoral system. This influence ranges from direct causal determination to latent support, due, for instance, to the structural affinities between political agents such as MEPs. In the hierarchy of embassies in the Finnish Ministry for Foreign Affairs, for example, the most important posts have traditionally been Moscow, Stockholm and Washington. With the advent of the European Union, Brussels henceforth is the most important post, according to some diplomats (Raivio 1996).

The integration of the Finnish political field into a European political field means that political agents construct various strategies that reflect different ways of appropriating the levers of power and dealing with the transformations that integration imposes. These strategies are simultaneously reactions and local anticipations, that is, rationalisations linked with political careers and political discourses, which are seen, for instance, in the adoption of a European political vocabulary. Generally speaking, 'Europe' functions for many as a mechanism for the multiplication of political power, especially at the level of the national political executive. National executives can now present themselves not only as national but as European politicians, relatively independent of the national level. Politicians are eligible for supranational posts and integrated into European and global networks, such as at Davos and other meetings with European Union representation. In a world that has become smaller, the value of this European type of political resources increases in relation to traditional, national political resources, without however simply substituting the latter. The example of the political trajectory of a Finnish Commissioner is illustrative. Social Democratic politician, former minister, Erkki Liikanen was nominated to Brussels in 1995 and re-nominated in 1999. Liikanen's stature has grown, and his investment in a European career has clearly enabled him to rise and stay at the top of Finnish national politics, standing above the fray.

Elections to the European Parliament play a key role in the collective construction of Europe and Union institutions. As the 1999 French elections have demonstrated, they give political organisations such as parties and social movements the opportunity to construct their 'their own visions of' Europe and in this way influence popular perceptions concerning Europe. European elections also partake in the restructuring of national political fields by presenting political agents with a new structural basis for political action. How should one conceptualise the role of European elections in these national fields?

German political scientists Karlheinz Reif and Hermann Schmitt have presented the most influential interpretation of the role of European elections to date (Reif 1997; Reif and Schmitt 1980). According to this interpretation, elections to the European Parliament are second-order elections as compared to national elections. These second-order elections have the following characteristics:

1 Politically there is less at stake in these elections than in other national elections.
2 Second-order elections are protest elections, which explain the high level of abstentions.
3 Small and new parties are more successful in second-order elections than in first-order elections.
4 Second-order elections result in a decreased popularity of parties in power.

While examining the campaigns and the Finnish elections of 1999 I will also 'test' these ideas.

The rules of the game

The Finnish national parliament chose the first contingent of Finnish Europarliamentarians (MEPs) in 1995 when Finland joined the European Union. In 1996, universal suffrage was introduced for European election voting. This instituted the practice that the sixteen Finnish MEPs (fourteen in 2004) are chosen in a single nationwide district, through *preferential* list voting. In the European elections, a voter casts votes for individuals and not lists. This favours small parties. Each party or list can present at most twenty candidates. In contrast, elections to the national parliament (the *eduskunta*) are conducted in fifteen districts, in direct and uninominal elections. As seen above, in France, on the other hand, elections to the European Parliament are essentially framed as a continuation of the politics of political parties (Perrineau 1996; Bidegaray and Emeri 1996). In this French mode of election, parties or lists decide on the serious candidates, which are placed at the top of the list. Candidates are pre-selected. In the Finnish European elections, as voters choose between individuals, the elections are not a continuation of party politics in the same way as in France. Rather, the Finnish European Parliament elections have acquired a character of their own. Because the country is one electoral district and the vote is preferential, given to individuals and not lists, the power of political organisations in the pre-selection of eligible candidates diminishes. This gives the advantage to the media, foremost among which are the four national television channels and the largest daily, *Helsingin Sanomat* (Majonen 1996).

The preferential voting system introduces further biases into the political game. Collective political organisations, parties and lists compete for the recruitment of candidates of national renown. Consequently, eligible candidates are most often individuals known to the national audience. Some of them might be total political novices. This manner of 'pre-selection' gives a new tone to political competition. First, the economic resources held by candidates reinforce the distance between the public and the political class. In 1999, the average taxable income of Finnish MEPs was three times that of the average voter (approximately €52,700 compared to €15,600) (Tilastokeskus 1999). It is interesting to note that considering all 140 candidates for the European Parliament, the average taxable income was €34,500, twice that of the average voter. Secondly, the role played by educational resources is evidently even more crucial for election to the European Parliament than in national elections. While 13.9 per cent of the electors hold a university diploma, 87.5 per cent of Finnish MEPs and 65 per cent of candidates to the European elections held a university degree. In contrast, 70 per cent of Finnish MPs have a university degree. Thirdly, the media, and especially television, favour oral presentation skills. This resource is of course unevenly distributed in the political class. The voters select on the basis of pre-selection criteria involving three types of resources: economic, educational and presentation of self. The higher per centage of holders of university diplomas and of persons enjoying national or regional renown show that the criteria of European political representation are different than those of traditional political representation. It is clear that parliamentary and local elections are more tightly controlled by political parties.

Compared to other elections, the Finnish elections to the European Parliament resemble presidential elections, because of their tendency to highlight individuals. In France, as we have seen, some politicians, such as Michel Rocard for instance, use the European elections as a testing-ground for presidential elections. In Finland, several factors linked to national political culture emphasise the individual nature of European elections. For some while, electors have become increasingly mobile and party loyalty has become an affair of the past (Pesonen et al. 1993, 53–69). In lieu of jealously guarding their voters, parties attempt to attract new voters by recruiting to their lists well-known individuals. Like in other small member-states of the European Union, the limited number of candidates (140) and parliamentarians (16) favours the individualisation of the election. The preferential voting system channels political stances inside the parties themselves. This process, and the strategy of the national political executive to delegitimise the European Parliament, can prevent the formation of a strong, collective anti-European protest party or movement that would split the parties and the electorate. At the same time, however, the fragmentation of political opinion inside political parties prevents the constitution of a single party line.

The preferential voting system has numerous effects. It accentuates the divisions inside political parties between anti- and pro-Europeans, by forcing political duels between 'sovereignist' and 'federalist' candidates. It aggravates the division between political professionals representing the party, and amateurs – that is, individuals who aspire to represent Finland. With these rules of the game, the media becomes an arena of competition less between parties' political programmes than between celebrities that are recruited by parties, but present themselves as 'apolitical' or 'independent'. Preferential voting also sharpens the geographical division between the Helsinki region, where one quarter of the population lives, and the rest of the country. For this reason it is not uncommon for various regional interest groups to put their weight behind candidates who, if chosen, would represent their interests in Brussels. The role of the media and of television especially has sent political campaign budgets soaring (Majonen 1996). While the average budget for national parliamentary elections was between €25,000 and €34,000 in 1996, this rose to an average of €67,000 in the 1999 European election, i.e. about twice the amount. The budget of the Centrist regional candidate Kyösti Virrankoski from Pohjanmaa was astronomical by local standards, officially at €150,000 (see also Majonen 1996).

Since the first European Parliament elections in 1996, the Finnish parties' programmes have developed considerably. In 1996, the programmes could be described as lacking in political vision. Given the novelty of the elections this was not surprising (Anckar 1997, 262–5). Campaigns were neutral, partly because of the popular anti-European sentiment that prevented the candidates from developing their European visions. In 1999, the programmes were already more developed.

On the right, the Conservative Party and the Centrist Party (formerly called the Agrarian Party), conceptualised Europe in terms of a national project, of the protection of jobs and of fighting pollution. The Conservative Party emphasised the economic aspects. Europe would guarantee economic progress and stabilise Finland's economic position in the world. They also expressed the wish to rationalise the European decision-making system without giving more power to Union institutions. For its part, the Centrist Party resisted the federalisation of the European Union and wanted to give more power to the regions. Protagonists of a neutral Finland in terms of foreign policy, the Centrists wanted to see power decentralised in the European Union. Like the Social Democrats and the Left Alliance (the former Finnish Communist Party) on the left, the third party on the right, the Swedish People's Party, which represents Finland's Swedish-speaking minority (about 6 per cent of the population), was worried about European security and the creation of a peace project. However, in contrast to leftist parties, the Swedish Party emphasised the positive role of the market in this project of peace and prosperity. The programme of the ecologists also gained in precision since 1996. The Greens argued that Europe needed a supranational agency that would be responsible for environmental protection. They demanded a common European strategy that would lead to the abandonment of nuclear power. The programme of the Left Alliance was coloured by the ideas and policies of the Socialist Internationals. Less ideological in character, the Social Democrats acted as the protagonists of the principle of equality in European decision-making and for the elimination of unemployment.

Nevertheless, in the 1999 European elections, the party programmes resembled one another. There were more differences between individual candidates than between political parties. The most pro-European was the Conservative Party and the most critical the Centrists, which was in opposition at that time. Between these extremes one finds the critical Europeans, the Greens and the Swedish People's Party. Because of the mode of the elections, differences of political opinion on European policies were formed as much (or more) from inside the parties than between the parties. The largest 'party' by far is the Party of Finland: in 1999, as in 1996, the majority of candidates were chosen to represent the country more than for their political ideology.

The media debate

The electoral 'grand final debate' took place on 10 June 1999 on the main Finnish television channel TV1. The main political leaders Paavo Lipponen, Prime

Minister and leader of the Social Democrats, and Sauli Niinistö, leader of the Conservative Party and Minister of Finance, were conspicuously absent from the debate. Their parties, too, seemed to want to avoid talking about Europe. Why? The silence can be explained by the consensus that reigned among the Finnish national executive concerning Finnish European politics. According to this consensus, the European Parliament was insignificant. Another reason was the upcoming Finnish presidency of the European Union, to start two weeks after the elections. The message to the voters was clear: elections to the European Parliament were secondary. In the European Union, what really mattered was intergovernmental cooperation, especially for small member-states like Finland. It was of course true that the sixteen Finnish seats were but a small portion of the 626 seats in the European Parliament. But the contempt for European electoral politics demonstrated by Lipponen was also short-sighted and anti-democratic. His macho comment after the election results on television was revealing. In saying 'Häkkinen won!', Lipponen was referring to the Formula One victory of Finnish driver Mika Häkkinen. This result seemed to him more important than that of the European Parliament elections.

This delegitimation of the democratic process by political leaders had its corollary in the almost total absence of political parties in the explicitly political work of framing and initiating political debates during the campaign. This political and symbolic task was simply left to the candidates themselves and the media. Consequently, Finnish collective political enterprises did not develop their own visions of Europe or elaborate stances on issues tied to European politics. By abstaining from this kind of definition of platforms, the political parties and the political leaders deserted a wider public debate on Europe, Finland's place in it and in its future. Paradoxically, it was thanks to this unofficial delegation of power to forces outside political party control that the media debates during the campaigns could focus on European questions and not those of internal politics, as was the case in most other European Union member-states. This contempt for the process, and the retreat of parties and leaders from the campaign that accompanied it, ironically enabled real discussion to develop on issues such as the enlargement to the East, the European monetary system, the development of supranational decision-making, as well as the roles of the European Parliament and the Council of Ministers. These debates were initiated by candidates and journalists without the blessing of political parties.

The results

On 13 June 1999, only 31.4 per cent of voters bothered to go to the polling booths. This was the second lowest voter turnout in Europe, after the UK. In 1996, voter turnout had been at 60.3 per cent. How can this be explained? Had

152 Democracy, social resources and political power in the European Union

the novelty of these elections already faded away? Without doubt the parties and leaders bear a great deal of the responsibility for this democratic catastrophe. They signalled to voters that, 'It's OK not to vote'. This message was linked to a well-known feature of Finnish political culture according to which foreign affairs (in which European affairs are included) are the domaine reservé of the political and economic executive elites. The people should not meddle with such issues. 'Election fatigue' was an additional reason for a dramatic drop in voter turnout. National parliament elections had taken place in March three months earlier, with a voter turnout of 68.3 per cent.

According to a study by Statistics Finland (Tilastokeskus 1999), non-voters in the European elections were more likely to be found among voters from the lower classes. This abstention was directly reflected in the electoral turnout of leftist parties, the Social Democrats and former Communists, both of which lost seats. Of voters under 26 years of age only 26 per cent voted. The highest turnout was in the region around the capital (40.5 per cent voted), and the most phlegmatic voters were to be found in the north eastern part of the country, in the Kuopio province (25.7 per cent).

The sixteen elected MEPs are shown in Table 6.3. One can see that a slight majority of MEPs were Europeanists. The prototypical Finnish MEP was male, forty-seven years old, of the capital region, and a university graduate whose taxable yearly income was about €52,000. From an economic and educational point

Table 6.3 Finnish MEPs; 1999–2004 (Left/Right, Europeanists/Anti-Europeanists)

Left	Right
Europeanists	
Riitta Myller (SDP, PSE)	Piia-Noora Kauppi (Conservatives, PPE)
Ulpu Iivari (SDP, PSE)	Ari Vatanen (Conservatives, PPE)
Heidi Hautala (Greens, V)	Marjo Matikainen-Kallström (Conservatives, PPE)
	Ilkka Suominen (Conservatives, PPE)
	Astrid Thors (SPP, ELDR)
Reino Paasilinna, (SDP, PSE)	
Matti Wuori, (Greens, V)	Eija-Riitta Korhola (Christian Party, PPE)
Anti-Europeanists	
Esko Seppänen (Left, GVE-NGL)	Mikko Pesälä (Centre Party, ELDR)
	Samuli Pohjamo (Centre Party, ELDR)
	Kyösti Virrankoski (Centre Party, ELDR)
	Paavo Väyrynen (Centre Party, ELDR)

of view, he was a member of the social elite. He was known to the general public and had important linguistic resources and experience living abroad.

Three of the sixteen MEPs were total political novices: the former rally world champion Ari Vatanen a resident of Monaco who was recruited by the Conservative Party (Kokoomus, KOK); the television journalist Eija-Riitta Korhola, elected on the list of the conservative Christian Party (Suomen Kristillinen Liitto, SKL, that changed its name to Christian Democrat Union of Finland in 2001); and the former director of Greenpeace International and renowned human rights lawyer Matti Wuori, who was elected on the list of the Greens (Vihreät, VIHR). All three present themselves as patriots ready to fight for the country's interests in the European Parliament. Wuori declared he would concentrate on human rights and environment issues. Vatanen exhibited the profile of an ordinary person who is at the same time also a man of the world. In an interview to the French daily *Libération* he stated:

> I am not a political person. Ordinary people trust me and listen to me when I talk to them about Europe, which I know well. I fell in love with the *Provence*. We live on a continent of incredible richness. I hope to build bridges between people, to be a sort of ambassador. (Merchet 1999, 15)

In the previous elections to the European Parliament in 1996, four amateurs were elected, among them former cross-country skiing Olympic champion Marjo Matikainen-Kallström (Conservative Party). She was re-elected in 1999. Among the MEPs elected in 1999, we find, as in 1996, three former ministers and nine former MPs (56 per cent of the total Finnish contingent). This indicated the solid link of direct recruitment from the national parliament to the European Parliament. 39.3 per cent (55/140) of European Parliament candidates and 44 per cent (7/16) of the elected were women, a good average in a member-state like Finland. 37 per cent of the elected could be called regional representatives, the remaining 63 per cent, national representatives. For instance, Ari Vatanen, candidate of the Conservative Party, received most of his votes from Southern Finland and only 1,000 votes from Lapland, the northernmost district. In contrast, Kyösti Virrankoski, Centrist regional candidate from the Vaasa district in the Western part of the country, received 67.7 per cent of his votes from his region.

Among Finnish MEPs, regional representatives were the Centrists Paavo Väyrynen from Lapland, Kyösti Virrankoski from Ostrobothnia, Samuli Pohjamo from Oulu, Mikko Pesälä from the region of Kymi, and the Social Democrat Riitta Myller from Northern Karelia in the eastern part of the country. The first four of these, running on the Centrist list, a party in governmental opposition, were convinced anti-Europeans. This went especially for Väyrynen, a former prime minister and former leader of the Centrist Party. Myller, on the other hand, portrayed herself during the campaign as a pro-European social democrat, working not only in the interest of the party but also for her region and of the country as a whole.

Twelve of the sixteen MEPs were elected thanks to votes from the southern part of the country, which is the most populous. The Green Heidi Hautala received the most votes, 9.3 per cent of the national total. The conservative Marjo Matikainen-Kallström got 6.8 per cent of the vote and Astrid Thors, Euro-parliamentarian from the Swedish People's Party, 6.5 per cent of the vote. This ranking list revealed several interesting facts, such as the continuity between old and new representatives, the role of gender (as those that received the most votes were women) and the dominance of candidates from the south of Finland. Especially Hautala was elected thanks to votes from large southern cities like Helsinki, Turku and Tampere, the regions where electors voted the most and where practically all national elections were decided. In 1999, the lack of strong popular anti-European sentiments prevented the Centrist Paavo Väyrynen and the former Communist Esko Seppänen from a repeat of their overwhelming victories of 1996.

In terms of the distribution of votes, the European elections confirmed some long-term tendencies in Finnish election cycles. Table 6.4 indicates that since 1995, among the larger parties, the Social Democrats have lost seats whereas the Conservatives have won seats. Compared to the previous European elections of 1996, the Conservative Party gained 5.1 per cent in 1999. The position of the fourth largest party, one which often tends to participate in coalition governments, seems to have shifted from the Left Alliance to the Greens. Compared to the previous elections, the Greens received 5.8 per cent more of the vote. Thanks to their very media friendly candidate, MEP Astrid Thors, the Swedish Party succeeded in raising their list's proportion of votes to 6.8 per cent, which is above the official per centage of Swedish-speaking Finns of the total population (6 per cent). In terms of seats, the losers were the Social Democrats (from four to three seats) and the Left Alliance (former Communists) (from two to one seat). The

Table 6.4 Results of the Finnish European Parliament elections in 1999 in percentages and seats (in parenthesis)

	Soc	Cent	Cons	Left	Swed	Green	Christ
NP95	28.3	19.8	17.9	11.2	5.1	6.5	–
EP96	21.5(4)	24.4(4)	20.2(4)	10.5(2)	5.8(1)	7.6(1)	2.8(0)
NP99	22.9	22.4	21.0	10.9	5.1	7.3	2.0
EP99	17.8(3)	21.3(4)	25.3(4)	9.1(1)	6.8(1)	13.4(2)	2.4(1)

NP= National Parliament, EP= European Parliament

winners were the Greens (from one to two seats) and the Christian Union (from zero to one seat). All of those elected from winning parties were well-known to the nationwide public. These figures do not confirm the thesis of Reif and Schmitt, according to which the governmental opposition and protest parties usually win in European elections: the Centrist Party lost, and protest parties were virtually nonexistent in the Finnish case.

A structural model of transformations in national political fields in the context of the European political field as an emerging, multilevelled and multipolar political order should take into account the structural and temporal position of European elections. Scholars should analyse the social and political characteristics of politicians working in the European Parliament – a marginal institution in the context of the internal politics of all European Union member-states and their national political hierarchies – in order to evaluate the effects of integration on these domestic fields. Can one speak of the formation of a new political elite arising from these developments?

It seems that in Finland certain politicians have monopolised these posts. The following individuals succeeded in retaining their seats in 1999: Paavo Väyrynen, Samuli Pohjamo and Kyösti Virrankoski of the Centrist Party; Riitta Myller and Reino Paasilinna of the Social Democratic Party; Heidi Hautala of the Green Party; Marjo Matikainen-Kallström of the Conservative Party; Esko Seppänen of the Left Alliance; and Astrid Thors of the Swedish Party. Overall, 56 per cent (9/16) retained their seats.

How did these MEPs use Europe, what kind of political strategies did they apply? For many, particularly Väyrynen and Seppänen, the European Parliament served as a basis for attacks against the leaders of their own respective parties, the Centrist Party and the Left Alliance. Both were virulent critics of the European Union and of the Finnish national executive's 'pro-European pragmatism'. On the other hand, paradoxically, for many Centrist politicians the European Parliament was essentially a forum where they could defend the interests of their regions in the face of the nation-state. The other MEPs able to renew their mandates were pro-Europeans who used their political competence to forge a new career for themselves – a career which was regional, national and European at the same time. Many of them specialised in European issues. The Green's Heidi Hautala, for instance, distinguished herself in the European Parliament as a specialist on issues relating to environmental protection and transparency of the Union.

A new political type: the elected diplomat

According to a poll in 1999 by *Helsingin Sanomat*, the largest Finnish daily, 83 per cent of the respondents considered an MEPs most important task the conscious promotion of Finnish interests (Pennanen 1999, 2). Furthermore, a majority of the respondents thought that MEPs should be able to express themselves well and have international experience. With the advent of European elections, a new type of politician was born: the elected diplomat, a hybrid of cultural ambassador and political representative. The MEP was elected to represent the country or a region, not a political ideology, and to defend the interests of Finns in the European Parliament.

In the Finnish political field, the criteria for being a European representative were largely cultural, which, as we have seen, stands in contrast to the French political field. The person elected had to be presentable 'over there' in Europe: to be media-friendly, cultivated and well-mannered. In politics, as in other sectors of contemporary Finland, being 'international' seemed to be the monopoly of the middle and the upper-middle classes. The case of Eija-Riitta Korhola illustrates the significance of the 'personal' characteristics required. A popular TV journalist and mother of three children, she holds a Ph.D. and has never run for public office. She does not consider herself to be a politician: 'Rather, I consider myself to be a critical citizen' (Korhola 1999, B3). According to Korhola, the Christian Party was looking for a candidate from outside professional politics who could attract the votes of the Christian public (over 90 per cent of Finns are members of the official Lutheran Church). This she did this admirably. The daily *Iltalehti* described her in the following way: 'Eija-Riitta Korhola is an ideal representative for the Finnish Christian Party. She is a smooth talker, she smiles nearly all the time in the American style. She is elegant and sure of herself' (Ahokas 1999, B6).

The case of the regional Centrist candidate Kyösti Virrankoski is also exemplary in many respects. His campaign was largely financed by the regional daily *Ilkka* of Ostrobothnia in the western part of the country. His election was presented as a necessity for the region's future. The following profile of Virrankoski was published in *Ilkka*:

> He has a diploma of higher education and he is teacher of mathematics. Kyösti isn't a professional politician. On the contrary, he made his career as a teacher of mathematics. But he took care of public affairs for eight years, first as an assistant to Veikko Pihlajamäki, the Minister of Defence, then for four years as an MP. He knows the rules of the political game, how one takes care of public affairs and how they can be influenced ... Virrankoski knows how to operate in the European Union. He has studied the Brussels machinery during a month's visit and knows how regional initiatives make their way in the superbureaucracy ... He knows how to open the doors that help the region. An amateur should not go to (the European) parliament. One has to know at least one language – English is by far the most important one – fluently. Köpi [a nickname] speaks flawless English. Another thing is important, of which virtually nothing is said today. Kyösti

is an absolutely honest man ... If somebody doubts that in these wine [France, Italy and Spain] countries a simple man would not manage, well this suspicion is unfounded. On the contrary, the administration of our common affairs could not be in better hands than when our representative wakes up in the morning with a clear head. It is true that Köpi isn't a charmer or a charismatic orator. But he is a delegate one can count on. The region needs him for the job. (Hokkanen 1996)

Kyösti Virrankoski was thus a politician without being a professional of politics, an honest man one could count on, somebody who knew how things were done in Brussels. Virrankoski's personal qualities could be distinguished from the political qualities of representatives of the Centrist Party, qualities which were considered secondary and even *a priori* damaging in this context. Virrankoski was thus a representative for everybody from the region. The retreat of political parties and the delegitimation strategies of the national political executive, ministers and party leaders, had lead to a situation where a version of non-political representation could be developed.

Types of MEPs

If the European Parliament is a place where members of politically marginal groups can acquire political experience, for some politicians it is merely a stepping stone. For ambitious young politicians who have all the necessary credentials to make it to the top (such as alumni of the *Institut d'études politiques*, the *École nationale d'administration*, or of ministerial cabinets (Bourdieu 1996b), experience in the European Parliament has in the 1990s become a positive addition to the political curriculum vitae. More experienced politicians close to retirement age often also see the European Parliament as a temporary stagepost. According to a senior Finnish politician, the European Parliament is for many European politicians an 'elephant cemetery' to use the term of former Finnish Prime Minister Harri Holkeri. In the French case, Valéry Giscard d'Estaing, who long harboured hopes of becoming Europe's first President, is an excellent example of this use of the European Parliament. For Giscard d'Estaing, representation in the European Parliament was more symbolic than political in the traditional sense of the term.

More generally, MEPs can be divided into 'experts', 'novices', 'elephants' and 'tourists' depending on their political experience and level of involvement in European affairs. Experts like Jean-Louis Bourlanges share with 'elephants' a high level of political experience, whereas 'novices' such as Hélène Carrère-d'Encausse and unknown 'tourists' are beginners in political matters.

The significance of a seat in the European Parliament depends to some extent on the size of the member-state represented and on how long the

Table 6.5 Typology of MEPs

		Political experience	
		High	Low
Investment	High	A. Expert	B. Novice
	Low	C. Elephant	D. Tourist

member-state has been a member-state of the European Union. Accordingly, the dilemma of representation – party or member-state – takes a different form in Finland (a small, new European Union member-state) and France (a large, long-standing European Union member-state). For instance, the first European elections in Finland in 1996 consisted of two separate elections: one of political representatives and the other of cultural representatives. Political representatives were close to party leaders, relying on traditional collective political resources. Cultural representatives were media stars, often without political experience, and with important cultural or educational resources. In contrast to political representatives, they were more often women than men and relied on resources that escaped party control. In the popular mind, reinforced by political parties seeking to recruit celebrities, it was enough to be photogenic and cultured to be a competent Euro-parliamentarian. Although ski-champions and television hosts may not as such be competent for the job of MEP, the collective creation of such cultural representatives testifies to an effort on the part of the media to define what European competence could be. In France, on the other hand, traditional party politics rule the roost in selecting MEPs.

Conclusions

In the Finnish European elections of 1999, the strategy of the national political executive was clear from the beginning: delegitimise the elections by leaving the debates and campaigns to individual candidates and the media. In this way, the political monopoly of the national executive is protected. The effects of this laissez-faire approach are partly paradoxical: in the campaigns, the debates were substantial and dealt with European issues without, however, being a continuation of national political debates, as is the case in nearly all other member-states (Katz and Wessels 1999). At the same time, the construction of Europe in the campaigns diminished the power of Finnish political parties as initiators of political debates – one of their key social functions – and reinforced the role of the national media. In this context, the figure of the popular diplomat as a type of national and cultural non-political representation in the traditional sense of the term was born. One effect of the delegitimation strategy of the European Parliament elections was that it prevented political parties from developing their collective conceptions concerning Europe.

The case of the Finnish European elections reveals several weaknesses in the model proposed by Reif and Schmitt. First, the model does not sufficiently take into account the structural features of European elections. The characteristics of European elections depend first and foremost on their meaning in the national political field in question, not only on their position in the national electoral cycle, as argued by Reif and Schmitt. As the Finnish case demonstrates, the European elections do not necessarily imply a sinking of the popularity of parties in power, or the success of protest parties or smaller parties (Härkönen 1996). The model proposed by Reif and Schmitt does not sufficiently take into account the nationally specific modes of election that frame political competition and determine the characteristics of campaigns. Second, the model neglects the qualitative effects of the European elections. Indeed Reif and Schmitt analyse only the quantitative effects, the popularity of parties and abstention rates. Perhaps unconsciously without realising it, they examine European elections as a simple extension of national politics. As the Finnish case indicates, the elections also make possible the social construction of new conceptions of political representation and of political delegation. Popular diplomacy is one of these novelties. These qualitative transformations are, in many ways, politically far more important than a few percentage changes in the popularity of political parties.

One of the most visible structural effects of the integration of the Finnish political field into a broader European political field has been the differentiation of elections and elites, of European elections and MEPs, from traditional elections and legislative elites. Integration takes place through structural differentiation (integration by differentiation). This collective strategy of integration, which is not intentional but rather adapted to certain conditions and constraints, can be distinguished from that evolving in the French political field, where the integration of the electoral system takes place through an extension of the power of political parties and thus by annexation into the national field of European elections (integration by extension). This enables French political parties to formulate their European policies and incorporate them into their political programmes.

In contrast to posts in the European bureaucracy, posts arising from legislative integration have been little valued. In both Finland and France, the European Parliament attracts mostly individuals with little or no legitimate political resources. The Finnish contingent in the European Parliament has consisted of a mixed bag of retiring politicians and celebrities with little political experience.

Although a marginal institution in domestic politics and at the supranational level, the European Parliament plays a significant political role in the sense that it provides politicians with career posts and anchors the domestic political class to European politics. Legislative integration involves participating in legislative politics, seeking office in the European Parliament. In France, the European Parliament has provided some politicians, such as women politicians, with an avenue of political promotion. But then transformations have to be examined in relation to broader processes that affect European civil societies.

In the next chapter, I will examine a key factor of French civil society, the role of French intellectuals, in relation to the European Parliament elections.

Notes

1 The new requirement that political leaders list as many female candidates as male candidates – gender parity – will, without a doubt, change elections somewhat.
2 France had rejoined NATO in 1996 on President Chirac's initiative.

7 Intellectual politics and Europe

> More than other societies, French society needs revolutionary totems. Next to the eponymous statuette of Pierre Bourdieu, great sociologist and first-class ultrabasist mandarin, will henceforth stand that of Arlette Laguiller, as a caryatid supporting *Lutte ouvrière* [a Trotskyist party]. Formerly the Communist party, symbol of an unattainable 'Great Evening', the torch of a frank and massive strategy of rupture with capitalist society, held this role. (Duhamel 1998, 4)

The often contradictory process of symbolic integration into the evolving European political field has had a significant impact on public debates concerning not only the politics of Europe but also concerning France as a whole and its political and intellectual heritage. Since the French revolution, French intellectuals have played an important role in the shaping of European and global political discourses that centre on democracy and public debate. It is crucial to understand the links between French intellectual traditions and the broader European trends that partake in the symbolic structuration of the evolving European political field. In this chapter, I will discuss some aspects of this symbolic structuration, which is relatively independent of institutional structuration, the figure of the intellectual in different European traditions, the issue of the European public sphere and the uses a leading French intellectual, Pierre Bourdieu, made of 'Europe' in his public interventions.

A neglected aspect of European democratic politics is the European Parliament's educational role and the effects European Parliament elections have on civil society and on the symbolic structuration of public debates. They provide an opportunity for a variety of groups – such as intellectuals, NGOs and various public associations – to elaborate their views on Europe concerning, for instance, the role of European institutions and the enlargement of the European Union to the East.

In France, the withering away of the state has alarmed many intellectuals and politicians. For them, globalisation and European integration are linked to the triumph of neoliberalism, which is for them the culprit of social misery and unemployment. The impact of French public debate on the symbolic structuration of 'Europe' can be dated back at least to the Dreyfus affair.

In the mid-1990s, Pierre Bourdieu (1930–2002) began to be seen by the media in France and abroad as the new French intellectual star following Michel Foucault and Jacques Derrida. Bourdieu became a vocal defender of the unemployed on the streets of Paris, and denounced neoliberal economic doctrine: a Sartrean intellectual in the full sense of the term. According to most commentators, this shift from the library to the street split Bourdieu's trajectory into two parts: academic sociologist on the one hand, and public activist on the other. Moral values, which seemed absent from Bourdieu's academic work, have taken a central role in his public activism. It is true that in his theory, strategies of resistance to the rule of the dominant classes reproduce more than challenge domination, creating a bleak picture of social reality. In contrast, in his intellectual activity, Bourdieu has demonstrated practically the effectiveness of strategies of resistance to domination and globalisation. His republican values enabled him to switch from a theory of practice to the practice of theory, revealing in the process the ambiguities and contradictions of both his scientific work and his political activism. Theory needs ethical grounding to become practice.

The political activity of intellectuals is nothing new in France. In fact, they form an integral part of the French political field. On the eve of the 1999 European Parliament elections, it looked like Bourdieu would run for office on a radical leftist platform, using his intellectual resources as political resources. Before discussing Pierre Bourdieu's intellectual and political activities, I will explore briefly the issue of the political status of intellectual discourse in different national political fields.

Intellectual and political power in France and Europe

Some years ago, a prominent mathematician wrote a book review on a philosophical book. He was shocked to find out that its author had made several false statements. According to the mathematician, natural scientists, among which he included himself, could not afford to make mistakes, because mistakes in the sciences have serious consequences. Satellites would drop from the sky, bridges would collapse, skyscrapers would come tumbling down. But in the humanities, error was without consequence and relevance. Therefore humanists could afford to be reckless.

This attitude is shared by many and it contributes to a general anti-intellectualist climate. Today's world is the world of specialists and technocrats. For their part, intellectuals are recruited mostly among humanists, social scientists, journalists and writers. They are notorious for discussing public issues in a non-specialised manner from a political or an ideological angle. What makes things even worse is that, most of the time, being an intellectual is not a profession but rather a part-time career or a hobby. From the point of view of a professional mathematician, it makes little sense to promote non-specialist discussions on often very complicated issues in front of a non-specialist audience. Why not have the experts discuss and decide about the standards and the policies we, the public, should adopt?

It is difficult to totally disagree with the mathematician. After all, it is thanks to specialised knowledge in the sciences that people's lives are made easier and even saved in some cases. However, I would argue that there is today an acute need for more, not less, intellectual discourse, for two reasons. The first reason has to do with intellectual autonomy, the second with the public character of knowledge. Both ideas were central to French sociologist and philosopher Pierre Bourdieu's career as a scholar and public intellectual in the French and European contexts.

Intellectual culture

Intellectuals are part of our common, democratic tradition. According to some American commentators critical of intellectuals, the problem is right there. Intellectuals like Daniel Bell and Michel Foucault played important political roles, but today intellectuals do not perform their social function as they should. For Mark Lilla, thinkers like German philosopher Martin Heidegger, notorious for having supported Hitler's regime in the 1930s, are dangerous and irresponsible individuals (Lilla 2001). The root of the problem is psychological, a weakness of character that leads to excess and lack of moderation. The naive adventures into politics of intellectuals such as Michel Foucault are explained according to the same formula. But can we be sure that Heidegger backed the Nazis because of an individual weakness of character? I am not sure historians like Daniel Goldhagen, author of *Hitler's Willing Executioners*, would agree with this. For Richard Posner (2002), here following authors like Russell Jacoby (1987), the problem has to do with the specialisation of American intellectuals. Previously, American intellectuals were writers and journalists, like fish in water in the public sphere. Today, intellectuals are university professors. According to Posner, they do their job poorly because they lack the journalists' and writers' educational background and broad perspective on public issues. I think both Lilla and Posner are partly right, but their approaches suffer from a too narrow political and cultural perspective.

Our democratic tradition demands that the public be informed and be able to think for itself about issues that affect it. This is why public intellectuals are needed. A quick historical reminder might be in place. Two thousand three hundred years ago on the southeastern tip of the European continent some philosophers and politicians developed the idea of autonomy or self-government (Castoriadis 1997). Until that time, human societies had been ruled by supreme commandments from the gods who were represented on earth by priests, pharaohs and kings. Their words were the will of God, and they had to be obeyed: an unjust God was a contradiction in terms. The revolutionary idea consisted in thinking that humans have to rule their societies themselves. They have to think for themselves what is good for them and what they should strive for. How did they come up with that idea? Perhaps they found out that the best opinion is the one discovered together through public discourse and critical scrutiny, not the one handed down by a god. At the root of this idea of public deliberation is that of independent, unsolicited thinking. The principle is simple enough. Citizens should, at any time and about any issue, be able to challenge those that rule them. This was a mixed blessing, of course. If something went wrong, the Greeks could not blame the gods, like they had done previously. They were themselves responsible for their mistakes and errors of judgment.

Two thousand years later elections and political representation as mechanisms that determine the popular will and allocate responsibilities and duties were invented. Free speech, an independent press and a written constitution as the founding text of a political society saw the light of day. During the Enlightenment, as the level of education rose in Europe, a learned public, a common European language and a public sphere developed (Habermas 1989). The common language was French. Intellectuals as a heterogeneous social group started to resist monarchies and the clergy; demanding that access to knowledge and political participation should be the right of every citizen, that is, available to all and not just a minority. Knowledge and public debate about issues relative to the *polis* were linked to the criteria of civic virtue. Self-government required that citizens had the right to publicly discuss the issues that had to do with them, and to be informed about them. The idea that autonomy signified independent thinking took a new twist. Fuelled by moral outrage in the face of the growing poverty and exploitation of the working classes, Communism and Socialism developed. Karl Marx came up with his theory of class struggle in the library of the British Museum in London. The political, economic and social effects of these ideas were to be enormous. In France, the Dreyfus affair in 1898 crystallised this development: the autonomisation of a stratum of well-educated individuals, the intellectuals, whose social function was to defend justice and freedom. Since those times, intellectuals have become a significant social force.

When discussing intellectuals we should be discussing intellectual culture, democracy and the public sphere, as they all go together. If two thousand years ago the producers of intellectual goods were also their consumers, today we have three functionally specialised groups, the producers, the intermediates and the consumers. The intermediates, more often than before, specialised journalists or pundits, are directly competing with the traditional providers of intellectual goods, writers and humanists. In France this tension is especially pronounced, which explains the success of books like Bourdieu's *On Television*, a critical analysis of the media. As information is easily available, the social function of symbolic goods has changed for the consumers. Intellectual goods have become goods that enable their consumers to reinforce a certain ideological outlook (neoliberal, leftist, feminist, postmodern, and so on).

Two models of political engagement for European intellectuals coexist today: the model of the oppositional intellectual and that of the functional intellectual. These models are embedded in different national political cultures and institutional configurations. The intellectual goes either against the stream or with it. The relationship between the two in different countries and public spheres varies, from the dominance of one over the other to a more or less equal relationship.

France is a country where intellectual culture is highly developed and where the oppositional intellectual rules. An example will illustrate this cultural characteristic. Pierre Bourdieu died on 23 January 2002 at the age of 71. The announcement of his death was published on the front page of the leading French daily *Le Monde*. Not since the death of former president of the republic, François Mitterrand, had an individual's death been published on its cover page. But Pierre Bourdieu was not just an ordinary academic. He was a celebrated public intellectual, part of the national heritage, somebody who embodied the French tradition of independent thinking. Typically, Bourdieu saw it as his duty as an intellectual to provide the dominated with instruments in their battle against exclusion. For him, sociology was a martial art, a technique of self-defence. This intellectual posture took many forms: the production of scholarly works, speeches, participation in public gatherings and demonstrations, and the signing of petitions. Paradoxically, in France an intellectual can be radical and a national icon. This cultural characteristic might partly explain the success of radicalisms of all kinds in France.

In Bourdieu's very Rousseauist political vision, each generation is faced with new challenges as new forms of exclusion and marginalisation are created. In our times, for instance, globalisation and European integration have promoted neoliberal economic policies, and he viewed the European Union as a mechanism of social exclusion and marginalisation. As a result of globalisation, many in the French public sector have lost their jobs. According to Bourdieu, the task of the militant scholar as a public intellectual is to invent new forms of social intervention based on his specialised knowledge of society. According to the traditional narrative that informed Bourdieu's intellectual activism, the task of the intellectual is to help the powerless in their struggle against those in power, or the dominant in Bourdieu's terminology.

Since his anthropological studies in Algeria at the end of the 1950s Bourdieu was conscience of the political nature of his academic work and of its political implications. He saw himself essentially as a critical observer of political life: of

French colonial policies in Algeria in the 1950s (*The Algerians*, 1962); of the French education system and its lack of egalitarianism in the 1960s (*The Inheritors*, 1964); of the class-aspects of French society in the 1970s (*Distinction*, 1979); and starting from the 1990s, of globalisation and neoliberalism (*Acts of Resistance*, 1998). A political subtext can be found throughout all of his works. Seeing Bourdieu's academic work as having a larger relevance makes sense in the French context, where intellectual culture is very much alive and books written by social scientists like Bourdieu are read by the general educated public. For this reason, social scientific texts like Bourdieu's *Distinction* can become best sellers. The general educated public takes an active interest in intellectual issues and shares with authors like Bourdieu an educational background (certain philosophical and sociological texts, Leibniz, Spinoza, Kant, Durkheim, Mauss ...) and, often, an ideological outlook (for instance, a leftist political outlook). Studies like the *Inheritors* or *Acts of Resistance* are thus read by other social scientists, students and members of the educated public. Since his appointment to the *Collège de France* in 1981, Bourdieu was increasingly seen as being part of the French national legacy, despite his iconoclastic leftist posture. Alongside Habermas and Giddens, he became a leading European intellectual.

In the French tradition, intellectuals are critical thinkers, not functional intellectuals in the service of political parties or ideologies or depoliticised interpreters of texts and discourses (Bauman 1987). Independence means autonomy vis-à-vis political authorities, and intellectual politics is seen as relatively detached from democratic party politics, although most French intellectuals are university professors, that is, servants of the state (state intellectuals). The intellectual is the carrier of universal ideas of equality and justice, but as the republican state embodies these values, there is no contradiction between universalism and particularism. The state is the temporal agent of universal values. Independence means that, in theory at least, that one can say what one has on one's mind. In fact, like the fool in a medieval court, the intellectual's public task is to say what nobody else dares say. He or she is by definition a troublemaker, whistleblower or party pooper (Elshtain 2001). The intellectual is free-floating, to use Karl Mannheim's term, an expert whose expertise is not wanted by society at large (Berger and Luckmann 1966, 126). In reality, intellectuals are of course not so free-floating as they like to think they are; like everybody, they have social interests. Mannheim might have had in mind more the independent, wealthy writer than the university professor.

Dissidents like Václav Havel or Alexander Solzhenitsyn are good examples of the critical or oppositional intellectual. In their cases, being 'irresponsible' and 'reckless' takes on a new meaning. Individuals who disagree with official truth can be labelled irresponsible, reckless or even insane. Under some political regimes, being irresponsible is the sign of a true intellectual. For critical intellectuals in many countries, the constant danger in their growing political significance is that they be turned into ersatz politicians, giving up their social function as independent critical observers for short-sighted political or personal gains. Here they become more *public* intellectuals representing certain interests than public *intellectuals* raising nasty questions and offering analysis.

The second model, that of the functional intellectual, challenges the model of the independent, critical intellectual. It is dominant in northern European countries, where intellectuals' public utility is seen in terms of service to the state and to elected public officials at national or local levels. In this model, intellectual politics is subordinate to democratic politics, the independence of intellectuals being less pronounced than in the critical intellectual model. Anthony Giddens in the UK is a good example of a functional intellectual who sees his mission as being not so much to criticise the system from the outside or from the margins but to contribute to the development of democracy by providing expert services to public officials. He served as Prime Minister Tony Blair's adviser and was one of the architects of the 'Third Way', an attempt to define an alternative to communism and capitalism.

Both the critical and the functional intellectual have a desire to contribute to the general interest. But while the critical intellectual sees exteriority as being the *sine qua non* condition of intellectual activity, the functional intellectual seeks to contribute to public issues by serving democratically elected officials. In terms of priority, the first serves unmediated universal values and the second universal values mediated by those democratically elected. The critical intellectual has a mental habit of seeking opposition and distinction, while the functional intellectual emphasises consensus and public service. Following Gustave de Coulanges, the critical intellectual's motto could be 'I do not propose anything. I expose' (*Je ne propose rien; j'expose*). For the functional intellectual, this is not enough.

Public spheres

In both models of public intervention, the social function of the intellectual – to provide insight from a political or ideological angle on topical issues in accessible language – is closely connected to the development of a public sphere which provides some of the conditions of existence of intellectual discourse. The size of this public sphere determines if intellectual goods are market goods and if being an intellectual can be a full-time professional activity (the market intellectual). The Finnish market for intellectual goods, for instance, is so small that this is impossible. In practice, intellectuals are academics. But the expanding English-language global public sphere does provide some with the material conditions for full-time intellectual activity. Another key issue is the quality of the learned public. Its interests, social and educational characteristics will influence which issues will be discussed and how they will be discussed, as Bourdieu's career and changing political interests demonstrate.

The globe consists of a multitude of public spheres of varying sizes. While all public spheres are limited by the language used in them, some are limited to national borders and thus national political fields, while others are not. Languages that are linked to cultures and countries with a colonial past, such as France, are spoken outside of their national borders. The French-speaking global public sphere, which centres on Paris, covers France, French-speaking Belgium, French-speaking Switzerland, French-speaking Canada, French-speaking West Africa plus all the French-speaking intellectual milieus in other countries. It includes the French-language press, books, TV (TV5), radio (Radio France Internationale, RFI), and so on. In contrast, European Union member-states that do not have a colonial or feudal past have public spheres that are national. For instance, the Finnish-speaking public sphere centres on Helsinki and is limited to national borders.

Since the 1990s, significant developments have taken place in various European public spheres, developments that Bourdieu did not take fully into account. The first development was the expansion of the English-language public sphere at the expense of some other public spheres, the German and the French mostly. English has become Europe's and the world's *lingua franca*. It is the most studied foreign language in European schools. European professional associations conduct their business in English. It is the official language of the European Central Bank, based in Frankfurt, Germany. English-language, Europe-wide media has developed: 'Euronews' on television (which is also produced in French, German, Russian ...), dailies such as the US-owned *International Herald Tribune*, publications of the European Commission (some of them are published in other languages as well), and so on. NGOs organise gatherings of European intellectuals – in English. This development has its advantages and disadvantages. The advantage is that there finally is a common language. The disadvantage is that the dominance of English favours certain interests and groups – those whose mother-tongue is English.

The second significant process of de-territorialisation since the 1990s is the Internet, which has created a virtual public sphere where debate is conducted on all kinds of issues. New social movements have succeeded in using the Internet to further their messages, redefining politics and creating fora for a 'world opinion'. The expansion of the English-language public sphere and the Internet *de facto* unify the national European public spheres and create a common European public sphere by connecting Europe to global cultural and political post-Cold War processes. Knowledge of English opens up the world.

Intellectual politics and Europe

Some French intellectuals see this as meaning that Europe is becoming less European. In a way, this is true. But everything has its price. The larger the public sphere, the greater the global influence of the issues that are discussed in it and of the intellectuals who discuss these issues. This is not necessarily bad for European democracy.

At the same time as European public spheres have been transformed, the European Union bureaucracy in Brussels has become stronger, creating a problem of legitimacy, as supranational decision-making is not coupled with supranational opinion-formation. In the evolving European political field, political and economical decisions are increasingly taken on the European level while input legitimacy remains at the level of the national political fields. The European Union has been unwilling to support the creation of a European public sphere. Culture is seen as a national, not European issue. According to Jürgen Habermas, what Europe needs is an effective public sphere that would mediate between European decision-making and national audiences (Habermas 2001). But there is a lot of resistance. Some national cultures still harbour hegemonic ambitions. Economic integration has developed the most, cultural integration the least. But it is difficult to see how we can have a developed European democracy if we do not have an effective European public sphere. This would require, paradoxically, depoliticising the role of national languages and cultures and politicising that of a common European language and culture. Until now, perhaps with the exception of India, political culture has been that of the majority culture. A multinational, multiethnic, multilinguistic and multireligious European public sphere and political field that would correspond to it would decouple political culture from majority culture in one country. A multicultural civil society would have to accept groups with different linguistic and cultural backgrounds. In Habermas's vision, a constitutional patriotism based on the values of liberal democracy might be the solution to the problems of European democracy (Habermas 2001). Citizens would have to shift their loyalties from the nation-state and the usual common historical descent tied to the nation and a common language, to an abstract foundation, a European constitution (which is 'in the works'). Developing a European public sphere would require the creation of common practices of opinion formation and public debate in a Europe-wide public arena.

Some scholars have criticised Habermas's conception of the public sphere according to which Europe requires a unified European public sphere. Europeans should develop a new model and not duplicate the nation-state model on the European level. In reality, the media of different European countries already now discuss the same issues in very similar manner (van de Steeg 2002). Furthermore, in reality the national public spheres are not so homogeneous as we think. In many European countries public debate is conducted in several languages: in Belgium in French and Flemish and in Finland in Finnish and Swedish, for instance. Many intellectuals also follow the English-language media, or in some cases, the French-language media. The role of international news agencies such as Reuters and the Associated Press is absolutely central. For many European dailies, international news is translated from English. The concept of the public sphere as homogeneous, as bound by national borders and restricted by language, has to be modified. European intellectual discourses constitute a bundle of dynamic, multilingual public spheres, where individuals, fed by international news agencies, discuss to a certain extent the same issues. These might include the danger posed by oil shipments to the environment, the enlargement of the European Union to the East, or the rise of the extreme right, for instance.

In the concluding chapter of his analysis of the irresponsible intellectual, Mark Lilla writes that the first job of the intellectual is to master the tyrant within. Once self-mastery is achieved, freedom and happiness will follow. I wish it were so simple. Lilla concentrates on a few individuals, psychologises their mistakes, and turns them into a moral lesson: don't support tyrants. I think we need more analysis rather than moralising judgment of this type. But analysis has to have the perspective of a few thousand years. Autonomy is above all a public invention, an invention as important for us as natural scientific inventions like the theory of relativity. But in contrast to inventions such as the theory of relativity, social inventions such as democracy need constant upkeep. Because they are public inventions they do not exist without human intervention. Yearly check-ups do not happen by themselves.

If ideas were as meaningless as the mathematician mentioned in the first section of this chapter would have it, ideas would not be talked about. Why do ideas have relevance? Because theories about reality, be they democratic, authoritarian or revolutionary theories, have the nasty habit of having self-fulfilling properties. Karl Marx's ideas about class struggle were not only descriptive, but also prescriptive. Because they appeared to describe nineteenth century reality rather well and some people started to believe in them, they created reality. People started seeing reality through the spectacles provided by Marx's theory. In this sense intellectual goods are always, but to varying degrees, credence goods.

Ideas are dangerous for the simple reason that social reality does not exist 'out there' independently of our activities and thoughts. Facts of society are not facts of nature, *paideia* is not *physis*, given once and for all. We create society, twenty-four hours a day, using concepts and ideas produced by professionals of ideas, intellectuals who mediate between the world of ideas and the public world. Qualifying public debate as unnecessary for our democracies reinforces the decline of civil society, which becomes a self-fulfilling prophecy that leads to a vicious circle of doubt, mistrust and powerlessness. Autonomy is not easy.

It is collectively fought for and never achieved once and for all. The notion of being doomed to be free (Sartre) takes its full meaning from here.

Viewing intellectual independence in terms of moral failure, as Mark Lilla does in his book, reinforces the decline of civil society in two ways. First, concentration on individual moral failure de-historicises and de-socialises intellectual activity. The danger of Lilla's book is that by focusing on the perils of independence it reinforces and legitimises a trend that has been developing in the Western world since the 1980s, the decline in civil society. Citizens do not take part in public affairs in the same way as they did before. Second, the capacity of citizens to govern themselves is weakened by their belief that the dangers of independence (being wrong) outweigh its positive effects. Lilla is saying not only that it is dangerous to think independently but that, given his examples, mistakes have disastrous consequences. Errors of judgment are of course inevitable, but they should not prevent us from trying to improve our lot and thinking critically.

In their classic book on the social construction of reality, Berger and Luckmann talk about intellectuals not so much as heroic or tragic individuals but as a social group. With the onset of modernisation, the division of labour developed. Certain groups could devote themselves full-time to the creation of symbolic universes and of public spaces where issues could be raised and discussed. As the division of labour and a demand for specialised knowledge developed, communication between different providers of knowledge became more complicated, and the function of a general, non-specialist discourse on public issues became more crucial to the proper functioning of society as a whole. The decline of the public sphere is an effect of, among other factors, the specialisation of knowledge. For Niklas Luhmann, specialisation and differentiation is total, leaving no room for common spaces between specialised fields. Sociologists talk to sociologists, historians to historians, journalists to journalists. Reality contradicts Luhmann's assessment as the media provides a public space where topical issues are discussed. In this age of fragmented knowledge and growing disenchantment, society needs public debate more than ever. But instead of reproducing an ideological outlook, public intellectuals should be encouraged to adopt the iconoclastic posture characteristic of the independent minded, who are not afraid to change their mind if necessary. Bourdieu's legacy is to continue to create the conditions of possibility for a truly independent intellectual movement that crosses national borders. This requires developing links between intellectuals in different countries and bringing into question developments that inhibit public debate, such as the uncritical acceptance of European regional integration, or economic doctrines like neoliberalism.

I will next examine some of the political and cultural characteristics of French intellectual mentality.

French intellectuals: a short history of a political totem

In the eighteenth century, a new type of figure, the *philosophe*, became the defender of reason. In the nineteenth-century journalists and academics inherited this mission. For many of them, reason served morality, and vice versa. Indeed, reason and morality merged to such an extent that the philosopher Maurice Merleau-Ponty once declared that 'the political convictions of French writers are nothing but moral attitudes' (quoted in Rémond 1959, 867). According to Jacques Julliard and Michel Winock among others, the modern intellectual appeared with the Dreyfus affair (Rémond 1959, 868; Bodin 1962; Julliard and Winock 1996, 13–14). Christophe Charle has argued that the notion of 'intellectuals' first appeared in France at the end of the nineteenth century, and that other European countries copied this usage from France (Charle 1996, 20). But scholars have had trouble determining exactly how intellectuals as a group differ from previous groups of intellectuals in other countries such as Poland and Russia. Surprisingly, Michel Winock mentions as the main distinguishing feature of the intellectuals as a group 'the massive mobilisation of those who henceforth would be the intellectuals' (Winock 1996, 371). The Dreyfus affair has become an imagined inaugural event and the intellectuals involved a reference point for French and foreign intellectual and cultural historians. In popular and scholarly writing, this symbolic *tour de force* transformed Zola and his friends from writers and academics, representatives of the educated classes, into members of a new social group, the intellectuals, now considered a French invention and part of the politico-national cultural heritage. Through this semantic appropriation, by the end of the twentieth century, the notion of the intellectual can only be 'taken in the sense of the Dreyfus affair', to the extent that some think the term cannot be used in any other context (Jurt 1995, 1; Charle 1996, 283).

These processes of national appropriation of the idea of the intellectual and construction of a national mythology were already well underway during the Dreyfus affair. After all, France was the country of the Great Revolution, and many considered human rights to be a French invention. The defence of universal values had become a French specialty, and France had a reputation to defend. A few members of the educated classes, including Lucien Herr, librarian at the *École normale supérieure*, were convinced of the innocence of Captain Alfred Dreyfus, who had been tried for treason. Indeed, the imprisonment of the innocent Dreyfus was felt by many members of the educated classes, including Émile Zola, to be a blemish on the prestige of France as the country that had, in their minds, invented freedom in the modern sense of the term. In his numerous public interventions, Zola defended the legacy of France as the country of human rights and justice and the duty of the intellectual as a citizen to defend republican virtues. According to Zola, the Dreyfus affair was France's 'moral Sedan' (refers to the French town of Sedan, where Bismarck's army gave the decisive blow to the French in 1870) and the intellectual's mission was to 'give to our people this lesson of truth and equity, to re-establish the honour of France's moral being in front of the world' (Zola 1901, 153, 210). To save the national reputation, redeem France's honour in the eyes of the world, all means were legitimate. In his task of the defence of the universal values of 'light', Zola's most frequent weapons were blackmail and denunciation. Zola himself was ready to become a martyr for justice. In his letter to President Félix Faure, published in George Clemenceau's *L'Aurore* on 13 January 1898, Zola challenged Faure publicly. In his letter to Faure's successor Émile Loubet, likewise published in *L'Aurore* on 22 December 22 1900, Zola warned that if the president did not publicly denounce those who were responsible for the Dreyfus mess, his reputation would be forever tarnished, just in the way that of the deceased Faure had been (Zola 1901, 205).

Although the signatories of the Manifesto of the Intellectuals, published in *L'Aurore* on 14 January 1898, reacted as citizens defending the public's moral values, over 80 per cent of them added to their university qualifications their name. The appeal to the principles of the Revolution was partly legitimised by academic credentials. According to Winock's calculations, 261 of the petitioners were school and university teachers and 230 writers and journalists (Winock 1996, 373). During this inaugural event, then, it seems that the intellectual was, to use Max Weber's terminology, a priest presenting himself as a prophet, rather than a pure prophet or an outsider. Indeed, in many subsequent popular and academic texts, intellectuals have been portrayed more as prophets than as priests, that is, representatives of an institution. Through this collective retroactive construction the educated classes have identified the intellectuals as Mannheimian free-floating altruistic defenders of universal values. Academics or journalists in civil life, intellectuals have a more noble cultural and political mission, the defence of the legacy of the Great Revolution.

In contrast to Zola, who went from being an unknown author to becoming the celebrated defender of republican virtues, Jean-Paul Sartre who came to fame after World War Two was like many turn-of-the-century intellectuals, a philosopher by training and an alumni of the *École normale supérieure*. In accordance with the qualities of the Dreyfusard-petitioner-intellectual, both Zola and Sartre were on the left and anti-clerical. For them, human rights took precedence over reasons of state. Today, Sartre epitomises French intellectuality even more fully than Zola.

J.-P. Sartre started his career teaching at various high schools, and in the 1930s became a well-known playwright. His career as a leading intellectual figure started after the Liberation from the Nazis. The mythologisation of the figure of the intellectual took place largely through the persona of Sartre, by then the leader of the Existentialists. In 1960, the 'Manifesto of the 121' marked an important step in the development of intellectual politics in France. The affair of the 121 reminded the French public of the Dreyfus affair. Essentially the signatories of the manifesto defended the right to civil disobedience in Algeria, and supported the cause of the Algerian people and the destruction of the French colonial system. The manifesto was followed by the creation of new petitions and counter-manifestos. In the minds of the signatories and the public, the intellectual activity that developed was a repeat of the battle of the intellectuals of the turn of the century.

During the trial of the so-called Jeanson network in 1960, in which the atrocities of the French army in Algeria were revealed to the whole world, the defence lawyers used Sartre's name as a symbolic shield to protect their clients. General de Gaulle, then France's president, is alleged to have responded to demonstrators who were demanding that Sartre be imprisoned, saying: 'One does not imprison Voltaire!' (quoted in Cohen-Solal 1988, 415). Sartre had become untouchable, and both the symbol and the cultural totem of French intellectuals. De Gaulle felt he had to protect the intellectuals' freedom of thought and expression. In fact, he gave them a blank cheque to write their claims on. The fear of cultural sacrilege had partly replaced the fear of the mob that had been very much in the minds of the educated classes at the turn of the twentieth century. Through his political activities, Bourdieu developed many of the central features of the French critical intellectual, which has also provided an example to follow for intellectuals from other European countries.

Intellectual politics à la Bourdieu

Specific historical traditions of the status of sociology as an academic discipline enabled Bourdieu to elaborate his particular political vision of society. In France, starting with Auguste Comte and later Émile Durkheim, sociology has been the intellectual heir of metaphysics, philosophy and religion. This heritage places specific pressures on French sociology's mission, different than the pressures on sociology in the US. In France, sociology has the larger mission of public defence of republican ideals such as equality and liberty. Bourdieu combines this republican mission with the more conventional one of the French intellectual's defence of society's underdogs. Bourdieu's critique of Jürgen Habermas's philosophy as too idealistic, and of Richard Rorty's as too directly assimilating science and power, can be understood in the light of this background, in which theory is always mediated by practical concerns that have to do with social inequality and class domination (whose eradication is a tenet of republican values). Who in society is authorised to determine what is right and just? Bourdieu sees intellectuals as constituting a relatively autonomous group, and as such, the defenders of universal values, equality and freedom.

In his history of French education published in 1938, Émile Durkheim had noted that French cultural particularism had traditionally taken the form of universalism, with philosophy as the privileged vehicle of this universalism. Bourdieu's ambitions can be understood only against this cultural background – its models inculcated by the school system, invisible to the unaccustomed eye. Emulation requires surpassing these models in ambition and scope, though sometimes reproducing them in form. One need only consider the scholastic structure of *Reproduction* and the philosophical scope of *Distinction*.

The philosopher Jacques Derrida, a schoolmate of Bourdieu's at the *École normale supérieure*, characterised his friend's intellectual project in these terms: 'It seems to me that he has always been in a love–hate relationship with philosophy' (Derrida 1990). Between philosophy and sociology, Bourdieu's theory joins two worlds: the world of theory and the world of fact. The two are subject to different requirements: the former those of danger and urgency, the latter those of caution and verification. This combination is central to Bourdieu's project, in which the sociologist ruler becomes the modern heir to Plato's philosopher ruler (Rancière 1983, 239–88). Sociology's mission is not constrained by disciplinary limits. Bourdieu has legitimised sociology's universal mission in Durkheimian terms: 'There is nothing more universal than the project of objectifying the mental structures associated with the particularity of a social structure' (Bourdieu 1984, xiv).

This scientific and moral mission sets the formal tone of Bourdieu's writings, as demonstrated, for instance, in the preface to the second edition of *Reproduction*. In this study, Bourdieu and Passeron dismiss as irrelevant variations in the position of cultural capital in relation to other types of capital in different countries. However, they do not present any data to support this assumption. Paradoxically, this kind of universalist stance highlights Bourdieu's embeddedness in a specific intellectual culture, that of France, of which he himself is one of the most brilliant representatives. Having risen from modest origins to occupy a Chair at the *Collège de France*, Bourdieu is an example of the ideals of the French republican educational system.

In the context of contemporary French and European culture, he represents both French sociology as the successor to figures like Émile Durkheim, and French intellectual culture as heir to the throne left vacant by Jean-Paul Sartre and Michel Foucault. In the US, too, he is seen as both a sociologist and a European intellectual (see for example Swartz 2004). In France, Europe and the US, then, Bourdieu is more than just a successful scholar. In the French cultural press he is presented as a dangerous person, one of the few with the courage to bite the bullet on questions of political and intellectual power. In this sense, Bourdieu's public image in France reproduces the characteristics of the French intellectual hero, the romantic individual alone against collective prejudice and illusion. Only he has the courage to reveal how things really are. He is both politically radical and a scientific myth-breaker.

From the 1960s until his death, Pierre Bourdieu denounced the illusions of intellectuals in relatively traditional terms, reproaching them for taking their world as *the* world and for trying to represent something they are not – the people. In May 1968, he backed the students, which led to a break in his relations with the sociologist Raymond Aron. Until the 1980s, Bourdieu continuously criticised French intellectuals such as Bernard-Henri Lévy and Philippe Sollers for their habit of getting involved in matters that did not belong to their realm of expertise – literature. During the presidential elections of 1981, he backed the comedian Coluche, who presented himself as a populist counter-force to established parties and to presidential candidates such as François Mitterrand and Valéry Giscard d'Estaing. Coluche's populism struck a cord with Bourdieu, whose own vision of society and politics also contained populist elements. During the 1980s, Bourdieu was close to the independent left represented by Michel Rocard's *Parti socialiste unifié* (PSU), though he remained critical of professional politics in general.

Whereas Bourdieu kept his distance from the arena of professional politics until the 1990s, from 1995 onward he came to embody political intellectuality *à la francaise*, and actively defended the underdogs of French society against neoliberal globalisation. His techniques of political intervention were very similar to Zola's: participation in public meetings and interventions on topical issues in the press. Very quickly Bourdieu became the intellectual reference of the 'French social movement' (Chemin 1998, 6). In 1995, at the Lyon Station in Paris, he stood up for the unemployed railroad workers, supporting their strike. The same year, a group of intellectuals led by Bourdieu signed an appeal of solidarity in support of the Movement of December (*Mouvement de décembre*), created to defend public services threatened with cutbacks and massive layoffs. The petition was published in *Le Monde* (15 December 1995), proclaiming the signatories' solidarity and defence of public service. They were against the rightist Juppé government's plan to reform social security, which contributed to splitting the left into two camps that had diametrically opposed views of economic and social modernisation, the radical left versus the Socialists and the Communists.

In 1996, Bourdieu attacked the media in his little book *On Television*, which came out in January 1997 and sold over 100,000 copies by May 1998. In this booklet, Bourdieu denounced the symbolic oppression exercised by the media. Later in *Acts of Resistance*, he expressly denounced the triumph of neoliberal economic doctrine. Neoliberalism was portrayed as a fatalistic economic doctrine that was now becoming a political programme. This iconoclastic profile came through in Bourdieu's theory, too, in which danger and urgency reigned over common sense and prudence, creating an apocalyptic atmosphere of inevitable domination – a necessary condition for the existence of intellectual heroes and liberators. In contrast to figures such as Zola and Sartre, however, Bourdieu explicitly combined scientific legitimacy as a professor at the *Collège de France* with his more traditionally prophetic political interventions. Many of these touched on the various social problems about which, as a sociologist, he had expertise. But in contrast to intellectuals like the historian Pierre Vidal-Nacquet, who intervened on specific issues at specific times, Bourdieu combined the Sartrean all-around intellectual with the Foucaultian specific intellectual. Like Zola, Sartre and Foucault before him, Bourdieu blended populist and intellectualist conceptions of politics in his discourse. On the one hand, Bourdieu denounced in elitist terms the mediocrity of politics, the media and his intellectual competitors; on the other hand, he considered politicians crooks who lived off the backs of ordinary people. Like Zola, who publicly attacked President Félix Faure, Bourdieu challenged Hans Tietmeyer, chief of the German Central Bank, who to him represented the forces of evil, neoliberalism and globalisation.

For Bourdieu, as for Zola and Sartre, the intellectual cannot possibly contribute to political activity through democratic or party politics. As a result the political left accused him of being an anti-democrat, and the right of reviving the tradition of the intellectual rebel. But for Bourdieu as for Sartre, the people in power were bastards (*salauds*). At the end of 1998, it looked like Bourdieu might head a protest list to run in the European Parliament elections of June 1999, following the example of Bernard-Henri Lévy and Léon Schwartzenberg in 1994. He did not, but at the time the Socialists and the Communists were especially alarmed. Not surprisingly, the press began talking about the 'Bourdieu affair', making parallels with the Dreyfus affair. With this kind of increased public visibility, Bourdieu became the most prominent French intellectual of the outgoing century.

Like Sartre before him, Bourdieu founded a series of books, *Le sens commun*, at the Éditions de Minuit publishing house in 1965; a social scientific journal, *Actes de la recherche en sciences sociales* (of which he was the director) in 1975; and a European review of books, *Liber*, published in several European languages [1989–]. Bourdieu launched a new publishing venture in 1996, *Liber/Raisons d'agir*, from his *Collège de France* office. In the *Raisons d'agir* series he published 30-franc pamphlets on topical issues such as the public service, Europe, the media and the 'neoliberal invasion'. Bourdieu also took part in founding the so-called Parliament of Intellectuals, an attempt to create an association of intellectuals. The *Liber/Raisons d'agir* series could be described as a collection of political or 'militant-scientific' interventions. The booklets sought to be both scientific and polemical. They did not have a scientific apparatus, but rather testified to the pressure exerted on academics like Bourdieu to wield influence in society. For instance, *Le décembre des intellectuels* (Liber/Raisons d'agir, 1998) was not only an analysis of the petitionist movement of 1995 in which the authors described in detail the process of constitution of the lists of signatories, but also an attack on intellectual enemies and competitors, including those at the popular review *Esprit* led by Olivier Mongin and Pierre Nora and the powerful Fondation Saint-Simon. The authors of the pamphlet blamed the Fondation Saint-Simon for contributing to social *pensée unique* – alternativeless, second-class reflection.

In contrast to Zola and Sartre, the mythical figure of the solitary intellectual has been transformed in Bourdieu to that of an intellectual manager who reigns not only over an academic empire (*Collège de France, École des hautes études en sciences sociales*) but also over a publishing empire and more. Until his death in 2002, this intellectual network extended to popular publications such as *Télérama*, a weekly television guide, *Les inrockuptibles*, a supplement of *Le Monde* directed at young people, and the influential weekly *Le Monde diplomatique*, which also came out in other European languages including English and Spanish. It further extended to social movements such as ATTAC (*Association pour la taxation des transactions financières pour l'aide aux citoyens*), an association started by journalists from *Le Monde Diplomatique* and now spreading globally, which is fighting for the introduction of a Tobin tax on the movement of capital.

The initiator of ATTAC was the editor-in-chief of *Le Monde Diplomatique*, Ignacio Ramonet. It was he who first mentioned the idea of creating an NGO to further the adoption of a Tobin tax on global financial transactions (Ramonet 1997). The taxation of financial revenues was said to be a minimal democratic requirement. At 0.01 per cent of global revenues, this would amount to 166 billion US dollars yearly, that is, 'twice the sum necessary for the eradication of extreme poverty from now to the end of the century'. Following the call for the creation of a Tobin tax on a global scale, soon other French publications such as *Charlie hébdo, Politis, Transversales science culture* and *Témoignage chrétien*, organisations such as *Agir ensemble contre le chômage* (Ac!), individuals like Danielle Mitterrand, wife of former president François Mitterrand, trade unions such as the *Fédération internationale des ouvriers de métallurgie* (FIOM), as well as the collection *Raisons d'agir* led by Pierre Bourdieu, joined Ramonet's ranks.

Bourdieu's network extended beyond French borders. On a European scale, Bourdieu openly presented himself as the leader of intellectuals, who now more clearly than before form a globalised interdisciplinary collective led by the French. From the above one can see that symbolic power is no longer reducible to personal charisma, but rather means the capacity to mobilise individuals in a flexible and expanding web, the ascending nodes of which are individuals, institutions, associations and publications promoting a similar *Weltanschauung* to Bourdieu's own.

Intellectual politics and European democratic politics

In Bourdieu's view, political parties, and especially the French Socialist Party, have neglected social movements and intellectuals. Hence, for intellectuals the only alternative was to side with extreme leftist forces like Alain Krivine's Lutte communiste révolutionnaire and Arlette Laguiller's Lutte ouvrière. The European Parliament elections provided an opportunity to denounce the political elite, and bring into public debate issues, such as the dominance of the neoliberal doctrine, that were not discussed by the mainstream. The nature of intellectuals' political power meant exercising influence and pressure through public interventions into the substance of party campaigns and political debates.

As I will show in this part, the pressures exerted by intellectuals like Bourdieu on politics revealed both the limits of French intellectual politics and the weaknesses of the French political field. As we shall see, according to many critics intellectuals were not tied to democratic principles and democratic accountability. They could engage in subversion without bearing the responsibility. Indeed, the denunciation of politicians and the delegitimation of the democratic process had perverse effects, and might even hasten the destruction of the republican ethos that Bourdieu set out to save.

According to sociologist Daniel Bensaïd, who shares many of Bourdieu's opinions, what we are seeing with Pierre Bourdieu's public activism was a renewal of earlier French social movements (Bensaïd 1998, 80). Bourdieu was against economic globalisation and monetary unification of Europe, and for a political and social Europe created in the spirit of a new internationalism. The target of Bourdieu's interventions during the European election campaigns was the leftist political establishment. In an article entitled 'La gauche de gauche'('The left of the left') published in *Le Monde* (Bourdieu 1998b, 1, 13), Bourdieu criticised politicians' instrumental and cynical conception of politics, which reduced democracy to political electoral calculation. This cynicism had, he said, led to the victory of Le Pen's *Front National* and to the explosive rise of the right. In Bourdieu's mind the main reason for the success of the *Front National* is a political class that is blind and deaf to the helplessness of the people. The 'gauche plurielle', the left governmental majority at the time, had demobilised the militants and thereby unwittingly incited some of its supporters, including the unemployed, the 'sans-papiers', and the school teachers among others, to take to the streets. According to Bourdieu, the French left was to try to get rid of the heritage of *mitterrandism*, the legacy of the Socialist President Mitterrand, an elitist and snobbish attitude toward ordinary people.

> The rank and file left still believes in the social Republic. It is time the Jospin, Chevènement, Hue, and Voynet quartet remember that leftist majorities have led to disaster every time they have wanted to apply the policies of their opponents and have taken the voters for amnesiac idiots. (Bourdieu 1998b, 13)

The social movements that had formed since 1995 were the only alternative Bourdieu would support. He believed that they provided a form of collective resistance to obtuse politics that, in the name of a struggle against the extreme right, often took its ideas and weapons from Le Pen himself. For Bourdieu, the movement of the unemployed and the movement for a Tobin tax were examples of international movements that could practically resist the fatalism of economic laws, and in this way humanise the social world. 'The aim of the social movement is to form an International of resistance to neoliberalism and to all forms of conservatism' (Bourdieu 1998, 13).

The Socialists were not happy with Bourdieu's increasing involvement in democratic politics. In an article entitled 'Pierre Bourdieu, l'imprécateur' ('Pierre Bourdieu, the imprecator') published in the Socialist Party's monthly cultural and artistic review *L'Ours*, the late Pierre Guidoni reviewed Bourdieu's pamphlet *Acts of Resistance* (1998). While praising Bourdieu's pamphlet for its incisive style, Guidoni lamented the incoherence of its author's discourse. Was Bourdieu a sociologist or a pamphleteer? What seemed foreign to Bourdieu was democracy. Guidoni did not refer only to European elections, to the vote, the delegation and the representation of power, but also to public debate and to discussion, to the received mandate one is responsible for, to the ethics of conviction and responsibility. According to Guidoni, this was the whole difference between intellectuals such as Bourdieu and anthropologist Marcel Mauss, who had been a member of the Socialist Party. Reading Bourdieu's pamphlet, Guidoni continued, the reader found a savvy denunciation of neoliberalism, largely shared by all on the left, especially by leftist 'old timers' that adhered to the motto, 'the social movement against the state'. What was deemed missing, however, was a political message that would take into account economic and social realities. What was fundamentally lacking in Bourdieu's discourse, he claimed, was a commitment and belief in universal suffrage. Armed with contempt for democratic rules (such as negotiation and compromise), Bourdieu intervened in electoral politics. 'One does not run in elections to denounce, prophesise or testify, but to act'. (Guidoni 1998)

Bourdieu's activities caused a great deal of uneasiness also in the Communist camp. A young Communist leader, Michel Laurent, published a critical review of Bourdieu's intellectual activism in the party's internal information booklet *Échanges* (28 April 1998). Bourdieu's left was 'protestataire', anti-political and romantic. It was incapable of seeing differences in the 'Jospin, Chevènement, Hue, and Voynet quartet'. To endow social movements with the political mandate to implement social and economic change would be to renounce democratic principles and the republican ethos.

During the Dreyfus affair, instead of merely being a member of an intellectual profession, the intellectual became the privileged defender of republican virtues. Since Zola's time, scholars, writers and journalists have collectively constructed an entity called 'the intellectuals' based on this inaugural event, the Dreyfus affair. By creating a categorical break between French intellectuals and their historical antecedents and equivalents in other countries, this construction reified the intellectual into a romantic hero, a self-appointed watchdog of public virtue, who operated in the timeless realm of justice. It reinforced the belief that truth was to be found in the marginalised: among the oppressed, the disfavoured and the weak, and against the political establishment. Intellectual culture and politics appeared as French particularities that could nevertheless and at the same time serve as yardsticks of universal historical development. The legitimate qualities of intellectuals were identified with those of an idealised, retrospectively retouched image of the Dreyfusard intellectual.

The French intellectuals of the beginning of the new millennium shared with those of the late nineteenth century a moral narrative that could be summarised in three words: alone against injustice. This heroic scenario inspired Sartre and Bourdieu, and before them Zola. For Zola, the *misérables* were Dreyfus and the ordinary working people; for Sartre, the colonised, proletarians and Jews; and for Bourdieu, the poor, unemployed and foreign workers. In this grand narrative, the oppressed needed a liberator, the intellectual, who was turned by moral outrage into a hero of mythical proportions and who altruistically denounced those in power and liberated the oppressed from their misery.

Intellectuals like Sartre and Bourdieu reproduce the myth of the altruistic intellectual in the service of justice and ask to be valued in relation to this ethical mission. At the beginning of the new millennium, this historical legacy has again become a cultural and political weapon in the struggle over the legitimate function of the European intellectual. In contrast to France, where intellectuals see themselves as a counterforce, in other European countries such as Germany, the Nordic countries and the UK the intellectual is often in the service of the elites, and evaluates his or her power in relation to its pragmatic utility to democratically elected political leaders. In these cases, intellectual politics is subordinate to party politics, whereas in the first case intellectual politics is relatively independent of it.

Although Bourdieu followed French intellectual traditions in his emphasis on philosophical and literary discourse and in developing an all-encompassing theory, he renovated these traditions in three significant ways. First, what set this heir apparent of Cartesian, positivist sociology, apart from his intellectual (rather than academic) predecessors was his insistence on his achievements as a sociologist and the scientific nature of his work. Secondly, his theoretical project was embedded, perhaps more than for authors like Sartre, in a normative one: the creation of a society based on republican values. In a manner reminiscent of Plato, Bourdieu attached a universal moral project, the creation of a just society, to a scientific one, the search for truth. Thirdly, partly consciously and partly unconsciously, Bourdieu replaced the romantic scenario of the intellectual alone against the world with one of the intellectual patron who functioned as a central node in a transnational intellectual network. For as his case demonstrated in today's globalised society, symbolic power meant occupying a dominant node in a central locality such as Paris which also formed part of a transnational network encompassing several language groups, most notably the English-language group. Such a global network enabled Bourdieu both to transmit his ideas and to coordinate his public interventions.

Both Pierre Bourdieu's theory and public activism were informed by a larger republican mission – the creation of a just society. In pursuit of this goal, the sociologist's task was the scientific study of social inequality; the intellectual's task, the symbolic struggle for justice and equality. A particular set of values united the various elements of Bourdieu's intellectual activity as a scientist, activist, publisher and editor. In his theoretical work, class determined moral attitude. In his public activities, republican values united theory with practice, transforming theory into symbolic power. While his public activism revealed the mechanistic aspects of his theory, i.e. the theory did not allow for the type of non-mechanistic agency found in practice, his theory highlighted the voluntaristic aspects of his public activism, i.e. that agency is possible.

Conclusions

The symbolic integration of French intellectual debate into a broader European discursive space offered avenues for major transformations in the domestic political life of France. The 1999 European Parliament elections empowered political parties and voiceless, previously unrepresented, anti-establishment movements to imagine a European future for France. Because the elections were viewed as being of secondary importance, politicians and civic activists could innovate and transform French politics. For the first time in French political history, each list had an equal number of male and female candidates – a revolutionary occurrence in a country that, despite its self-image as the inventor of human rights, has lagged behind in all indicators relative to women in politics. For the first time some lists, such as that of the Communists, included activists of colour who were not members of the Party. By elaborating the idea of double parity (between men and women, and Communists and non-Communists), the Communists tried to bring previously unrepresented groups such as France's Muslims and the unemployed into the political process. For the first time, despite the fact that France was one of the originators of the European Communities in the 1950s, political parties had to elaborate a European dimension on issues such as defence policy, European taxation and immigration. As a result of European regional integration, political parties and lists such as the regional 'hunters' were compelled to imagine their own Europe and, in the process, challenged the official notion of 'French Europe' elaborated by the government and president (see Chapter 3). The candidates running in the European Parliament elections constructed an alternative Europe to the one presented by official discourse concentrating on a unified, republican France. A Europe was imagined where non-Christians, the unemployed, women and regional representatives would also have a public voice. In these ways, the elections contributed to a qualitative transformation of French politics.

The European Parliament elections provided French intellectuals with an opportunity to wield power and reaffirm their role in the French and international public debate. As Pierre Bourdieu's case demonstrates, intellectuals play an important role in French politics: the politics of the street has always been an important part of French political life. No doubt intellectual politics reveals the fragility of the French omnipotent state, and the vulnerability of political legitimacy. At the same time, however, democratic political practices such as elections disclose the weaknesses of French intellectual politics. Free from the chains of democratic accountability, intellectuals engage in the politics of denunciation, in which they unmask politics and politicians and the political establishment more generally. Revitalising the link between citizens and civil society through the charismatic figure of the intellectual did not provide answers to the problems of representative democracy and the challenges of European integration and globalisation.

Through an analysis of sociologist and philosopher Pierre Bourdieu as an intellectual, I scrutinised in this chapter one dimension of symbolic structuration of the evolving European political field: the political uses of 'Europe' to legitimise political stances and to construct an alternative European Union to the one existing now. In this way, Bourdieu's example provides for some critical European intellectuals a model to follow, for others a model to be contested.

Conclusions

In this work, I set out to study the democratic stalemate in European politics through an examination of European integration as a general transformation of practices, norms and identities. I conceptualised this process as that of the structuration of an evolving, multilevelled European political field – a common space for political action composed of a relatively heterogeneous supranational level and more established national political fields - that is reinforcing specific mental and objective structures of political domination. In this process, certain political agents have become more powerful while others have lost power.

This study has shown that the structural reasons for the democratic stalemate are twofold. First, as I have demonstrated through Finnish and French case studies, in the European political order executive-type political resources held by state executives and European bureaucrats prevail over legislative types of political resources. Supranational executive networks have become more autonomous, reinforcing the dominance of the resources they control in the dimensions 'supranational–national' and 'executive–legislative' that structure the political fields studied and the actions of political agents. Second, while the evolution of the European political field has furthered integration by creating common institutions, practices and norms, the relatively more established domestic political fields constrain the development of European democracy. This is because, for individuals and groups, the political culture embedded in domestic political fields determines the political value of European political resources and the desirability of posts in various European institutions. The combined effect of the dominance of executive resources and of domestic political culture has prevented the development of democratic accountability.

I divided this study into two broad parts that correspond to the two types of political legitimacy and resources. In Chapters 3 and 4, I examined certain aspects of executive legitimacy, while in Chapters 5, 6 and 7, I studied legislative legitimacy. I concentrated mostly on symbolic and institutional structuration, that is, on the uses political agents make of 'Europe' and on the differentiated integration of European Union institutions into domestic political fields. The general process of European political field formation induces individuals to integrate themselves into the institutional supranational level and, through different political strategies, to transform themselves and their environment as they move from one practical regime to another.

In Chapter 3, I interpreted France's European policy as an executive political strategy that attempts to influence the shaping of European institutions and

Conclusions

common European interests. Despite the formation of a European political field, France's European strategy has not changed since de Gaulle's times. It is still based on a heroic scenario the aim of which is to bring back to France its lost superpower status. As we have seen, European integration has presented French executive politicians with new resources, and especially the opportunity to speak in the name of 'Europe' and to represent common European interests.

In Chapter 4, I studied the integration of French politicians and civil servants into European institutions, the European Parliament and the European Commission. For French civil servants and politicians, European careers have been integrated into domestic career structures. The posts of Commissioner and MEP represent two modes of career integration and political legitimacy, the first as an avenue to executive legitimacy and the second as a means to legislative legitimacy. As we have seen, in the French political field European Commissioners are ministerial-level politicians, while MEPs are situated between regional politicians and deputies. The two types of European political resources have been increasing unevenly in value since the first elections to the European Parliament in 1979. Today, European parliamentary experience is still at most a secondary appendix to a politician's curriculum vitae. In contrast, experience as a Commissioner is increasingly seen as necessary for an ambitious politician, enabling him or her to be classified as a 'European statesman.' As we have seen, French executive political groups utilise 'Europe' as an extension of the domestic ministerial cabinet system, whereas legislative political groups such as MEPs use 'Europe' as a means to enter national electoral politics through the back door provided by the European Parliament.

In the second part of Chapter 4, I examined the constitutional reforms of 2000 in the only two semi-presidential political systems in the European Union, France and Finland. In France, the reform seems to have strengthened the president's powers whereas in Finland power was transferred from the president to the government. In both cases, domestic political culture, the power interests of executive politicians – partly in relation to European decision-making - and the window of opportunity presented by political circumstances explain the form the constitutional reforms took.

In Chapters 5 and 6, I analysed the European Parliament elections of 1999 in Finland and France. Despite the limited political value of the European Parliament in the French and Finnish political fields and of legislative legitimacy in the European political field as a whole, the European Parliament has played a significant role in the structuration of the French and Finnish political fields. It has enabled dominated groups such as female politicians, regional politicians and political novices to build political careers for themselves and legitimise issues that would otherwise have been eliminated from the political agenda. The demonising of Europe practiced by those on the far left and far right is also an integral part of the symbolic and institutional structuration of domestic political fields.

Political agents use 'Europe' to legitimise or delegitimise a wide array of political goals. In the cases studied here political mimesis - that is, action enacted following a model provided by a legitimate idea, historical or contemporary - was the strategy that these agents applied to cope with changing circumstances. As in the case of French executive politicians clinging to a certain conception of France in Europe, agents projected to the European level models they perceived as legitimate. They also reformed domestic institutions such as national constitutions to better fit a perceived European pattern which was actually also a national pattern. In Finland, this pattern was that of parliamentarism, whereas in France it was still that of presidentialism.

When political agents reproduce domestic structures and their in-built power relations, they also innovate. Because elections to the European Parliament are secondary elections, politicians, civil activists and intellectuals can use them to challenge dominant French political values. Political parties and lists such as the regional 'hunters' imagined their own Europe and, in the process, questioned the official, executive vision of a 'French Europe'. The candidates to the European Parliament constructed an alternative Europe to the one presented by official discourse that concentrates on a unified, republican France: a more democratic Europe where non-Christians, the unemployed, women and regional representatives would also have a public voice. In the Finnish elections, institutional and symbolic structuration led to the social construction of a specific type of non-political European representative that stands in contrast to the traditional political representative. The elected diplomat is chosen more on the basis of her or his personal cultural resources than of the traditional collective political resources she or he controls.

The elections of 1999 played a crucial role in French political history. For the first time, lists and parties elaborated their own vision of Europe and of France's place in it. 'Europe' became an important element in the legitimation of political action. French intellectuals also got involved in this process of symbolic construction of Europe. By criticising the leftist forces represented by the Socialists and the Communists, Trotskyist movements represented by Arlette Laguiller and Alain Krivine won seats in the European Parliament. The elections empowered small political parties and voiceless anti-establishment movements to imagine a European future for France. For the first time in French political history, each list had an equal number of male and female candidates, a revolutionary occurrence in a country that, despite its self-image as the inventor of human rights, has lagged behind in all indicators relative to women in politics. For the first time, some lists such as the Communist Party list included social activists of colour who were not members of the French Communist Party (PCF). By elaborating the idea of

Conclusions

double parity (*double parité*), the Communists tried to bring into the political process voiceless groups such as France's Muslims and the unemployed. For the first time, despite the fact that France was one of the originators of the European Communities in the 1950s, political parties had to elaborate a European dimension in issues such as defence policy, European taxation and immigration.

As Chapter 7 demonstrated, the European Parliament elections have also provided French intellectuals with an opportunity to reaffirm their role in public debate. I have tried to show that, given the prestige in Europe of the French intellectual tradition, these individuals are able to participate in the shaping of European discourses on 'Europe'. As Pierre Bourdieu's case demonstrates, intellectuals are important players in French politics: the politics of the street has always been a key part of French political life. However, paradoxically, by delegitimising the political process, intellectuals contribute to the crisis of the republican ethos they set out to save. The politics of denunciation reveals the weaknesses of the political field without presenting an alternative way out of the democratic stalemate.

This study has analyzed how political agents, integrated within European institutions yet clinging to a political habitus tied to national culture, cope with integration. Many state executives openly deride European electoral politics, while the majority of MEPs reproduce through their career choices and political actions national political hierarchies and cultural values. Consequently, and given the structures of political domination in the evolving European political field outlined in this work, the development of a more democratically accountable European polity has, for the time being, stalled.

Bibliography

Books, chapters and articles

Abegaz, Berhanu, Patricia Dillon, David H. Feldman, and Paul F. Whiteley. 1994. *The challenge of European integration: internal and external problems of trade and money*. Boulder: Westview Press.
Abélès, Marc. 1992. *La vie quotidienne au parlement européen*. Paris: Hachette.
Addi, Lahouari. 2001. 'Violence symbolique et statut du politique dans l'oeuvre de Pierre Bourdieu', *Revue française de science politique* 51(6): 950–4.
Ahokas, Tarja. 1999. 'Kiva juttu', *Iltasanomat*, 14 June: B6.
Allen-Mills, Tony. 1995. 'School for scandal', *The Sunday Times magazine* (London), January 22: 22–4.
Anckar, Dag. 2000. 'Jäähyväiset semipresidentialismille', *Politiikka* 1.
Ansart, Pierre. 1990. *Les sociologies contemporaines*. Paris: Seuil.
D'Arcy, François and Luc Rouban, eds. 1996. *De la Ve République à l'Europe: hommage à Jean-Louis Quermonne*. Paris: Presses de Sciences Po.
Assemblée nationale. 1999. 'La conférence des présidents', available at www.assemblee-nationale.fr.
Attali, Jacques. 1993. *Verbatim I: 1981–1986*. Paris: Fayard.
Bachelard, Gaston. 1983. *La formation de l'esprit scientifique: contribution à une psychanalyse de la connaissance objective*. Paris: Vrin.
Badie, Bertrand and Pierre Birnbaum. 1979. *Sociologie de l'état*. Paris: Grasset.
Badie, Bertrand and Marie-Christine Smouts. 1992. *Le retournement du monde: sociologie de la scène internationale*. Paris: Presses de la Fondation Nationale des Sciences Politiques.
Baecque, Francis de. 1982. 'L'interpénétration des personnels administratifs et politiques'. 19–60. In de Baecque and Quermonne. 1982.
Baecque, Francis de and Jean-Louis Quermonne, eds. 1982. *Administration et politique sous la Cinquième République*. Paris: Presses de la Fondation Nationale des Sciences Politiques.
Bailey, F. C. 1969. *Stratagems and spoils: a social anthropology of politics*. Oxford: Basil Blackwell.
Bashevkin, Sylvia. 1984. 'Changing patterns of politicization and partisanship among women in France', *British journal of political science* 15(1): 75–96.
—— ed. 1985. *Women and politics in Western Europe*. London: Frank Cass.
Baudoin, Jean. 1994. 'Sociologie critique et rhétorique de la déploration', *Revue française de science politique* 44(5): 881–93.
Bauman, Zygmunt. 1987. *Legislators and interpreters: on modernity, post-modernity, and intellectuals*. Cambridge: Polity.
Bazin, François. 1999. 'Gauche rouge: Arlette porte la culotte', *Le Nouvel Observateur*, 20–26 May: 34–5.

Beauvallet, Willy. 1998. *Les eurodéputés français: logiques différentielles d'investissements au sein d'un espace politique périphérique.* DEA, science politique. Institut d'études politiques, Strasbourg.

—— 2003. 'Institutionnalisation et professionnalisation de l'Europe politique: le cas des eurodéputés français', *Politique étrangère* (hiver).

—— and Sébastien Michon. 2004. 'Les femmes au Parlement européen: structures sociales de recrutement et stratégies d'investissement à l'Europe', *Regards sociologiques*, Octobre.

Bellier, Irène. 1993. *L'ENA comme si vous y étiez.* Paris: Seuil. (L'épreuve des faits)

—— 1995. 'Moralité, langue et pouvoirs dans les institutions européennes', *Social anthropology* 3(3): 235–50.

Ben-David, Joseph and Randall Collins. 1966. 'Social factors in the origins of a new science: the case of psychology', *American sociological review* 31(4): 451–65.

Bensaïd, Daniel. 1998. 'Désacraliser Bourdieu', *Magazine littéraire* 369: 69.

Berger, Peter and Thomas Luckmann. 1966. *The social construction of reality: a treatise in the sociology of knowledge.* Harmandsworth: Penguin Books.

Bibes, Geneviève, Françoise de la Serre, Henri Ménudier and Marie-Claude Smouts. 1979. 'Dimensions partisanes et affinités croisées', *Revue française de science politique* 29(6), Décembre: 986–1063.

Bidégaray, Christian and Claude Emeri. 1996. 'Enjeux européens et système de partis politiques français'. 61–76. In D'Arcy and Rouban. 1976.

Birnbaum, Pierre. 1977. *Les sommets de l'état: essai sur l'élite du pouvoir en France.* Paris: Seuil.

—— 1985. *Les élites socialistes au pouvoir: les dirigeants socialistes face à l'état 1981–1985.* Paris: Presses Universitaires de France. (Politique d'aujourd'hui)

Birnbaum, Pierre, Charles Barucq, Michel Bellaiche and Alain Mairé. 1978. *La classe dirigeante française.* Paris: Presses Universitaires de France.

Bodiguel, François. 1978. *Les anciens élèves de l'E.N.A.* Paris: Presses de la Fondation nationale des sciences politiques.

Bodin, Jean. 1962. *Les intellectuels.* Paris: Presses Universitaires de France.

Bon, Frédéric and Yves Schemeil. 1980. 'La rationalisation de l'inconduite: comprendre le statut du politique chez Pierre Bourdieu', *Revue française de science politique* 30(1).

Boniface, Pascal. 1998. *La France est-elle encore une grande puissance?* Paris: Presses de la Fondation nationale des Sciences Politiques.

Börzel, T. A. 2000. 'Europeanization and domestic change: centralization and deparlamentalization', *Politische Vierteljahresschrift* 41(2).

Bottin administratif 1990–1991. Paris.

Bourdieu, Pierre. 1971a. 'Une interpretation de la théorie de la religion selon Max Weber', *Archives européennes de sociologie* XII: 3–21.

—— 1971b. 'Genèse et structure du champ religieux', *Revue française de sociologie* XII: 295–334.

—— 1977. *Outline of a theory of practice.* Cambridge: Cambridge University Press. Trans. Richard Nice.

—— 1980. *Le sens pratique.* Paris: Minuit.

—— 1981a. 'La représentation politique. Éléments pour une théorie du champ politique', *Actes de la recherche en sciences sociales* 36(37): 13–21.

—— 1981b. 'La délégation et le fétichisme politique', *Actes de la recherche en sciences sociales* 52(53): 49–55.

—— 1984. *Distinction: a social critique of the judgment of taste.* Cambridge: Harvard University Press. Trans. Richard Nice.

—— 1989. 'Social space and symbolic power', *Sociological theory* 4: 18–26.

—— 1990. *In other words: essays toward a reflexive sociology.* Cambridge: Polity Press. Trans. Richard Nice.

—— 1991. *Language and symbolic power.* Cambridge: Polity Press.

—— 1993. *Sociology in question.* London: Sage.

—— 1994. *Raisons pratiques.* Paris: Seuil.

—— 1996a. 'Champ politique, champ des sciences sociales, champ journalistique', *Cahiers de recherche* 15, GRS (Lyon).

—— 1996b. *The state nobility: grandes écoles et esprit de corps.* Cambridge: Polity Press.

—— 1996c. *Sur la télévision.* Paris: Liber/Raisons d'agir.

—— 1997a. *Contre-feux.* Paris: Liber/Raisons d'agir.

—— 1997b. *Méditations pascaliennes.* Paris: Seuil.

—— 1998a. 'L'essence du néolibéralisme', *Le Monde diplomatique*, March: 3.

—— 1998b. 'La gauche de gauche', *Le Monde* 8.4: 1, 13.

—— 2000. *Propos sur le champ politique.* Lyon: Presses Universitaires de Lyon.

Bourdieu, Pierre and Jean-Claude Passeron. 1970. *Reproduction in education, society, and culture.* Beverly Hills: Sage. Trans. Richard Nice.

—— 1979. *The inheritors. French students and their relation to culture.* Chicago: University of Chicago Press.

Bozo, Frédéric. 1995. 'France and security in the new Europe: between the Gaullist legacy and the search for a new model'. 213–32. In Flynn. 1995.

Braudel, Fernand. 1985. 'L'identité française est à rechercher en dehors de toute position partisane', *Le Monde.* 24–25 March: 1 and 7.

Brigouleix, Bernard. 1986. *C.E.E. Voyage en Eurocratie.* Paris: Alain Moreau.

Bulmer, Simon. 1983. 'Domestic politics and European Community policy-making', *Journal of Common Market studies* 21(4): 349–63.

Bulmer, Simon and Martin Bruch. 2001. 'The "Europeanization" of central government: the UK and Germany in historical institutionalist perspective'. In Schneider and Aspinwall, 2001.

Canard enchaîné, Le. 1999a. 'La mare aux Canards'. 14 April: 2.

—— 1999b. 21 April: 2.

—— 1999c. 19 May: 21.

Caro, Jean-Yves. 1980. 'La sociologie de Pierre Bourdieu: éléments pour une théorie du champ politique', *Revue française de science politique* 30(1): 1171–97.

Cartou, Louis. 1989. *Communautés européennes.* Paris: Jurisprudence Générale Dalloz. (9th edition)

Cassese, Sabino. ed. 1987. *The European administration/L'administration européenne.* International Institute of Administrative Sciences/European Institute of Public Administration.

Castoriadis, Cornelius. 1997. *Magma. Tutkielmia yhteiskunnan imaginaarisista instituutioista*. Helsinki: Hanki ja jää.
Chadron, Martine, Charles Suaud and Yves Tertrais. 1991. 'Les Français, entre crainte et désir d'Europe', *Esprit* 176, November: 34–46.
Champagne, Patrick. 1991. *Faire l'opinion*. Paris: Minuit.
Charle, Christophe. 1996. *Les intellectuels en Europe au XIXème siècle*. Paris: Seuil.
Checkel, Jeffrey T. 1999. 'Social construction and integration', *Journal of European public policy* 6(4): 545–60.
Chemin, Ariane. 1998. 'Pierre Bourdieu devient la référence intellectuelle du "mouvement social"', *Le Monde*, 8(5): 6.
Chevallier, Roger-Michel. 1975. 'Le contentieux des Communautés et le droit administratif français'. 459–72. In Rideau et al. 1975.
Chirac, Jacques. 1995. 'Pour une Europe forte', *Revue des affaires européennes* 1: 28–9.
—— 2000. 'Présentation du programme de la présidence française de l'Union européenne'. Strasbourg, July 4. Available at www.elysee.fr/cgi-bin/auracomm/aur...il?aur_file' discours/2000/PROG"/ html.
Christiansen, Thomas. 1994. *European integration between political science and international relations theory: the end of sovereignty*. EUI working papers RSC no.94/4. Florence: European University Institute.
Christiansen, Thomas, Knud Erik Jørgensen and Antje Wiener. 1999. 'The social construction of Europe', *Journal of European public policy* 6(4): 528–44.
Chryssochoou, Dimitris N. 2001. *Theorizing European integration*. London: Sage.
Cicero. 1997. *Le bien et le mal: de finibus, III*. Paris: Les belles lettres.
Cohen, Samy. 1982. 'Le Secrétariat général de la présidence de la République'. 104–28. In de Baecque and Quermonne. 1982.
Cohen-Solal, Annie. 1988. *Sartre: a life*. London: Heinemann.
Cole, A. 2001. 'National and partisan contexts of Europeanization: the case of the French Socialists', *Journal of Common Market studies* 39(1): 15–36.
Condorelli-Braun, Nicole. 1972. *Commissaires et juges dans les Communautés Européennes*. Paris: Librairie Générale de Droit et de Jurisprudence. (Bibliothèque de droit international 68)
—— 1975. 'Les commissaires français'. 415–26. In Rideau et al. 1975.
Coombes, David. 1970. *Politics and bureaucracy in the European Community: a portrait of the Commission of the E. E. C.* London: George Allen & Unwin.
Corbey, Dorette. 1995. 'Dialectical functionalism: stagnation as a booster of European integration', *International organization* 45.2: 253–84.
Coutrot, Aline. 1982. 'Les membres des cabinets du Premier ministre et du président de la République, 1959–1974'. 61–7. In de Baecque and Quermonne. 1982.
Couve de Murville, Maurice. 1971. *Une politique étrangère 1958–1969*. Paris: Plon.
Cowles, Maria Green, James Caporoso and Thomas Risse, eds. 2001. *Transforming Europe: Europeanization and domestic political change*. Cornell: Cornell University Press.
Criqui, Etienne. 1994. 'Qui sont les nouveaux députés?' *Revue politique et parlementaire* 974: 28–35.

Daley, Suzanne 1999. 'Under attack, Premier offers France's Left an embrace', *New York Times*. 2 October: 7.
De Clercq, Willy and Leo Verhoef. 1990. *Europe, back to the top*. Brussels: Roularta Books.
Delors, Jacques and Clisthène. 1988. *La France par l'Europe*. Paris: Grasset.
Denetz, Jean-Michel. 1999. 'Commission européenne: le prix de la démocratie', *L'Express* 18(3): 68–9.
Denetz, Jean-Michel, Fabrice L'homme, Jean-Marie Pontant and François Geoffroy. 1999. 'L'affaire Cresson', *L'Express*, 11(3): 88–94.
Derrida, Jacques. 1993. *Spectres de Marx: l'état de la dette, le travail du deuil et la nouvelle Internationale*. Paris: Galilée.
Dietler, Michael. 1994. '"Our Ancestors the Gauls": archeology, ethnicity, nationalism, and the manipulation of Celtic identity in modern europe', *American anthropologist* 96(3): 584–605.
Diez, Thomas. 1999. 'Speaking "Europe": the politics of integration discourse', *Journal of European public policy* 6(4): 598–613.
Dinan, Desmond. 1993. *Historical dictionary of the European Community*. Metuchen and London: The Scarecrow Press. (International Organization Series, no.1).
Dogan, Mattei. ed. 1975. *The mandarins of Western Europe: the political role of top civil servants*. New York: Halsted Press.
Donat, Marcell de. 1979. *Europe: qui tire les ficelles?* Paris/Nice: Presses d'Europe. Trans. Louis C. D. Joos. (2nd edition).
Doulcet, Caroline. 1994. *Les femmes hauts fonctionnaires et la politique*. DEA de sciences économiques. Université Panthéon-Assas. Paris II. Septembre.
Druon, Maurice. 1998. 'Les listes maudites', *Le Monde*. 10 October.
Duchêne, François. 1994. *Jean Monnet: the first statesman of interdependence*. London and New York: Norton.
Duhamel, Olivier. 1994. 'Arrêter le n'importe quoi', *Le Monde*, 1 June: 2.
Durkheim, Émile. 1950. *Leçons de sociologie: physique des moeurs et du droit*. Paris: Presses universitaires de France.
Duverger, Maurice. 1974. *La monarchie républicaine*. Paris: Laffont.
—— 1994. 'Une nouvelle alliance franco-allemande', *Le Monde*, 26 October: 2.
École nationale d'administration. 1999. 'Les anciens élèves dans le secteur public', available at www.ena.fr.
The Economist. 1992. 'The race to succeed Delors'. 25 January: 46.
—— 1993. 'An unequal opportunity employer'. 20 March: 60.
—— 1995. 'Keeping mum'. 18 March: 5.
Egeberg, Morten. 2001. 'An organization approach to European integration', ARENA Working Papers WP01/18.
Ehrnrooth, Jari and Niilo Kauppi, eds. 2001. *Europe in flames*. Helsinki: Helsinki University Press.
Eick, C. van der and M. N. Franklin, eds. 1996. *'Choosing Europe': the European electorate and national politics in the face of Union*. Ann Arbor: University of Michigan Press.

Elias, Norbert.1978. *The civilizing process: the history of manners. Vol. 1*. Oxford: Blackwell.
Elshtain, Jean Bethke. 2001. 'The future of the public intellectual: a forum', *The Nation*, 12 February. Available at www.thenation.com/docprint.mhtml?i=20010212&s=forum.
Emptaz, Erik. 1999. 'Victoires intérieures', *Le canard enchaîné* 28.4: 1, 8.
European Commission. 2001. White paper on European governance. COM 428.
European Database. 1999. 'Women in decision-making', available at www.db-decision.de.
European Parliament. 1996. *List of members*. Luxembourg: Office des publications officielles des Communautés Européennes.
Evropeiskoe soobshchestvo. Perspektivi edinovo rinka. 1992. Moskva: Rossiiskaia Akademia Nauk.
Fabre, Clarisse. 1999. 'Les propositions des principales listes', *Le Monde*. 8 June: 7.
Featherstone, Kevin. 1994. 'Jean Monnet and the "democratic deficit" in the European Union', *Journal of Common Market studies* 32(2): 149–70.
Le Figaro. 1994. 'Europe: le réquisitoire de Claude Cheysson'. 7 May.
—— 1995. 'La "liste des 100"'. 25 September: 16.
Fligstein, Neil. 2001. 'Social skill and the theory of fields', *Sociological theory* 19(2): 105–25.
Fligstein, Neil and Alec Stone Sweet. 2002. 'Constructing polities and markets: an institutional account of European integration', *American journal of sociology* 107(5): 1206–44.
Flynn, Gregory, ed. 1995. *Remaking the hexagon: the new France in the new Europe*. Boulder: Westview Press.
Forcari, Christophe. 1999. 'Arlette ou le poids des "mots justes et naturels"', *Libération*. 11 June: 18.
Foucault, Michel. 1977. *Discipline and punish*. New York: Vintage.
—— 1997. *The archaeology of knowledge*. London: Routledge.
Fouillée, Alfred. 1893. *La psychologie des idées-forces*. Paris.
Fréchet, Jean-Gabriel and Martine Gilson. 1999. 'Strauss-Kahn: voir l'Europe en rose!' *Le Nouvel observateur*, 3–9 June: 34–5.
Gallagher, Michael, Michael Laver and Peter Mair. 1995. *Representative government in modern Europe*. New York: McGraw-Hill. (2nd edition).
Garcia, Alexandre. 1999. 'Les chasseurs présentent une liste aux européennes résolument "anti-Verts"', *Le Monde*, 20 April: 10.
Gaulle, Charles de. 1970. *Discours et messages. Dans l'attente. Février 1946–Avril 1958*. Paris: Librairie Plon.
Gaxie, Daniel. 1973. *Les professionnels de la politique*. Paris: Presses Universitaires de France. (Dossiers thémis).
—— 1978. *Le cens caché. Inégalités culturelles et ségrégation politique*. Paris: Seuil.
—— 1980. 'Les logiques du recrutement politique', *Revue française de science politique* 30(1), February: 5–45.
—— 1994. 'Déni de la réalité et dogmatisme de la doxa', *Revue française de science politique* 44(5): 894–912.

—— 2000. *La démocratie représentative*. Paris: Montchrestien.
Gaxie, Daniel and Michel Offerlé. 1985. 'Les militants associatifs et syndicaux au pouvoir? Capital social et carrière politique'. 105–38. In Pierre Birnbaum, ed. *Les élites socialistes au pouvoir*. Paris: Presses Universitaires de France.
Georgakakis, Didier, ed. 2002. *Les métiers de l'Europe politique: acteurs et professionnalisation de l'Union Européenne*. Strasbourg: Presses Universitaires de Strasbourg.
George, Stephen. 1991. *Politics and policy in the European Community*. Oxford: Oxford University Press. (2nd edition)
Gerth, H. H. and C. Wright Mills, eds. 1991. *From Max Weber: essays in sociology*. London: Routledge.
Goetz, K. H. 2000. 'European integration and national executives: a cause in search of an effect?' *West European politics* 23.4: 211–31.
Goldsmith, James. 1994. *The trap*. New York: Carroll and Grat Publishers.
Gorce, Paul-Marie de la. 1999. 'Les cinquante ans de l'Alliance Atlantique', *Le Monde diplomatique* 23.4. Available at: www.monde-diplomatique.fr.
Graham, Robert. 1998. 'Jospin drops election reform plans', *Financial Times*. 3 July.
Gramsci, Antonio. 1971. *Selections from the prison notebooks*. Ed. and trans. Quintin Hoare and Geoffrey Nowell Smith. New York: International Publishers.
—— 1978. *Selections from political writings 1921–1926*. London: Lawrence and Wishart.
Grosjean, Blandine, 1999a. 'Européennes: les faux nez de la parité', *Libération*. 19.5.
—— 1999b. 'Pour les chasseurs du Béarn, "l'Europe, c'est toujours l'interdit"', *Libération*, 15 June: 9.
Guérivière, Jean de la. 1992a. *Voyage à l'intérieur de l'eurocratie*. Paris: Le Monde Éditions. (Actualité)
—— 1992b. 'Les mal-aimés de Bruxelles', *Le Monde*. 13 October: 9.
Guidoni, Pierre. 1998. 'Pierre Bourdieu, l'imprécateur', *L'Ours* 280.
Guiral, Antoine. 1999. 'Un scrutin sans enjeux visibles', *Libération*. 15 June: 8.
Habermas, Jürgen. 1989. *The structural transformation of the public sphere: an inquiry into a category of bourgeois society*. Trans. Thomas Burger. Cambridge: MIT Press.
—— 2001. *The postnational constellation. Political essays*. Cambridge: MIT Press.
Hall, Peter and Rosemary Taylor. 1996. 'Political science and the three new institutionalisms', *Political studies* 44: 936–57.
Hallstein, Walter. 1972. *Europe in the making*. New York: Norton. Trans. Charles Roetter.
Härkönen, Elina. 1996. 'Ensimmäiset europarlamenttivaalit Suomessa: toisen asteen vaalit?' In Tuomo Martikainen and Kyösti Pekonen, eds. *Eurovaalit Suomessa 1996: vaalihumusta päätöksenteon arkeen*. Helsinki: Department of political science.
Harmsen, Robert. 1993. 'European integration and the adaptation of domestic institutional orders: an Anglo-French comparison', *Revue d'intégration européenne* 18(1): 71–99.
Harvie, Christopher. 1994. *The rise of regional Europe*. London: Routledge.

Hayward, Jack. 1996. 'La Cinquième République et l'intégration communautaire'. 23–44. In D'Arcy and Rouban. 1996.
Henry, Natacha. 1995. 'Gender parity in French politics', *Political quarterly*: 177–80.
Hirschman, Albert O. 1970. *Exit, voice, and loyalty*. Cambridge: Harvard University Press.
Hoagland, Jim. 1999. 'France coping with globalization', *International herald tribune*. 23 September: 10.
Hobbes, Thomas. 1991. *Leviathan*. Edited by Richard Tuck. Cambridge: Cambridge University Press.
Hoffmann, Stanley. 1963. 'Paradoxes of the French political community'. 1–117. In Hoffmann et al. 1963.
—— 1982. 'Reflections on the nation-state in Western Europe', *Journal of Common Market studies* 21: 21–37.
Hoffmann, Stanley, Charles P. Kindleberger, Lawrence Wylie, Jessie R. Pitts, Jean-Baptiste Duroselle and François Goguet. 1963. *In search of France: the economy, society, and political system in the twentieth century*. New York: Harper Torchbooks.
Hokkanen, Kari. 1999. 'Hyvä mies', *Ilkka*, 17 October.
Hollande, Francois. 1999. 'L'Europe de la défense, un exigence', *Libération* 10–11 April: 13.
Hooghe, Liesbet and Gary Marks. 1999. 'The making of a polity: the struggle over European integration'. In Kitschelt, Herbert, Peter Lange, Gary Marks and John Stephens, eds. *Continuity and change in contemporary capitalism*. Cambridge: Cambridge University Press.
Howorth, Jolyon and Philippe C. Cerny, eds. 1981. *Elites in France: origins, reproduction and power*. New York: St. Martin's Press.
L'Humanité. 1999a. Interview of André Campana. 9 April.
—— 1999b. 1 June: 6.
Humblot, Catherine. 1996. 'Arte, la télé-Maastricht au quotidien', *Le Monde*, 18–19 February: 2–4.
International herald tribune. 1996. 'British anti-European demands referendum'. 12 March: 5.
Izraelewicz, Erik. 1996. 'Jacques Chirac prophète de l'Europe?' *Le Monde*, 26 March: 1 and 15.
Jacobs, Francis, Richard Corbett and Michael Schackleton. 1990. *The European Parliament*. Harlow: Longman. (Current Affairs)
Jacoby, Russell. 1987. *The last intellectuals: American culture in the age of academe*. New York: Basic Books.
Jakobson, Max. 1995. 'Viisi vuotta Brysselissä', *Helsingin sanomat*, 8 October: B2.
Jamar, J. and Wolfgang Wessels, eds. 1985. *Community bureaucracy at the crossroads/ L'administration communautaire à l'heure de choix*. Bruges: De Tempel/Tempelhof.
Janova, Mira and Mariette Sineau. 1992. 'Women's participation in political power in Europe: an essay in East–West comparison', *Women's studies international forum* 15(1): 115–28.
Jarreau, Patrick. 1999. 'France: le choc du Kosovo sur le débat européen', *Le Monde*, 11–12 April: 13.

Jenson, Jane and Mariette Sineau. 1995. *Mitterrand et les françaises. Un rendez-vous manqué*. Paris: Presses de Sciences Po.

Jepperson, R., Alexander Wendt and Peter Katzenstein. 1996. 'Norms, Identity, and Culture on National Security'. In Peter Katzenstein, ed. *The culture of national security: norms and identity in world politics*. Chicago: University of Chicago Press.

Johnson, R. J. 1995. 'The conflict over Qualified Majority Voting in the European Union Council of Ministers: an analysis of the UK negotiating stance using power indices', *British journal of political science* 25(2): 245–88.

Jospin, Lionel. 2001. 'Zur Zukunft des erweiterten Europa', Die Zeit, 28.5. Available at www.europa-digital.de/aktuell/dossier/reden/Jospin.shtml.

Journal Officiel. 2003. Loi no.2003-327 relative à l'élection des conseillers régionaux et des représentants au parlement européen ainsi qu'à l'aide publique aux partis politiques. 12 April, 6488. Available at www.legisfrance.gouv.fr.

Jouve, Edmond. 1984. *Les nouveaux parlementaires européens*. Paris: Economica. (Perspectives économiques et juridiques)

Julliard, Jacques and Michel Winock, eds. 1996. *Dictionnaire des intellectuels français. Les personnes. Les lieux. Les moments*. Paris: Seuil.

Jurt, Joseph. 1995. *Das Literarische Feld: Das Konzept Pierre Bourdieus in Theorie und Praxis*. Darmstadt: Wissenschaftliche Buchgesellschaft.

Jyränki, Antero. 2000. *Uusi perustuslakimme*. Turku: Iura nova.

Kahn, Annie. 1999. 'Trois scénarios pour le Vieux Continent à l'horizon … 2008', *Le Monde* 20(4): IV.

Kato, Junko. 1996. 'Institutions and rationality in politics: three varieties of neo-institutionalists', *British journal of political science* 26(4): 553–82.

Katshanov, Yu. L. and Natalia Shmatko. 1996. 'Kak vosmozhna sotsial'niia gruppa? (k probleme real'nosti v sotsiologii)', *Sotsiologitsesnie issledovaniia* 12: 90–104.

Katz, Richard S. 1999. 'Role orientations in parliaments'. In Katz and Wessels. 1999.

Katz, Richard S. and Bernhard Wessels, eds. 1999. *The European Parliament, national parliaments, and European integration*. Oxford: Oxford University Press.

Kauppi, Niilo. 1996. *French intellectual nobility: institutional and symbolic transformations in the post-Sartrian era*. Albany: State University of New York Press.

—— 1997. 'Kohti postabsolutistista valtiota? EU-tutkimuksen haaste politiikan tutkimukselle', *Politiikka* 39(1): 60–3.

—— 2000. *The politics of embodiment: habits, power, and Pierre Bourdieu's theory*. Frankfurt am Main/New York: Peter Lang.

Keeler, John T.S. 1987. *The politics of neocorporatism in France: farmers, the state, and agricultural policy-making in the Fifth republic*. Oxford and New York: Oxford University Press.

Kende, Pierre. 1979. 'La France et l'intégration européenne', *Commentaire* 2(6), été: 181–8.

Keohane, Robert O. and Stanley Hoffman. 1990. 'Conclusion: community politics and institutional change'. 276–300. In Wallace. 1990.

Kerwer, D. and M. Teutsch. 2001. 'Elusize Europeanization: liberalizing road haulage in the European Union', *Journal of European public policy* 8(1): 124–43.

Kessler, Marie-Christine. 1982. 'Le cabinet du Premier ministre et le Secrétariat général du gouvernement'. 69–103. In de Baecque and Quermonne. 1982.
—— 1986. *Les grands corps de l'état*. Paris: Presses de la Fondation Nationale des Sciences Politiques.
—— 1999. *La politique étrangère de la France: acteurs et processus*. Paris: Presses de Sciences Po.
Kirchner, Emil J. 1984. *The European Parliament: performance and prospects*. Aldershot: Gower.
Kohn, Walter S.G. 1981. 'Women in the European Parliament', *Parliamentary affairs* 24(2): 210–20.
Korhola, Eija-Riitta. 'Asiat kiinnostavat politiikkaa enemmän', *Helsingin sanomat*, 15 June: B6.
Kovar, Robert and François Wendling. 1975. 'Les parlementaires français au Parlement Européen'. 427–54. In Rideau et al. 1975.
Kozyrev, Andrei V. 1995. *Preobrazhenie*. Moskva: Mezhdunarodnie otnoshenia.
Labrie, Normand. 1993. *La construction linguistique de la communauté européenne*. Paris: Honoré Champion Éditeur.
Lacouture, Jean. 1990. *De Gaulle. Vol. 3. Le souverain, 1959–1970*. Paris: Le Seuil.
Lamy, Pascal. 1991. 'Choses vues ... d'Europe: entretien avec Pascal Lamy', *Esprit* 175, October: 67–81.
Lassman, Peter. 2000. 'Politics, power, and legitimation'. 83–98. In *The Cambridge Companion to Weber*, ed. Stephen Turner. Cambridge: Cambridge University Press.
Laurent, Michel. 1998. Sur Pierre Bourdieu. *Échanges*, 28 April.
Laursen, Finn and Sophie Vanhoonacker, eds. 1992. *The Intergovernmental Conference on political union: reforms, new policies and international identity of the European Community*. European Institute of Public Administration. Maastricht: Martinus Nijhoff Publishers.
Lavroff, Dmitri-Georges. 1979. *Le système politique français: la Vème République*. Paris: Jurisprudence Générale Dalloz. (2nd edition)
Lequesne, Christian. 1993. *Paris-Bruxelles: comment se fait la politique européenne de la France*. Paris: Presses de la Fondation Nationale des Sciences Politiques.
Le Theule, François-Gilles and Daniel Litvan. 1993. 'La réforme de la PAC: analyse d'une négociation communautaire', *Revue française de science politique* 43(5), October: 755–87.
Lévy, Bernard-Henri. 2000. *Le siècle de Sartre: essai philosophique*. Paris: Bernard Grasset.
Libération. 1999. 15 June: 2.
Lilla, Mark. 2001. *The reckless mind*. New York: New York Review of Books.
Lindberg, Leon N. 1965. 'Decision making and interpretation in the European Community', *International organization* 19(1): 56–80.
—— 1970. 'Political integration as a multidimensional phenomenon requiring multivariate measurement', *International organization* 24(4), Autumn: 649–731.
Lipset, Seymour M. 1962. 'Introduction'. In Michels, Robert. 1962.

Lipset, Seymour Martin and Stein Rokkan. 1967. 'Cleavage structures, party systems, and voter alignments: An introduction'. 1–64. In Lipset and Rokkan, eds. *Party systems and voter alignments: cross-national perspectives*. New York: Free Press.
Lodge, M. 2000. 'Isomorphism of national policies? The 'Europeanization' of German competition and public procurement law', *West European politics* 23(1): 89–107.
McBride Stetson, Dorothy. 1987. *Women's rights in France*. Greenwood: Greenwood Press.
McIlroy, John. 1995. *Trade unions in Britain today*. Manchester: Manchester University Press. (2nd edition)
Maclean, Mairi and Jolyon Howorth, eds. 1992. *Europeans on Europe: transnational visions of a new continent*. Preface by Edgard Pisani. New York: St. Martin's Press.
McNamara, Kathleen R. 1998. *The currency of ideas: monetary politics in the European Union*. Ithaca and London: Cornell University Press.
McRae, Susan. 1990. 'Women at the top: the case of British national politics', *Parliamentary affairs* 43(3): 341–47.
Majonen, Pia. 1996. 'Kauniita ja rohkeita vai aatteellisia ammattipoliitikkoja?' In Tuomo Martikainen and Kyösti Pekonen, eds. *Eurovaalit Suomessa 1996: vaalihumusta päätöksenteon arkeen*. Helsinki: Department of political science.
Mangenot, Michel. 1998. 'Une école européenne d'administration? L'improbable conversion de l'ENA à l'Europe', *Politix* 43: 7–32.
March, James G. and Johan P. Olsen. 1984. 'The new institutionalism: organizational factors in political life', *American political science review* 78: 734–49.
Marjolin, Robert. 1986. *Le travail d'une vie. Mémoires 1911–1986*. Robert Laffont: Paris.
Marks, Gary, Liesbet Hooghe and Hermit Blank. 1995. 'Integration theory, subsidiarity and the internationalisation of issues: the implication for legitimacy', EUI Working Papers RSC no.95/7, Robert Schuman Centre, Florence.
Marsden, Chris and Steve James. 2000. 'Denmark: referendum rejects euro heightening Europe's currency crisis', *World socialist web site*, 30 September, available at www.wsws.org/articles.
Marx, Karl. 1954. *Capital: a critical analysis of capitalist production. Vol. 1*. Moscow: Foreign Languages Publishing House.
Mény, Yves. 1986–1987. 'Les restrictions au cumul des mandats: réforme symbolique ou changement en profondeur?' *The Tocqueville Review* 8: 279–90.
—— 1996. *Le système politique français*. Paris: Montchrétien.
Merchet, Jean-Dominique. 1999. 'Trois questions à Ari Vatanen', *Libération*, 8 June: 15.
Michels, Robert. 1962. *Political Parties*. New York: The Free Press.
Middlemas, Keith. 1995. *Orchestrating Europe: the informal politics of the European Union 1973–95*. London: Fontana.
Milési, Gabriel. 1985. *Jacques Delors*. Paris: Belfond.
Milward, Alan S. 1994. *The European rescue of the nation-state*. London: Routledge.
Moïsi, Dominique. 1985. 'L'épreuve de la réalité', *Politique étrangère* 50(2), été: 317–19.
Le Monde. 1994. 14 June. Special issue on European elections.
—— 1998. 'Pour les élections européennes, M. Jospin reprend la proposition de M. Barnier'. 15 May: 44–5.

—— 1999a. 'François Bayrou plaide pour une Europe fédérale'. 16 March: 7.
—— 1999b. 'Les socialistes et les chevénementistes confirment leur alliance'. 10 April: 9.
—— 1999c. 'M. Jospin au journal de France-2'. 28 September: 6.
—— 1999d. 'Une union librement consentie de nations et de peuples'. 10 April: 9.
—— 1999e. 'François Bayrou plaide pour une Europe fédérale'. 16 March: 7.
—— 1999f. 'L'intérêt général, et non les intérêts nationaux ou partisans'. 18 May.
—— 1999g. 15 June: 4.
—— 2004. 'Une mode de scrutin d'une grande compléxité'. 22 March.
Monnet, Jean. 1976. *Mémoires*. Paris: Fayard.
Moravcsik, Andrew. 1983. 'Why the European Community strengthens the state: a Liberal intergovernmentalist approach', *Journal of Common Market Studies* 31: 473–524.
—— 1990. *Negotiating the Single Act: national interests and conventional statecraft in the European Community*. Cambridge: Harvard University, Center for European Studies Working Papers # 21.
—— 1993. 'Preferences and power in the European Community: a liberal intergovernmentalist approach', *Journal of Common Market studies* 31: 473–517.
—— 1998. *The choice for Europe*. Ithaca: Cornell University Press.
Moravcsik, Andrew and Andrea Sangiovanni. 2002. 'On democracy and the "public interest" in the European Union'. Center for European Studies Working Papers no.93/2002, Harvard University, available at www.fas.harvard.edu/ces/papers.
Moreau Defarges, Philippe. 1985. '... J'ai fait un rêve ... Le Président François Mitterrand, artisan de l'union européenne', *Politique étrangère* 50(1), été: 359–77.
Morse, Edward L. 1973. *Foreign policy and interdependence in Gaullist France*. Princeton: Princeton University Press.
Mörth, Ulrika and Malena Britz. 2002. European integration as organizing: alternative approaches to the study of European politics', Score Rapportserie 2002:1, Stockholm University, available at www.score.su-se/pdfs/2002–1.pdf.
Mossuz-Lavau, Janine. 1992. 'Women and politics in France', *French politics and society* 10(1): 1–8.
—— 1993. 'Le vote des femmes en France (1945–1993)', *Revue française de science politique* 43(4), August: 673–89.
Muel-Dreyfus, Francine. 1996. *Vichy et l'éternel féminin*. Paris: Seuil.
Muller, Pierre. 1992. 'Entre le local et l'Europe: la crise du modèle français de politique publique', *Revue française de science politique* 42(2), April: 275–97.
—— 1994. 'La mutation des politiques publiques européennes', *Pouvoirs* 69: 63–75.
Murgazina, E. N. 1992. 'Vedenie: Evropeiskoe soobshchestvo odna iz osnov "obshcheevropeiskovo doma"'. 5–9. In *Evropeiskoe soobshchestvo*.
Murto, Eero, Pekka Väänänen and Raimo Ikonen. 1996. *Sisäpiirit EU-Suomessa*. Helsinki: Edita.
Nonon, Jacqueline and Michel Clamen. 1991. *L'Europe et ses couloirs: lobbying et lobbyistes*. Preface by Michel Albert. Paris: Dunod.
Norris, Pippa. 1985. 'Women's legislative participation in Western Europe'. 90–101. In Bashevkin. 1985.

Northcutt, Wayne and Jeffra Flaitz. 1985. 'Women, politics and the French Socialist government'. 50–70. In Bashevkin. 1985.
Norton, Philip, ed. 1996. *National parliaments and the European Union.* London: Frank Cass.
Nousiainen, Jaakko. 1992. 'EY-jäsenyyden vaikutus Suomen valtiollisten laitosten keskinäisiin toimivaltasuhteisiin', *Politiikka* 34(3): 262–70.
—— 2001. From semi-presidentialism to parliamentary government: political and constitutional development in Finland', *Scandinavian Political Studies* 24: 2: 95–110.
Nouvelles Questions Féminines. 1994.
Nugent, Neill. 2003. *The government and politics of the European Union.* Houndmills: Palgrave.
Nye, Robert. 1968. 'Comparative regional integration: concept and measurement', *International organization* 19(4): 855–80.
Olivi, Bino. 1998. *L'Europe difficile: histoire politique de la Communauté européenne.* Trans. by Katarina Cavanna. Paris: Fayard.
Pasqua, Charles. 1999. 'Un signal pour tout le continent', *Le Monde.* 12 June: 23.
Pennanen, Erkki. 1996. 'Herätys, vaalit ovat ovella', *Helsingin sanomat,* 1 June: 2.
Percheron, Annick. 1991. 'Les français et l'Europe: acquiessement de façade ou adhésion véritable?' *Revue française de science politique* 41, June: 382–406.
Perrineau, Pascal. 1996. 'L'enjeu européen, révélateur de la mutation des clivages politiques dans les années 90'. 45–60. In D'Arcy and Rouban. 1996
Pesonen, Pekka, Risto Sänkiaho and Sami Borg, eds. 1993. *Vaalikansan äänivalta.* Helsinki: WSOY.
Pisani, Edgar. 1980. 'La pratique de la négociation européenne', *Pouvoirs* 15: 71–7.
Pitette, Yves. 1998. 'Faiblesses françaises', *La Croix.* 3 July.
Plato. 1974. *The Republic.* Harmondsworth: Penguin Books. Trans. Desmond Lee.
Posner, Richard A. 2002. *Public intellectuals: a study in decline.* Cambridge: Harvard University Press.
Powell, William and Paul J. DiMaggio, eds. 1991. *The new institutionalism in organizational analysis.* Chicago: University of Chicago Press.
Rabier, Jacques-René, Ronald Inglehart, Ian Gordon and Carsten Lehman Sørensen. 1980. 'Quelle Europe: coopération ou intégration? Les préférences des candidats à l'élection de juin 1979 et des membres élus du Parlement européen', *Pouvoirs* 15: 139–51.
Raivio, Jyri. 1996. 'Ulkoasiainhallinnon Stahanov', *Helsingin sanomat,* 10 October.
Ramonet, Ignacio. 1997. 'Désarmer les marchés', *Le Monde diplomatique,* December.
Rancière, Jacques. 1983. *Le philosophe et ses pauvres.* Fayard: Paris.
Raunio, Tapio and Teija Tiilikainen. 2002. *Finland in the European Union.* London: Frank Cass.
Reif, Karlheinz. 1997. 'Reflections: European elections as member state second-order elections revisited', *European journal of political research* 31: 115–24.
Reif, Karlheinz and Herman Schmitt. 1980. 'Nine second-order national elections: a conceptual framework for the analysis of European election results', *European journal of political research* 8: 3–44.

Rémond, René. 1959. 'Les intellectuels et la politique', *Revue française de science politique* 9(4): 860–90.
Rideau, Joël, Pierre Gerbet, Maurice Torrelli and Roger-Michel Chevallier, eds. 1975. *La France et les Communautés Européennes*. Preface by Jean-René Dupuy. Paris: Librairie Générale de Droit et de Jurisprudence.
Riemenschneider, Rainer. 1992. 'The two souls of Marianne: national sovereignty versus supranationality in Europe'. 141–59. In *Europeans on Europe: transnational visions of a new continent*, ed. Jolyon Howorth and Mairi Maclean. London: Macmillan.Risse-Kappen, Thomas. 1996. 'Exploring the nature of the beast: international relations theory and comparative policy analysis meet the European Union', *Journal of Common Market studies* 34: 53–80.
Rivais, Rafaël. 1995. 'L'ENA veut oublier sa tradition jacobine', *Le Monde*, 26 January: 6.
Rosamond, Ben. 1999. *Theories of European integration*. London: Palgrave.
Ross, George. 1994. 'Inside the Delors cabinet', *Journal of Common Market studies* 32(4): 499–523.
—— 1995. *Jacques Delors and European integration*. New York: Oxford University Press.
Rouban, Luc and Jacques Ziller. 1995. 'De la modernisation de l'administration à la réforme de l'état', *Revue française d'administration publique* 75, July–September: 345–54.
Safran, William. 1995. *The French polity*. White Plains: Longman. (4th edition)
Sartori, Giovanni. 1994. *Comparative constitutional engineering*. London: Macmillan.
Sauvage, Pascale. 1999. 'Nicolas Sarkozy au RPR parisien "Si je perds, vous perdrez aussi!"'*Le Monde*, 2 June: 7.
Saux, Jean-Louis. 1999a. 'Charles Pasqua et Philippe de Villiers feront liste commune', *Le Monde*, 11–12 April: 7.
—— 1999b. 'MM. Sarkozy et Madelin présentent une liste rajeunie et féminisée pour les européennes', *Le Monde*. 5 May.
—— 1999c. 'La campagne de la droite pour les élections européennes', *Le Monde*. 14 May.
Sbraglia, Alberta M., ed. 1992. *Euro-politics. Institutions and policymaking in the 'new' European Community*. Washington D.C.: The Brookings Institution.
Scarrow, Susan. 1997. 'Political career paths and the European Parliament', *Legislative studies quarterly* 22: 253–63.
Scharpf, Fritz. 1999. *Governing Europe*. Oxford: Oxford University Press.
Scheinman, Lawrence and Werner Feld. 1972. 'The European Economic Community and national civil servants of the member states', *International organization* 26(1), Winter: 121–35.
Schlama, Alain-Gérard. 1995. 'Democratic dysfunctions and republican obsolescence: the demise of French exceptionalism'. 31–48. In Flynn. 1995.
Schlesinger, Philip R. 1994. 'Europe's contradictory communicative space', *Daedalus* 123(2), Spring: 25–52.
Schmitter, Philippe C. 2000. *How to democratize the European Union ... and why bother*. Lanham: Rowman & Littlefield.

Schneider, Gerald and Mark Aspinwall, eds. 2001. *The rules of integration. Institutionalist approaches to the study of Europe*. Manchester: Manchester University Press.

Schneider, Gerald and Lars-Erik Cederman. 1994. 'The change of tide in political cooperation: a limited information model of European integration', *International organization* 48: 633–62.

Schneider, Vanessa. 1999. 'L'UDF enfin d'accord sur 87 candidats', *Libération*. 13 May.

Schröder, Gerhard. 2001. 'Verantwortung für Europe', *Die Zeit*, 30.4. Available at www.europa-digital.de/aktuell/dossier/reden/schroder.shtml.

Scrivener, Christiane. 1984. *L'Europe. Une bataille pour l'avenir*. Preface by Simone Veil. Paris: Plon. (Tribune libre)

Sennett, Richard. 1998. 'The egotism of the spokesman', *Times literary supplement*, 4 December: 14–15.

Sidjanski, Dusan. 1992. *L'avenir fédéraliste de l'Europe. La communauté européenne, des origines au traité de Maastricht*. Paris: Presses Universitaires de France. (Publications de l'Institut universitaire d'études européennes, Genève)

—— 1996. 'Eurosphère. Dirigeants et groupes européens'. 279–98. In D'Arcy and Rouban. 1996.

Simon, A. H. 1982. *Models of bounded rationality*. Cambridge: MIT Press.

Sineau, Mariette. 1988. *Des femmes en politique*. Paris: Economica. (La vie politique)

Siwek-Pouydesseau, Jeanne. 1975. 'French ministerial staffs'. 196–209. In Dogan. 1975.

Smith, Keith A. 1973. 'The European Economic Community and national civil servants of the member states – a comment', *International organization* 27 (4), Autumn: 563–69.

Spinelli, Altiero. 1966. *The Eurocrats. Conflict and crisis in the European Community*. Baltimore: The Johns Hopkins Press. Trans. C. Grove Haines.

Stetson, Dorothy McBride. 1987. *Women's rights in France*. New York: Greenwood Press.

Stevens, Anne. 1981. 'The contribution of the Ecole nationale d'administration to French political life'. 134–52. In Howorth and Cerny. 1981.

Stolz, Klaus. 2001. 'Parliamentary careers in Europe: between the regional, national and supranational level', paper delivered at the ECPR Joint Session of Workshops, 6–11 April 2001, Grenoble.

Streeck, Wolfgang and Philippe C. Schmitter. 1991. 'From national corporatism to transnational pluralism: organized interests in the Single European Market', *Politics & society* 19(2): 133–46.

Suleiman, Ezra. 1978. *Elites in French society: the politics of survival*. Princeton: Princeton University Press.

—— 1997. 'Les élites de l'administration et de la politique de la France de la Vè République: homogénéité, puissance, permanence'. 19–47. In Suleiman, Ezra and Henri Mendras, eds. *Le recrutement des élites en Europe*. Paris: La Découverte.

Swann, Dennis. 1990. *The economics of the European Community*. Harmondsworth: Penguin Books. (6th edition)

Swartz, David. 2004. 'Pierre Bourdieu's political sociology and governance perspectives'. In Henrik Bang, ed. *Governance as social and political communication*. Manchester: Manchester University Press.
Thénard, Jean-Michel and Pascal Virot. 1999. 'La mutation Hue à l'heure du verdict', *Libération*. 9 June, 14–15.
Thuillier, Guy. 1982. *Les cabinets ministériels*. Paris: Presses Universitaires de France. (Que sais-je? no. 1985)
Tiersky, Ronald. 1994. *France in the new Europe: changing yet steadfast*. Belmont: Wadsworth.
Tiitinen, Seppo. 2000. 'Perustuslakiuudistus 2000, sen tausta ja keskeinen sisältö'. Available at www.om.fi/perustuslaki/6493.htm.
Tilastokeskus. 1999. Statistics Finland. Available at www.tilastokeskus.fi.
Tsebelis, George. 1994. 'The power of the European Parliament as a conditional agenda setter', *American political science review* 88(1): 128–42.
Tsinisizelis, Michael J. and Dimitri N. Chryssochoou. 1998. 'The European Union: trends in theory and research'. In Albert Weale and Michael Nentwich, eds. *Political theory and the European Union: legitimacy, constitutional choice and citizenship*. London: Routledge.
Uimonen, Risto. 2001. *Riisuttu presidentti*. Helsinki: WSOY.
United Nations. 1992. *Women in politics and decision-making in the late twentieth century*. Dordrecht: Martinus Nijhoff Publishers.
Vaïsse, Maurice. 1998. *La grandeur: la politique étrangère du Général de Gaulle, 1958–1969*. Fayard: Paris.
Vallance, Elizabeth and Elizabeth Davies. 1986. *Women of Europe: women MPs and equality policy*. Cambridge: Cambridge University Press.
Valett, Odin. 1991. *L'école ou la vanité considerée comme un mode de gouverment*. Paris. Albin Michel.
Van de Steeg, Marianne. 2002. 'Rethinking the conditions of a public sphere in the European Union', *European journal of social theory* 5(4): 499–519.
Vigan, Thomas le. 1990. 'Les finances et "Bruxelles"', *Pouvoirs* 53: 73–88.
Vignes, Daniel. 1975. 'Les fonctionnaires communautaires de nationalité française'. 515–24. In Rideau et al. 1975.
Virot, Pascal. 1999a. 'Robert Hue plie pour ne pas rompre', *Libération*. April 26.
—— 1999b. 'La mutation Hue à l'heure du verdict', *Libération* 9 June: 14.
Wallace, Helen. 2000. 'The institutional setting'. 3–38. In Wallace and Wallace.
Wallace, Helen and William Wallace, eds. 2000. *Policy-making in the European Union*. Oxford: Oxford University Press. (4th edition)
Wallace, William, ed. 1990. *The dynamics of European integration*. London: Pinter.
Waltz, Kenneth. 1979. *Theory of international politics*. Reading: Addison-Wesley.
Weber, Max. 1922. *Gesammelte Aufsätze zur Religionssoziologie I*. Tübingen: J.C.B. Mohr.
—— 1966. *Staatssoziologie: soziologie der rationalen Staatsanstalt und der modernen politischen Parteien und Parlamente*. Ed. Johannes Winckelmann. Berlin: Duncker & Humblot. (2nd edition)

—— 1978. *Economy and society.* Two volumes. Ed. Günther Roth and Claus Wittich. Berkeley: University of California Press.
Wendt, Alexander. 1992. 'Anarchy is what states make of it: the social construction of power politics', *International organization* 46: 391–425.
—— 1999. *Social theory of international politics.* Cambridge: Cambridge University Press.
Wessels, Bernhard and Richard S. Katz. 1999. 'Introduction: European Parliament, national parliaments, and European integration'. 3–18. In Katz and Wessels. 1999.
Wessels, Wolfgang. 1997. 'An ever closer fusion: a dynamic macropolitical view on integration processes', *Journal of Common Market studies* 35/2.
Whiteley, Paul F. 1994. 'Comments: has European integration started?' 301–8. In Abegaz et al. 1994.
Who's Who in France. 1979–1994. Several volumes. Paris: Éditions Jacques Laffitte.
Wickham, Alexandre and Sophie Coignard. 1986. *La nomenklatura française: pouvoirs et privilèges des élites.* Paris: Pierre Belfond.
Willis, Virginia. 1983. *Britons in Brussels: officials in the European Commission and Council Secretariat.* London: Policy Studies Institute. (Studies in European Politics 7)
Winock, Michel. 1985. 'Les affaires Dreyfus', *Vingtième siècle* 5: 19–37.
—— 1996. 'Dreyfus'. 371–4. In Julliard and Winock. 1996.
Ysmal, Colette. 1999. 'Les Français peu motivés', *Le Figaro*, 31 May: 6.
Zeitlin, Jonathan and C. F. Sabel. 2003. 'Networked governance and pragmatic constitutionalism: the new transformation of Europe'. Paper presented at the workshop on the 'Open method of coordination and economic governance in the European Union', Minda de Gunzburg Center for European Studies, Harvard University, 28 April.
Zola, Émile. 1901. *L'affaire Dreyfus: la vérité en marche.* Paris: Bibliothèque Charpentier.

Interviews, speeches, public appearances on television and radio

Anonymous Communist hardliner. 1999. F-2. 20 May.
Derrida, Jacques. 1990. 'Le bon plaisir de Pierre Bourdieu'. France-Culture, 23 June. (recording)
Duhamel, Alain. 1998. 'Interview'. Antenne 2, 3 December. (recording)
Kortunov, Andreï. 2001. Intervention. Paris: CERI.
Laguiller, Arlette. 1999. Public debate. FR-3. Politique Dimanche. 16 May.
Lamassoure, Alain. 1999. Interview with the author, Paris. 11 June.
Mitterrand, François. 1994. 'New year's speech'. Antenne 2, 31 December. (recording)
Nordley, Stanislas. 1999. Public debate. Université Saint Denis. 18 May.
Rocard, Michel. 1994. 'Interview'. Antenne 2, 5 December. (recording)
—— 1999. Intervention at the Théatre Veziley. Paris. 17 May.
Scylla, Fodé. 1999a. Public debate. Université Saint Denis. 18 May.
—— 1999b. Débat sur l'Europe. FR-3. 22 May.
Stasi, Bernard. 1994. 'Interview'. Antenne 2. 12 December. (recording)
Zeller, Adrien. 1999. Interview with the author. Paris. 6 May.

Index

Ac! (Agir ensemble contre le chômage) 178
acquis communautaire 5, 21, 54, 116n.3
Actes de la recherche en sciences sociales 177
Acts of Resistance (Bourdieu) 166, 176, 180
Adenauer, Konrad 53, 69
Agency *see* kairos
Ahtisaari, Martti 7, 85
alienation 26
Alliance pour la France 142
Alliot-Marie, Michèle 102, 109
Aron, Raymond 176
Association européenne des anciens élèves de l'ENA 70
see also École nationale d'administration
ATTAC (*Association pour la taxation des transactions financières pour l'aide aux citoyens*) 178
Attali, Jacques 69
Aubry, Martine 71
L'autre Europe 90–1, 96
Avec l'Europe, prenons une France d'avance 128

Balladur, Edouard 55, 113, 139, 141–3
Barnier, Michel 75
Barre, Raymond 78, 109
Bayrou, François 125, 127–8, 130, 139–43, 145
Bismarck, Otto von 57, 173
Blair, Tony 61, 128, 167
Bonapartism 75
Bouge l'Europe! 130, 132–5
bounded rationality 31
Bourdieu, Pierre 2, 11, 13–15, 21–50, 98, 110, 115, 132, 161–6, 168, 171, 174–83, 187

Bourlanges, Jean-Louis 126–7, 157
Braudel, Fernand 53
Briet, Lodewijk 75, 78
Brittan, Sir Leon 77, 109
Bundestag 79
Bush, George 7, 61

capital
  political 30–8
  symbolic 29
  see also resources
Centre National du Patronat Français 93
Centre Party (*Keskustapuolue*) 149–50, 152–7
Charzat, Gisèle 102, 105
Chasse-Pêche-Nature-Tradition (CNPT) 11, 90, 96, 123, 129, 143–5
Chevènement, Jean-Pierre 96, 122, 129–32, 136–7, 180–1
Cheysson, Claude 76, 78, 109
Chirac, Jacques 7, 52, 55–66, 76, 78–81, 86, 91, 94, 121–3, 125, 128, 130–2, 139–41, 145
Christian Democrat Union of Finland (*Suomen Kristillinen Liitto, SKL*) 152–6
civil society 87, 117, 133, 136, 160–1
class ethos 24–6
Cohn-Bendit, Daniel 9, 102, 128–9, 133–7, 145
Collège de France 166, 175, 177–8
Common Agricultural Policy (CAP) 73
Conseil d'état 68, 71, 77, 93–4, 102, 109–10, 114
  see also Cours des comptes; Inspection des finances
Conservative Party (Kokoomus, KOK) 150–5

Constitutional reform
   Europe 78, 169
   Finland 10, 81–7
   France *see* Referendum Gallicus
   see also Giscard d'Estaing, Valéry
Constructivism
   social 159, 171
   structural 3, 22–50
   see also European integration, theories
Cours des comptes 71, 93–4, 110
   see also Conseil d'état; Inspection des finances
Couve de Murville, Maurice 53
Cresson, Edith 58, 67–8, 73, 103, 106

De Gaulle, Charles 52–66, 69, 78–9, 122, 125, 128, 130, 139–41, 145, 174, 185
delegitimation 145–51, 157–9, 184
Delors, Jacques 14–15, 41, 52, 54–5, 68–78, 86, 98, 112
democratic deficit 1, 63, 113, 115
Démocratie libérale (DL) 121, 128, 130, 139–44
Deniau, Jean-François 78, 109
Derrida, Jacques 161, 175
Deutsche Bundesbank 177
diplomacy
   electoral 155–7
   see also legitimacy, executive and legislative
Directorates-General 73–6, 109
domination 46, 74, 184–7
Dreyfus, Alfred 161, 164, 172–4, 181
Durkheim, Émile 22, 26–7, 35, 166, 174–5
Duverger, Maurice 55, 82
dynamic topography
   structural constructivism 14
   topographical time 15

École des hautes études en sciences sociales (EHESS) 178
École nationale d'administration (ENA) 18, 32, 48, 67–71, 73, 75, 78, 86, 93–5, 100–1, 107, 109–11, 157

École normale supérieure (ENS) 94, 172–3
École polytechnique 18, 93–4
eduskunta 83, 84, 98, 125, 148, 152, 153, 154
   see also legitimacy
Énergie radicale 90, 96, 129
Eurocrats 67, 71–6
European Atomic Energy Agency (EURATOM) 77
European Bank of Investment (EIB) 71
European Bank of Reconstruction and Development (EBRD) 69
European Commission 21, 48, 52, 54–5, 68–9, 71–8, 86–9, 97–8, 103, 109–13, 126, 135–6, 138–40, 185
European Commissioners 67–9, 71–8, 86, 97–8, 103, 105–12, 115, 126, 147, 185
European Constitutional Convention 110, 169
European Council 62, 65
European Council of Ministers 19, 48, 62, 116, 131, 136, 138–40, 143, 151
European Economic Community (EEC) 54–5, 76–7, 93
European Employers Union (UNICE) 19
European integration 51 5, 57, 61–2, 65–8, 70, 76, 78, 81–2, 86, 97, 108, 114–15, 117, 127, 129–31, 146–7, 159–61, 183–5
   structuration of the European political field 51, 68
   theories 4–21
European Monetary Union (EMU) 72, 151, 179
European Parliament 2–3, 19–20, 48, 56, 59–60, 64, 88–162, 177, 179–80, 182–3, 185–7
   typology of parliamentarians 88–116
European political field 51, 67, 68, 78, 86–8, 95–8, 112, 115, 117–20, 146, 155, 159, 161, 169, 184–5, 187
   main cleavages 4–8
   structuration 1–3, 78, 161
European president 142, 157

Index

European Regional Development Fund (ERDF) 113
European Trade Union Confederation (ETUC) 19
Europe of people (*l'Europe des hommes*) 63
L'Europe pour la France 121
Europeanisation 8, 98, 131, 146
Eurosphere 5–6
executive networks 71

Fabius, Laurent 91, 109, 127, 137
Faure, Félix 173, 177
federalism 52–3, 97, 113–14, 129–30, 136–7, 140, 142, 149–50
Fédération internationale des ouvriers de métallurgie (FIOM) 178
field theory 35–7
   see also political field
Figaro, Le 107
Fifth Republic 52, 61, 78–82, 99, 125–6, 140
Fondation Saint-Simon 178
Fontaine, Nicole 103, 143
Foucault, Michel 27, 161–3, 175, 177
Fouchet Plan 53
Fouillée, Alfred 28
Fourth Republic 80
Front National (FN) 91, 97, 122, 129–31, 137, 144, 179
   see also Le Pen
functionalism 12

gender
   Finnish political class 152–4
   French political class 67, 94, 98–107, 108, 141, 143
   political value hierarchies 88
Génération écologie (GE) 121, 141, 144
German Central Bank 177
Giddens, Anthony 40, 166–7
Giscard d'Estaing, Valéry 19, 43, 52, 57, 91, 110, 126, 128, 141, 157, 176
globalisation 117, 161, 165–6
   European integration 117, 161, 165
   neoliberalism 117, 161, 165–6

Goldsmith, James 16, 18, 55–6
Gorbatshov, Mihail 54
Gramsci, Antonio 10, 34
grandes écoles 71, 91, 93–4, 100–1, 106
grands corps 91, 93–5, 101, 110
Green party
   Finland (Vihreät, VIHR) 150, 152–5
   France 90, 102, 105, 122, 128–30, 132–7, 143–5

Habermas, Jürgen 166, 169, 174
habitus
   political culture 35
   see also identity
Hautala, Heidi 152, 154–5
Helsingin Sanomat 148, 155
Hitler, Adolf 57, 163
Holkeri, Harri 157
Hollande, François 128–9, 136–7
homo politicus europaeus 8, 66, 105
d'Hondt system 88
Hostalier, François 108, 142
Hue, Robert 129–30, 132–6, 144, 180–1
L'Humanité

identity 3, 8, 40–1, 56–66
inrockuptibles, Les 178
Inspection des finances 71, 93–4, 110
Institut d'Études Politiques (IEP) 32, 67, 71, 86, 93–4, 100, 110, 157
Institut international d'administration publique (IIAP) 68–9
institutional isomorphism 46–7, 81–7
institutionalization *see* structuration
integration
   differentiation 159
   European 51–5, 57, 61, 65–8, 70, 76, 78, 81–2, 86, 97, 108, 114–15, 117, 127, 129–31, 146–7, 159, 161, 183–5
   institutional 81–7
   social 67–81, 86–7
   strategies 159–60
   subsumption 159

intellectuals 52, 116–17, 134, 160, 161–87
    democratic politics 134, 161–83
    European public sphere 160, 167–71
intergovernmentalism 62, 151

Jospin, Lionel 7, 17, 55, 58–9, 63, 79–81,
    99–100, 113, 120–3, 125, 128–32,
    137, 145, 180–1
Juppé, Alain 109, 121, 126, 128, 141–3,
    176

kairos (opportune moment) 14–15
Kant, Immanuel 166
Kekkonen, Urho 10, 83
Keskustapuolue see Centre Party
Kohl, Helmut 14–15
Koivisto, Mauno 85
Korhola, Eija-Riitta 152–3, 156
Kosovo war 58, 59, 118, 127, 129, 131–2,
    135, 139, 142
Krivine, Alain 129, 134–5, 179, 186
    see also Lutte communiste
    révolutionnaire (LCR)

Laguiller, Arlette 129–30, 134–5, 161,
    179, 186
    see also Lutte ouvrière (LO)
Lamassoure, Alain 113, 143
Lamoureux, François 71–5
Lamy, Pascal 69, 71–3, 75, 78, 109
Left Alliance (*Vasemmistoliitto*) 150, 152,
    154–5
legitimacy
    charismatic 46
    executive and legislative 2–3
    political 17, 43, 46, 111, 131
Legras, Guy 69, 73
Leibniz, Gottfried Wilhelm von 166
Le Pen, Jean-Marie 11, 96, 122, 129, 131,
    137–8, 144, 179–80
Lévi-Strauss, Claude 30, 38
Lévy, Bernard-Henri 11, 90, 96, 176–7
Leygues, Jean-Charles 72, 75
Libération 153
Liber/Raisons d'agir (Bourdieu) 177–8

Lienemann, Marie-Noëlle 102, 109
Liikanen, Erkki 147
Lilla, Mark 163, 170–1
Lipponen, Paavo 7, 44, 60, 84, 145, 150–1
longue durée 13
    see also identity
Luckmann, Thomas 40, 171
Lutte communiste révolutionnaire (LCR)
    90, 122, 129–31, 133–6, 144, 179
    see also Krivine
Lutte ouvrière (LO) 90, 122, 129–31,
    133–6, 144, 161, 179
    see also Laguiller, Arlette

Maastricht Treaty 79, 91, 96, 127
Machiavellian Tradition 46
Madelin, Alain 121, 127–8, 130, 140–3
Manifesto of the Intellectuals 173
    see also Zola, Émile
Mannheim, Karl 166, 173
Marchais, Georges 130, 134
Marx, Karl 22–3, 38, 46, 164, 170
Matikainen-Kallström, Marjo 152–5
Mauroy, Pierre 55, 71
Mauss, Marcel 166, 180
Mégret, Bruno 126, 129, 131, 138–9, 144
Member of the European Parliament
    (MEP) 56, 60, 65, 71, 80, 87,
    88–116, 117–60, 185–7
    social characteristics 88–98, 155–7
    typology 155–160
    see also legitimacy
Merleau-Ponty, Maurice 172
Méry-scandal 81
Michels, Robert 22, 26, 46, 49
Mitterrand, Danièle 178
Mitterrand, François 14–15, 45, 52–4,
    57–60, 67, 76–9, 106, 165, 176, 178,
    180
Monde, Le 76, 165, 176, 178–9
Monde diplomatique, Le 178
Monnet, Jean 18, 52, 54, 58
Mosca, Gaetano 49
Mouvement de décembre (Movement of
    December) 176

Index

Mouvement des citoyens (MDC) (Chevènement) 122, 129–32, 136, 137, 144
Mouvement national (MN) (Mégret) 126, 129, 137, 144
Mouvement pour la France 131
Myller, Riitta 152–3, 155

Napoleon 54, 57
National Assembly (*Assemblée nationale*) 58, 61, 78–81, 92–5, 97, 99, 102–3, 105–6, 108, 119–21, 124, 126, 130, 137, 141–2
Nation-state 127, 155
Neoliberalism 116–17, 146, 161–2, 165–6
North Atlantic Treaty Organization (NATO) 52, 56–7, 60, 130, 135–6, 138–40, 160n.2

Ortoli, François-Xavier 68, 78, 109

Paasilinna, Reino 152, 155
pantouflage 78
parachutage 72
parity (*parité*) 10–11, 99–100, 102–3, 108, 160n.1
  Parti communiste français and double parity 133–4
Parliament
  European 2–3, 56, 59–60, 64, 88–160, 161, 162, 177, 179, 180, 182–3, 185–7
  Finnish 83–4, 98, 125, 149, 152–4
  national 98, 119, 125, 138, 140, 149, 152–4
  eduskunta 83, 84, 98, 125, 148, 152
  see also National Assembly
Parliament of Intellectuals 177
Parti communiste français (PCF) 90–1, 96–7, 106, 122, 129–30, 132–6, 143–5, 161, 176–7, 180, 182, 186
Parti Radical (PR) 143
Parti républicain (PR) 141
Parti républicain de gauche (PRG) 129, 131, 136, 144

Parti socialiste (PS) 74, 77, 79, 81, 90–1, 102, 105, 107–8, 110, 113, 120, 125–37, 140, 144–5, 176–7, 179–80, 186
Parti socialiste unifié (PSU) 176
Pasqua, Charles 81, 96, 129–31, 137–41, 144–5
Pesälä, Mikko 152–3
Pihlajamäki, Veikko 156
Pohjamo, Samuli 152–5
political culture 53, 59–61, 65, 105, 108, 114, 116–17, 126, 149, 152, 165
  European 114, 126
  national value hierarchies 114, 116, 149, 152, 165
political field
  European 4–5, 51, 67, 68, 78, 86–8, 95–8, 112, 115, 117–20, 146, 155, 159, 161, 169, 184–5, 187
  Finnish 85, 116, 146, 156, 159, 185
  French 53, 95, 97, 100, 107–17, 126, 156, 159, 179, 185
  national 51, 86, 111, 113, 117–18, 147, 155, 159, 162, 186
  structure 29–39, 78, 107–16, 126
political power 54–7, 59, 61, 65, 67, 71, 74–6, 78–9, 82–7, 88–9, 95–6, 99, 101, 103, 105–10, 113–15, 117, 119, 125, 130, 135, 138, 140, 146, 148, 150, 155, 159, 162–5
  social resource 47, 184–5
  see also resources
political representation
  delegation 24–6, 157
  see also alienation
Pompidou, Georges 52, 57, 68–9
post-imperialist syndrome (PIS) 51, 53, 65
Pour l'Europe des travailleurs et la démocratie 96
power-idea (*idée-force*) (Fouillée) 28
public intellectual 161–7
  functional 167
  independent 166
  social group 163–4

public sphere 151, 161, 164–5, 167–71
  democracy 164
  English 168
  European 161
  Finnish 167–8

Radio France Internationale 168
Raffarin, Jean-Pierre 113, 115
Rassemblement pour la France et l'indépendance de l'Europe (RPF) 90, 96, 129–31, 137, 138, 144–5
Rassemblement pour la République (RPR) 75, 79, 90–1, 96, 102–3, 108, 121, 124, 128–31, 137–44
rational choice 30–1
Referendum Gallicus 78–81
reinforced cooperation 62
Republican ethos 130, 137
resources
  cultural 158
  economic 148
  educational 148, 158
  European and national 6, 147
  executive and legislative 2–3
  intellectual 162
  linguistic 153
  political 17–18, 70, 75, 85–7, 102–6, 109–11, 115, 125, 147, 158, 159, 162
  social 107–16
Rocard, Michel 17, 89, 94, 102, 106, 125, 128, 137, 149, 176

Saint-Josse, Jean 129, 143, 145
'*sans papiers*' 132–7, 179
Sarkozy, Nicolas 121, 125, 128, 130, 139–43
Sartre, Jean-Paul 162, 171, 173–5, 177–8, 181–2
Saussure, Ferdinand de 29, 49
Schmitt, Hermann 147, 155, 159
Schröder, Gerhard 61, 88, 128
Scrivener, Christiane 78, 103, 109, 112
Scylla, Fodé 134, 144
  see also SOS-Racisme

second-order elections 147, 151
Séguin, Philippe 59, 121, 130, 137, 139, 141–2
semi-presidentialism 81–7
Seppänen, Esko 152, 154–5
Service général de coordination interministériel (SGCI) 19
Silguy, Yves-Thibault de 77–8, 109, 126
social capital
  political resources 18, 116n.1, 126
  see resources
social class 144, 152
  education 127
  see also class ethos
Social Democratic Party, Finnish (*Suomen Sosialidemokraattinen puolue*) 83, 145, 150–5
'social Europe' 135, 137
social movements 120, 132–7, 144
social spheres
  fields 29–30, 46–7
Sollers, Philippe 176
SOS-Racisme 134, 144
  see Scylla, Fodé
Strauss-Kahn, Dominique 6
structuration 9–15, 41–4, 127
  institutional 50, 127
  processual 9–15
  symbolic 50, 105, 108, 115, 117, 127, 161
Swedish People's Party (*Svenska folkpartiet*) 150, 152, 154–5
symbolic
  boundary 115, 117, 127, 161
  integration 161
  legitimacy 26, 125
  politics 133, 135, 151
  structuration 105, 108
  violence 28, 36

Tapie, Bernard 91, 96, 106, 108, 129
Thors, Astrid 152, 154–5
Tietmeyer, Hans 177
Tobin tax 135, 137, 178, 180
  see also ATTAC

Topographical time 15
  see also structuration

Union de la France 130
Union pour la démocratie française (UDF) 90, 91, 96, 113, 124–5, 128, 130, 139–44
L'Union pour l'Europe 128
Union pour la majorite présidentielle (UMP) 56

Vatanen, Ari 55–6, 152–3
Väyrynen, Paavo 152–5
Veil, Simone 103–4
Villiers, Philippe de 18, 81, 90–1, 96, 129–31, 137–41, 145

Virrankoski, Kyösti 149, 152–3, 155–7
voting systems
  Finland 147–8
  France 88–9, 121–2
Voynet, Dominique 11, 129, 143, 145, 180–1

Weber, Max 14, 22–3, 29, 31, 46, 49, 173
Western European Union (WEU) 136
Winock, Michel 172–3
Wuori, Matti 152–3

Zola, Émile 172–3, 176–8, 181

Lightning Source UK Ltd.
Milton Keynes UK
UKOW03f2235081013

218688UK00001B/4/P